Early Renaissance Architecture In England: A Historical & Descriptive Account Of The Tudor, Elizabethan & Jacobean Periods, 1500-1625, For The Use Of Students And Others

John Alfred Gotch

John S Humphreys

Dec 1900

EARLY RENAISSANCE ARCHITECTURE
IN ENGLAND.

PLATE I.

HENRY VII.'S CHAPEL, WESTMINSTER ABBEY.
INTERIOR VIEW, SHOWING VAULTING AND SCREEN.

EARLY RENAISSANCE
ARCHITECTURE
IN ENGLAND

A HISTORICAL & DESCRIPTIVE ACCOUNT OF THE
TUDOR, ELIZABETHAN, & JACOBEAN PERIODS,
1500—1625

FOR THE USE OF STUDENTS AND OTHERS

BY

J. ALFRED GOTCH, F.S.A.

AUTHOR OF "ARCHITECTURE OF THE
RENAISSANCE IN ENGLAND," ETC.

WITH EIGHTY-SEVEN COLLOTYPE AND OTHER PLATES AND
TWO HUNDRED AND THIRTY ILLUSTRATIONS IN THE TEXT

LONDON
B. T. BATSFORD, 94 HIGH HOLBORN

NEW YORK
CHARLES SCRIBNER'S SONS, 153-157 FIFTH AVENUE
MDCCCCI

PREFACE.

It should, perhaps, be observed that although this book is entitled *Early Renaissance Architecture in England*, it deals with much the same period as that covered by my former work *The Architecture of the Renaissance in England*, but with the addition of the first half of the sixteenth century. The two books, however, have nothing in common beyond the fact that they both illustrate the work of a particular period. The former book exhibits a series of examples, to a large scale, of Elizabethan and Jacobean buildings, with a brief account of each: whereas this one takes the form of a hand-book in which the endeavour is made to trace in a systematic manner the development of style from the close of the Gothic period down to the advent of Inigo Jones.

It is not the inclusion of the first half of the sixteenth century which alone has led to the adoption of the title *Early Renaissance*: the limitation of period which these words indicate appeared particularly necessary in consequence of the recent publication of two other books, one being the important work of Mr. Belcher and Mr. Macartney, illustrating buildings of the seventeenth and eighteenth centuries, under the title of *Later Renaissance Architecture in England*; and the other being Mr. Reginald Blomfield's scholarly book, *A History of Renaissance Architecture in England*, which, although it starts with the beginning of the sixteenth century, does not dwell at any length upon the earlier work, but is chiefly devoted to an exhaustive survey of that of the seventeenth and eighteenth centuries.

The value of a work on Architecture is greatly enhanced by

illustrations, and I am much indebted to the numerous gentlemen who, with great courtesy, have placed the fruits of their
pencil, brush, or camera at my disposal : their names are given
in the Lists of Plates and Illustrations.   More particularly I
desire to acknowledge the kindness of the Committee of that
very useful publication *The Architectural Association Sketch Book*,
in giving permission for some of their plates to be reproduced ;
and among other contributors I have especially to thank
Colonel Gale, Mr. W. Haywood, and Mr. Harold Brakspear;
while to Mr. Ryland Adkins I am indebted for several valuable
suggestions in connection with the text of the Introductory
chapter.   Mr. Bradley Batsford has rendered ungrudging assist-
ance at every stage of the undertaking, which has particularly
benefited from his broad and liberal views in regard to the
illustrations.   My thanks are also due to those ladies and
gentlemen who allowed me to examine, and sometimes to
measure and photograph their houses; and I am indebted to
Mr. Chart, the Clerk of Works at Hampton Court Palace,
for much useful information imparted during my investigations
there.

Each illustration is utilized to explain some point in the
text, but in many cases the reference is purposely made short,
the illustration being left to tell its own story.

J. ALFRED GOTCH.

West Hill, Kettering.
   August, 1901.

CONTENTS.

———◆———

LIST OF PLATES.

—◆—

NOTE.—The letters "A.A.S.B." denote that the subject is reproduced from *The Architectural Association Sketch Book*, with authority of the Draughtsman and by permission of the Committee.

LIST OF ILLUSTRATIONS.

———

NOTE.—The letters "A.A.S.B." denote that the subject is reproduced from *The Architectural Association Sketch Book*, with authority of the Draughtsman and by permission of the Committee.

———

.

A.R. *b*

EARLY RENAISSANCE ARCHITECTURE
IN ENGLAND

CHAPTER I.

INTRODUCTORY.

THE progress of style in the mediæval architecture of England was regular and continuous : so much so, that any one thoroughly acquainted with its various phases can tell the date of a building within some ten years by merely examining the mouldings which embellish it. These successive phases, moreover, merge into one another so gradually, that although it has been possible to divide them into four great periods—called Norman, Early English, Decorated, and Perpendicular—yet the transition from one to the other is unbroken, and the whole course of development can be traced as regularly as the change from the simplicity of the trunk of a tree to the multiplicity of its leaves. For about four centuries (A.D. 1100—1500) this growth continued, English architecture finding within itself the power of progression. But about the beginning of the sixteenth century it began to feel the influence of an outside power—that of Italy—which acted upon it with increasing force until, after two centuries, its native characteristics had nearly disappeared, and Italian buildings were copied in England almost line for line.

The object of the following pages is to display the effect of this foreign influence upon our native architecture up to the point when it became predominant, and stamped our buildings with a character more Classic than Gothic. But it will be desirable first of all to glance shortly at the causes which led to Italy having this extraordinary influence, and at the general effect which that influence produced upon England.

England, in common with the rest of North-western Europe, was the home of Gothic architecture, instinct with the mystery and romantic spirit of the Middle Ages. Italy was the home of Classic architecture, which it had cherished since the great days of Rome. The Gothic manner was never thoroughly acquired in Italy, even in those parts which lay nearest to France and Germany, although it affected their buildings to a certain extent. The best examples of Italian Gothic hold a low rank in comparison with the masterpieces of the northern style. Classic forms were those in which the Italian designer naturally expressed himself, and it was these which he employed when that great revival of the Arts which took place in the fifteenth century, set him building. The earlier Renaissance in letters "the spring before the spring," of which the great figures are Dante, Petrarch, and Boccaccio, heralded a great awakening of architectural energy, and Italian architects, in solving their new problems, mingled the results of a deep study of ancient examples with much of mediæval spirit and tendency. They set themselves resolutely to revive the architecture which had been one of the glories of ancient Rome; but they could not, even had they wished it, free themselves from the spirit of their own age, and the result was the development of a kind of architecture which used old forms in new ways, and which has gained the distinguishing title of the Renaissance style.

But the awakening in architecture was only one manifestation of the spirit which was abroad: in painting, sculpture, and all the applied arts, as well as in literature, the same vivifying tendency was at work. With the fall of Constantinople in 1453, an event which flooded Western Europe with Greek scholars and Greek literature, a tremendous impulse was given to the new aspirations. A new world of history and poetry had been discovered, just as, forty years afterwards, a new world of fact and reality was discovered by Columbus and Cabot. The two events combined to excite men's imagination to an extraordinary degree, and their stimulating effect was visible in all branches of mental activity. There was a marvellous mingling of the old and the new. In the past there was an inexhaustible well of knowledge and suggestion; in the present a boundless opening for enterprise and fresh experiences. Just at this juncture the invention of printing was being perfected, and it came at the precise time to help the dissemination of the new ideas. The result was that great movement of the human mind known as the Renaissance, which in the space of a century altered the life of Western Europe. In politics it shattered the international fabric of the Middle Ages; in religion it brought about the momentous change which we call the Reformation; in art it wedded faultless execution with an extraordinary fecundity of design. There followed an age richer, perhaps, than any other in original genius and fertility of mental products. Italy was at the centre of this upheaval. To her were attracted students from all parts of Europe, not excepting England. She herself was teeming with men of talent in all branches of learning and the arts. It was inevitable that she should part with some of her superfluous energy to the surrounding lands, touched as they were, though less intensely, with the new spirit. So general was the enthusiasm that her neighbours were only too glad to welcome whatever Italy could send, even if not of her very best. The new movement eventually reached the distant shores of England, but as the stream flowed across Europe it became tinged with the peculiarities of the various lands over which it passed, and each country can show its own version of the Italian Renaissance in architecture as well as in other matters. Spain has one version, France another, Germany another, and England yet another; and there is this peculiarity about the English version—that it is coloured by the two channels through which it came, France and the Netherlands.

The whole circumstances of the time being conducive to the spread of Italian ideas and forms (which are only the embodiment of ideas), how did they affect English architecture? They found in England a style long established, and still endowed with considerable vigour. At no period of its history had this style been so peculiarly English in its more elaborate efforts, the special development known as fan-vaulting, for instance—of which the finest examples are to be seen in the chapel at King's College, Cambridge, and Henry VII.'s chapel at Westminster (see Plate I.)—being found only in this country.

The Gothic style of England and the Classic style of Italy

had next to nothing in common. Their modes of expression were essentially different. The former was elastic, informal, readily adapted to different needs. Like Cleopatra, it was of infinite variety; its component parts were small and manifold, its tendency was towards well-marked vertical lines. Its outward appearance expressed its inward arrangement: a window more or less, a buttress here, a chimney there—so long as they were wanted—offered no difficulty to the designer. Classic architecture, on the other hand, was formal and restricted by considerations of symmetry; its component parts were simple and less mobile than those of Gothic; its tendency was towards strong horizontal lines. The Gothic string-course, for instance, could jump up and down to adapt itself to a door or window; it broke round projecting piers or buttresses without hesitation. But the classic cornice continued in the same straight line, neither rising nor falling, and only breaking forward round a pier or column after due deliberation. Its projection was far greater than that of any similar feature in Gothic work: it was consequently much less ductile. Compared to Gothic detail, Classic was unwieldy, even that more pliant version of it which had recently been evolved in Italy. The ornament, however, with which the Italian designers so freely adorned their architectural work, unlike that of the ancients, was generally small in scale and elastic in character. Here, therefore, was a feature common to both styles, and we shall find that it is in the ornament of buildings that the change first took place. It will be seen that the progress of the new style was very gradual: it showed itself first in small objects, such as tombs and chantries, and in the unimportant detail of larger buildings; then it affected the more significant detail; and ultimately, after many years, it controlled the organic conception and expression: but this final development did not take place till after the close of the period which we are to consider. That which we are to watch is the struggle of the old and the new: the encounter of the new spirit steeped in classical learning, with the old Gothic traditions and methods.

The great monuments of English Gothic architecture are to be found in ecclesiastical buildings; those of the succeeding phase are domestic in character. The change of thought in religious matters, which was proceeding all through the sixteenth century, was not favourable to church building, and

after the dissolution of the monasteries by Henry VIII. no
more churches were built.   But the new nobility, rich with the
spoils of the dissolved houses and the traffic of the Indies,
had acquired a taste for grandeur and dignity in outward life
that required great mansions for its display.   It is therefore
primarily in the Elizabethan mansion that we must watch the
contest between the old style and the new—a contest rendered
more piquant by the fact that the new style had no experience
of this particular kind of building in the land of its origin. ·
The English house had developed on lines widely different
from the Italian ; it had to meet other wants, it had to contend
with a different climate, it was subject to other traditions.
The new style when it came, had to harmonize these strange
traditions as well as its own, derived from a far distant past,
with the original and fertile spirit of the age.   The result
is one of abiding interest.   Almost any of the great houses
built in the reign of Elizabeth will show to the casual spectator
examples of crudity in detail and imperfect classical proportion,
mingled with reminiscences of Gothic notions ; but a deeper
scrutiny will disclose the fact that in spite of these short-
comings there is a national individuality and sense of genius
in the handling of materials sufficient to raise the result to the
dignity of a distinct style.   Just as the " Faërie Queen " shows
a jumble of heathen gods and cardinal virtues, Christian
knights and Pagan nymphs, and yet withal is a consummate
work of art, so the buildings of the period—

> "With many towers, and terrace mounted high,
> And all their tops bright glistering with gold,"

in spite of their inconsistencies, have a fertility of fancy, a
wealth of ornament, and a simplicity of treatment which
raise them to a similar high plane.   And just as the literature
of the period, as it became more in accordance with rule, lost
half its originality and more than half its fascination, so
Renaissance Architecture, as it passed from the Elizabethan
to the Jacobean, and so to the succeeding phases, became
more homogeneous, more scholarly, more true to its classical
origin, and yet withal lost vitality in the process.   The full
meaning of that great century which stretched from the
divorce of Henry VIII. to the accession of Charles I. cannot
be grasped unless it is always borne in mind that not only was

a new style supplanting an old one, but that it was doing so at a time when the originality and richness of men's minds were at their height.

But while in England the new style was winning its way, in Italy it was passing the zenith of its vigour. The continued study of ancient monuments enabled architects to reduce the old methods of design to a system which could be acquired with ease, and architectural design became less a matter of invention than a capacity for adapting new buildings to old rules. In course of time the same state of things established itself in England. The invention of printing brought to the eye of English craftsmen not only plans and pictures of buildings recently erected in foreign lands, but also the rules which celebrated Italian architects had laid down for the proportion of buildings generally—rules founded partly on the study of ancient fabrics and partly on the august authority of Vitruvius. The application of these rules to circumstances and needs which had never been contemplated by their authors was the problem which English designers set themselves to solve. During the earlier years of their attempt they were almost baffled. Then came Inigo Jones and Sir Christopher Wren, and by their commanding genius they made the rules bend to their will; but in the eighteenth century the rules triumphed completely, and, as already said, Italian buildings were copied in England almost line for line. It is the work of the men who were baffled that we are now to examine: work which, judged from the standpoint of their better tutored successors, may almost be regarded as a failure, but work which exhibits a vitality, a fancy, and a sense of romance for which we look in vain in the more correct architecture of the eighteenth century.

It is not surprising that England, in common with the rest of Europe, should have felt the influence of Italy. It is, perhaps, rather a matter for wonder that she should not have felt it earlier; that the architectural Renaissance should have continued for more than a century, and have reached its prime in Italy before it landed on our shores and began to touch the more susceptible places of our English stonework. But Brunelleschi, who crowned the cathedral of Florence with its dome, and reared the Pitti Palace, had been dead seventy years; the delicate sculpture on the façade of the Certosa of

Pavia was five-and-twenty years old ; and Venice was busy lining her canals with palaces, when Torrigiano brought the first Italian forms to England and applied them to the tomb of Henry VII. in Westminster Abbey.

But the way had been paved beforehand. For some fifty years it had been the custom of English scholars to repair to Italy to learn the humanities. They returned home familiar, if not in love, with Italian ideas and methods of expression, and if they themselves did nothing outwardly to hasten the impending change, it was their poverty and not their will which consented to inaction. Fine building requires money, and accordingly it is in the work of monarchs, noblemen, and great dignitaries of the Church that we find the first evidences of the Italian invasion. Henry VIII. was the outward and visible, although unconscious, agent who guided the new movement to our shores. His great Cardinal, Wolsey, was not less active in building, but Henry was the royal patron, vying with other monarchs in obtaining the services of distinguished artists to adorn his surroundings. Now most of the distinguished artists at that time were foreigners, hailing chiefly from Italy. There were plenty of excellent English workmen it is true, but it was the fashion to employ Italians. Henry's rival, Francis I. of France, had secured the services of several such men ; why not he ? So his efforts were frequent, although they met with comparatively small success. Italians were loth to leave their own sunny surroundings, where all men were in sympathy with them and their ways, for the chilly fogs and the barbarous manners of those " beasts of English," as Cellini called them. A few men complied with his requests ; of these, Torrigiano was the most celebrated. To him Henry entrusted the making of his father's tomb, discarding the design approved by the dead monarch, and taking the work out of the English hands already engaged upon it. None of the other Italians whose names have been preserved have left any great or permanent mark in the country to which they came unwillingly, and which they left gladly. The other great foreign figure which stands out among those of minor importance is that of a German, Holbein. But though Holbein did much work in England in different branches of art, he left no school, nor can the influence of his manner be traced far, if at all, beyond his death. Names of Italians appear occasionally as being employed by the King, and among them John of Padua occurs most frequently; but no one knows who he was, nor what work he left behind him. His name has often been attached to different buildings, and he has been confused with John Thorpe, but no evidence has yet been adduced actually connecting him with work that still survives. One of the curious and provoking facts about the early years of the Renaissance manner in England is the way in which Italian names elude pursuit. Work which looks as though it must have been done by a foreigner has no name that can be attached to it. Other work, which is almost as foreign in appearance, is found on investigation to be that of an Englishman.

Henry's rivalry with Francis I., his friendship and his feuds with that monarch, seem to have had some effect on architectural ornament, for much that was executed during Henry's lifetime has a French flavour about it. It is curious, indeed, to observe how little hold actual Italian detail obtained upon the fancy of English workmen. It was not direct from Italy that they would take it. The Italians were not liked by the English people at large; protests were raised by the more thoughtful against the Italianizing of our young nobles. The popular conception of the subtle Italian was embodied by Shakespeare in Iachimo and the more infernal Iago. What Italian detail we find in Henry VIII.'s time is chiefly superficial ornament, and even that is by no means of universal application. It is to be found up and down the country in considerable quantity, but side by side with work which is still thoroughly Gothic in character. Islip, the Abbot of Westminster, who laid the foundation stone of Henry VII.'s chapel, and who saw the erection of that monarch's tomb—the great central feature for which the chapel was built—was not sufficiently enamoured of the new ornament to cause his own tomb to be of the same character. On the contrary, the screen which encloses his chapel is free from any touch of actual Renaissance detail, although erected some fifteen years after Henry VII.'s tomb.

It was through Dutch and German channels that the Italian manner came to stay. This was the result partly of ties of race and religion, partly of commercial intercourse, and partly of the general imitation of Dutch methods which prevailed in England during the latter half of the sixteenth century. In commercial and political as well as naval and military matters this imitation is well known to students of that period. The character of Renaissance work in England during Henry VIII.'s time inclined to Italian and the French version of Italian. After his death it inclined towards the Dutch version. In both cases it was strongly infused with English feeling ; but there is this difference, that whereas the earlier phase ended abruptly, no merging of it into the latter being traceable, the second phase can be followed step by step into the pronounced Italian of Inigo Jones's mature manner. We can see how some features were dropped and others acquired, until, by the double process of shedding and assimilation, the style of Burghley House glides imperceptibly into that of the Banqueting Hall at Whitehall.

CHAPTER II.

THE INVASION OF THE FOREIGN STYLE.

In order properly to understand the position of the Elizabethan mansion in the story of architectural development, it is necessary to examine the work which intervenes between it and the last of the Gothic period.

1.—Tomb of Prince Arthur (d. 1502) in Worcester Cathedral.

The first work with Renaissance detail that was done in England was the tomb of King Henry VII.—the actual altar-tomb, not the metal screen enclosing it. There is no foreign influence to be detected either in the screen or in the wonderful fan-tracery vault that spreads itself above (Plate I). These are essentially English productions, and yet there are certain parts of them which would lend themselves readily to the new - fashioned detail which was about to invade our shores; parts which in subsequent buildings were actually affected by it. But so far, that is up to the year 1509, when the king died, the chapel being still unfinished, there is no Renaissance detail. Nor is there any in the fine chantry in Worcester Cathedral, wherein King Henry's eldest son, Prince Arthur, who died in 1502, lies buried (Fig. 1). The utmost that can be said is that here, as in the chapel at Westminster, the Gothic work is preparing to succumb to the new influence. It has been suggested that the king's own tomb was erected subsequently to that of his mother, the Countess of Richmond, who also lies in the Abbey.

But the question is one of little importance ; no long period can separate the two, and the important point is that the actual invasion of the foreign style is a well-marked event, the circumstances attending it are on record, its results still survive in an excellent state of preservation.

Henry VII. says in his will, dated 31st March, 1509, that he had arranged for his tomb to be made in a certain manner,* and

2.—TOMB OF ONE OF THE COKAYNE FAMILY, ASHBOURNE CHURCH, DERBYSHIRE. FIFTEENTH CENTURY.

from other sources we gather that the men who were to do the work were certain English craftsmen, of whom Lawrence Imber, carver; Drawswerd, sheriff of York; Humphrey Walker, founder; Nicholas Ewen, coppersmith; Robert Virtue, Robert Jenins, and John Lebons, master masons, were the chief. The last name is the only one with a foreign appearance, but it is a curious and rather significant fact that the design had been

* Britton's *Architectural Antiquities*, Vol. II.

made by one "Master Pageny," as he was called by his English acquaintances, but whom his own countrymen called Paganino. No other work of Master Pageny's is known in England, but it seems tolerably clear that he is the same

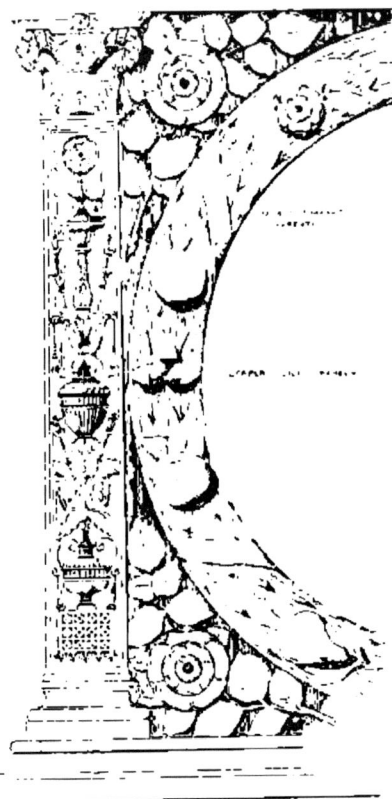

Paganino who designed the tomb of the French King Charles VIII. at St. Denis, and that Henry's tomb was to have been like it.* The project, however, fell through in consequence of the death of the king, and the passing of the control of affairs into the hands of his son, Henry VIII. The new monarch discarded the old design entirely, and entrusted the work to Pietro Torrigiano, or Peter Torrisany, as he became on English lips. Torrigiano's design departed widely from English traditions. The leading idea of recumbent figures upon an altar-tomb was retained—this idea indeed held the field for another three-quarters of a century—but the old practice of adorning the sides of the tomb with cusped panels, or figures of saints in niches, or angels holding shields

3.—HENRY VII.'s TOMB. DETAIL.

* _Archæological Journal._ 1894. " On the work of Florentine Sculptors in England." by Alfred Higgins, F.S.A.

of arms (Fig. 2), was abandoned; and instead of the restrained architectural treatment of the English tradition, where the figures were soli-

tary, and every fold of drapery harmonised with the main architectural members, Torrigiano gave us the free treatment of the Italian sculptors. The general arrangement of the panels is simple enough (Plate II.) There are three circular wreaths on each of the longer sides of the

4.—TOMB OF JOHN HARRINGTON (D. 1524), EXTON CHURCH, RUTLAND.

tomb, divided by Italian pilasters adorned with arabesques, into which the rose and portcullis of the Tudors are introduced.

A rose also fills each of the four spandrils formed by the circular wreaths. These wreaths were new to English eyes; so, too, was the treatment of the spandrils, where the flower is simply applied to the triangular space, instead of appearing to be

5.—TOMB OF THOMAS CAVE (D. 1558), STANFORD CHURCH, NORTHAMPTONSHIRE.

a growth on the structure itself in the old Gothic way (Fig. 3). The panels themselves contain figures in action, figures which have cast away conventional attitudes and stiffness of attire, and comport themselves in the most natural way imaginable. Henry's patron saints are there to the number of ten, but

6.—Tomb of Thomas Cave (d. 1558). End Panel.

instead of standing in niches, statuesque and motionless, they are grouped in pairs, every pair seeming interested in a common subject, instead of each individual being rapt in solitary contemplation. As there are six panels, the ten patron saints are supplemented by two other figures—the Virgin with the Child, and St. Christopher. Another novelty appears in the shape of the four cherubs

7.—Tomb of Sir George Vernon (d. 1567), Bakewell Church, Derbyshire.

poised at each corner of the tomb; they have no niches or other architectural background; they are detached pieces of sculpture, self-reliant ; their purpose, which they no longer fulfil, was to hold banners, but these have long disappeared.

The change of idea is complete, but it is a change that never took hold of English craftsmen. They adopted the circular wreaths and the arabesqued pilasters, and so far as those features are

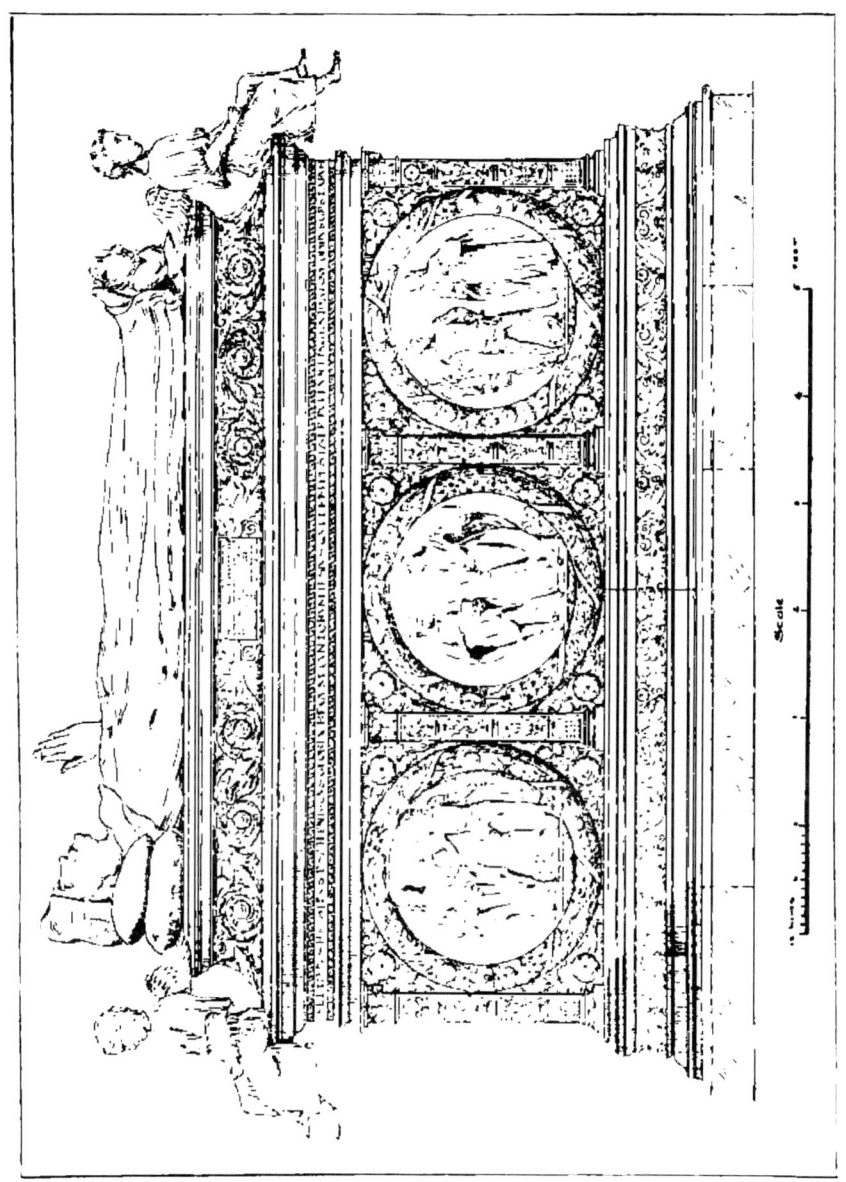

HENRY VII.'S TOMB IN WESTMINSTER ABBEY. SOUTH SIDE (1516).

concerned we see in this tomb the prototype of many that followed after. But the figures in action do not appear again. English tradition was too strong for the Italian influence to overcome it, and the principal way in which it was affected was that the panels became frequently divided by pilasters instead of by moulded members; and that the angels, which had hitherto been solitary and devout, took on the attitude of heraldic supporters, and assumed a more mundane

8.—TOMB OF SIR THOMAS ANDREW (D. 1563), CHARWELTON CHURCH,
NORTHAMPTONSHIRE.

appearance, or endeavoured to imitate the amorini of Italian craftsmen—an effort for which they were, as a rule, too elderly.

The dividing pilasters were sometimes nothing more than spiral columns, and such a column is occasionally the only sign of the new feeling. In the tomb of John Harrington, who died in 1524 (Fig. 4), a spiral column at the angles and a certain stiffness in the cusped panels indicate the impending change. This change is still more marked in the Cave tomb (Fig. 5) at Stanford Church, where (in 1558) the sides have three circular panels containing, however, shields of arms, not figures, and the upper end exhibits the family shield supported by two angels. On the other hand, the opposite end (Fig. 6) shows the family of the deceased gentleman in a number of figures treated with a stiffness of pose and a conventionality of attire that still belong to the ancient style. There is a very similar tomb at Charwelton to Sir Thomas Andrew, who died in 1563 (Fig. 8). In the tomb of Sir George Vernon (Fig. 7), who died in 1567, the angle pilasters, with their vases and portcullises in low relief, recall

those on Henry VII.'s tomb. The middle shield on the end is surrounded by a circular wreath, while the shape of the shield and the strange form of the dividing pilasters show a still further departure from the old detail. In the Bradbourne tomb of 1581 (Fig. 9) panels have disappeared altogether, and the sides of the tomb are occupied by figures of the children, who hold in a stiff and tiring manner, shields

9.—Tomb of — Bradbourne (d. 1581), Ashbourne Church, Derbyshire.

setting forth their marriages. There is a rather curious survival in the tomb of Elizabeth Drury at Hawstead Church, in Suffolk, where, as late as 1610, a shield of arms is supported by two amorini (Fig. 10). All these examples, selected from the tombs to be found in village churches, and covering a period of three-quarters of a century, tend to show that the Italianizing of the English workman, in this branch of art at any rate, was as incomplete as it was slow. The craftsman was, however, aware that a new influence was at work, and he was prepared to succumb to it where circumstances were favourable. In certain districts circumstances were favourable, and accordingly in parts of the eastern and southern counties, notably at Layer Marney, in Essex, there are tombs in which the detail is more decidedly wrought after Italian models (Fig. 11 and Plate III.), although even here the difference is so great that any of them would look strangely out of place if transported to a church in Italy.

The eastern and southern counties appear to have been specially affected by the new movement, for we find considerable traces of it scattered over wide areas, and affecting not only small objects like tombs, but permanent structures. We shall presently see it at Layer Marney Tower, and among other places at East Barsham and Great Snoring in Suffolk; while in Wymondham Church, in Norfolk, the sedilia is made of what appear to be fragments of a tomb much resembling those at Layer Marney in character (Fig. 12). In the southern counties, Sutton Place, near Guildford, abounds in Anglo-Italian

10.—FROM THE TOMB OF ELIZABETH DRURY (D. 1610), HAWSTEAD CHURCH, SUFFOLK.

detail; some of the woodwork at the Vyne, in Hampshire, is also affected by it. There is some very interesting work of the same nature at the Chapel of the Holy Ghost, at Basingstoke; while at Christchurch, in the same county, the chantry of the Countess of Salisbury is strongly touched with the Italian influence, and at St. Cross, near Winchester, are the very beautiful fragments of a Renaissance screen (Plate VII.). Winchester itself has some good work in the choir of the Cathedral; and still further west, at Bingham Melcombe, in Dorset, there is a charming gable of mixed English and Italian detail. At Lacock Abbey, in Wiltshire, there is a considerable amount of Renaissance work, wrought when the abbey buildings were converted into a dwelling-house soon after the dissolution of the monasteries.

Some of this work is in stone and some in wood, but some of it is in terra-cotta, and it would be an interesting task to

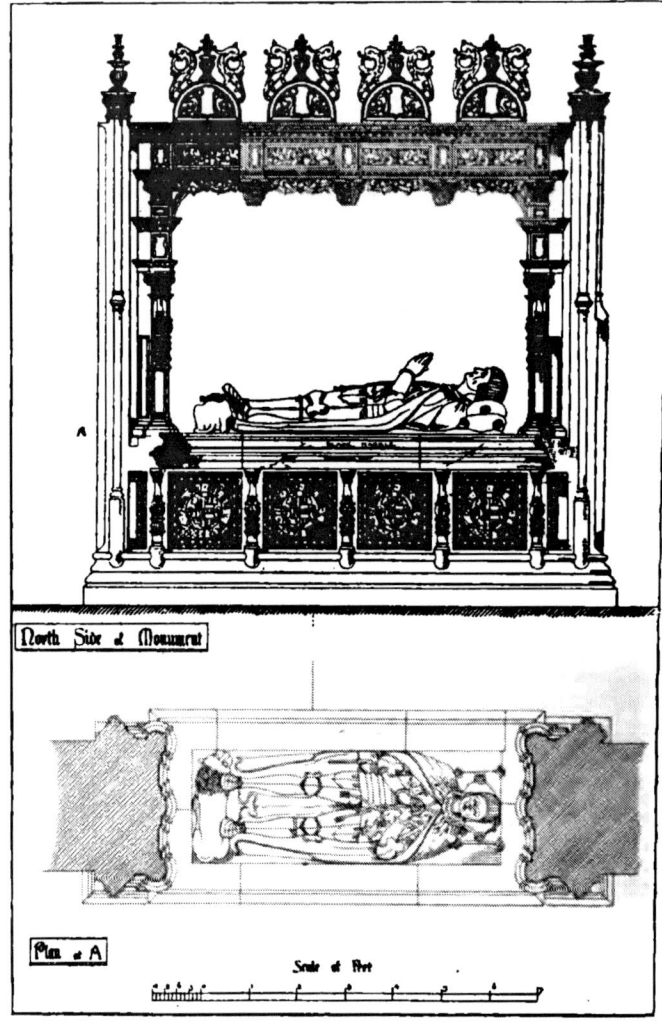

North Side of Monument

Plan of A   Scale of Feet

11.—TOMB OF HENRY, LORD MARNEY (D. 1523), LAYER MARNEY CHURCH, ESSEX.

ascertain why this pronounced detail should have been largely
confined to these particular districts. The stone and woodwork might have been carved by itinerant Italians wandering
some distance from their ports of debarkation; but the terra-

PLATE III.

DETAILS FROM THE TOMB OF HENRY, LORD MARNEY.

PLATE IV

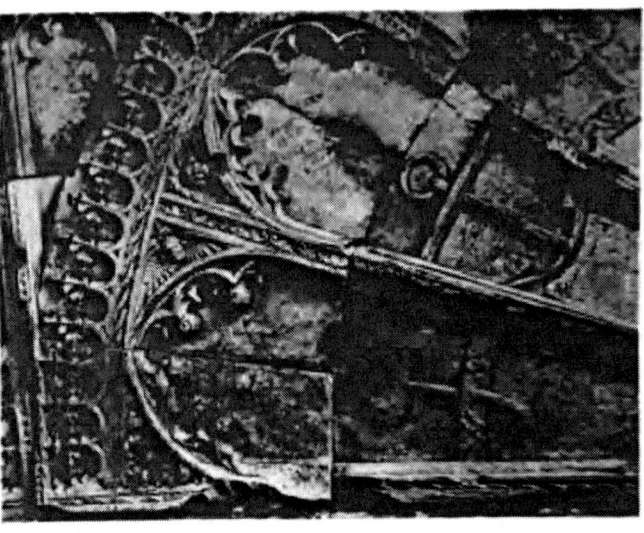

COWDRAY HOUSE, SUSSEX.
FAN VAULTING OF PORCH.

CHAPEL OF THE RED MOUNT, KING'S LYNN.
FAN-VAULTING.

cotta must have been cast, and need not have been cast close to where it was fixed, but abroad, and thence conveyed to almost any part of the country. Nevertheless, none of the work entirely loses its English character, whether it was done abroad or not.

Some of it must certainly have been wrought by Italians, but about much of it the general impression produced is that it was done by Englishmen with Italian proclivities, rather than by Italians under English orders.

12.—FROM THE SEDILIA, WYMONDHAM CHURCH, NORFOLK.

Nor was the foreign detail on the stone simply added to the English work after the native craftsmen had finished. It was not that the Englishman completed his work and then invited the Italian to come and do the carving after his own manner, but the two influences are curiously mixed. Take the fan-vaulting of the porch at Cowdray (Plate IV.), for instance. In general appearance it is of the same family as other fan-vaulting, of which the roof of the Chapel of the Red Mount at King's Lynn may be taken as a specimen. But, as might be expected, it is in the susceptible parts of the stone-

13.—COWDRAY HOUSE, SUSSEX. VAULTING RIB TO PORCH (CIR. 1540).

work that the foreign influence first shows itself,—not in the construction, but in the ornament. The spandrils at Cowdray are filled with carving; some of it is foliage, treated in the Late Gothic manner, but in one appears the head of a winged cherub, clearly not of English but Italian descent. The main ribs of the vaulting, too, have an Italian arabesque worked on them, and the point to be observed here is that the section of the rib is not of the usual type, but is expressly designed to receive the arabesque (Fig. 13).

In the Countess of Salisbury's chantry at Christchurch it is much easier to imagine the Italian carver following the English mason, and adding his ornament to the other's work, for nearly all of it lies in sunk panels, the highest parts of the carving being on the same face as the surrounding margin : that is to say, the Italian found plain surfaces between the moulded members left for him to carve, and one set of these plain surfaces, on the side next to the choir, he did not carve—they still remain bare. Take away the ornament, and the chantry in general design and treatment is Late English-

14.—Chantry of the Countess of Salisbury, Christchurch, Hampshire, from the North Aisle (cir. 1529).

Gothic (Fig. 14), such as no Italian would have produced, if we except the topmost stage on the choir side, where there are two domed pinnacles of rather clumsy and unintelligible design (Plate V.). One of these has a curious feature—the somewhat

PLATE V

THE SALISBURY CHANTRY, CHRISTCHURCH
VIEW FROM THE CHOIR.

15.—THE SALISBURY CHANTRY, CHRISTCHURCH. DETAIL OF CARVING.

16.—PRIOR DRAPER'S CHANTRY, CHRISTCHURCH. HEAD OF DOORWAY (1529).

vulgar product of the later Italian carvers—namely, the lower drapery and the feet of a figure ascending into clouds, all executed in complete relief. On the north side, next the aisle, are some shields in the spandrils between the niches (Plate VI.), carved in the Italian spirit, and these can hardly have been added afterwards, but must have been an integral part of the design. The arabesques on the vertical shafts and in the horizontal bands might very well have been carved by a man put on for that purpose only (Fig. 15). Altogether, it is difficult to adjust with any accuracy the claims of the English and Italian workmen; it would almost seem as though they worked together, or at any rate with a cordial understanding between them. The same may be said of the screen to Prior Draper's chantry (dated 1529) in the same church. The general design is Gothic, and while the arabesque enrichments may have been added afterwards, and the spandrils of the flat-pointed door, the same can hardly be said of the corbels to the niches over it (Fig. 16). The cresting along the top of this screen exactly resembles that over the screens at the sides of

17.—CHRISTCHURCH HAMPSHIRE. MISERERE SEATS.

PLATE VI.

THE SALISBURY CHANTRY, CHRISTCHURCH.
DETAIL OF NICHES ON NORTH SIDE.

the choir at Winchester Cathedral, except that the latter has
not a battlemented finish (Fig. 20).

Although it is not difficult to imagine an Italian carving this
stonework at Christchurch, it is not quite so easy to attribute
the interesting choir-stalls to him or a compatriot, for the
Gothic feeling is too pronounced, and the angel and cherubs
are not lissom and
graceful enough to have
descended from an
Italian sky.

The divisions be-
tween the miserere
seats (Fig. 17) are
thoroughly Gothic in
general treatment and
in their mouldings, but
in the carving the
Italian hand shows
itself, although sub-
dued to the Gothic sur-
roundings in which it
worked. Some of the
desk ends are traceried
and cusped, and some
have vases and foliage
after the Italian man-
ner. But here again the
two *putti* which turn
their backs in so uncere-
monious a way (Fig. 18)
can hardly be the work
of Italian chisels.

18.—CHRISTCHURCH, HAMPSHIRE. BENCH-END IN CHOIR.

It is equally difficult
to assign the beautiful panelling in the long gallery at the Vyne
to a foreigner (Fig. 19); there is so much English feeling about
it. The work conveys the impression that the carver was more
at home with his linen panels than with the Italian flourishes
with which he supplemented them; but the single panel over the
door is evidently the work of a hand thoroughly familiar with
the Italian method. We see the same mixed character wherever
we look; we can point to no work—not even Henry VII.'s

R.A.   C tomb—and say, " This is wholly Italian." There is always a strong English feeling, and sometimes it is only a touch here and there which shows the foreign influence.

The same remark applies to the stone screens at the sides of the choir at Winchester (Fig. 20). They are Gothic in general

19.—DOORWAY AND PANELLING IN THE GALLERY AT THE VYNE, HAMPSHIRE (BEFORE 1530).

treatment, but a little Italian carving is introduced in the cresting along the top. They were the work of Bishop Fox in 1525, who evidently had a hankering after the foreign ornament in his life, although his own chantry, in which he lies buried, is free from it ; for in the neighbouring church at St. Cross are the fragments of some very beautiful screens containing charming

Italian work (Plate VII.). The history of these fragments is not known, but from the occurrence in them of the pelican, which was Bishop Fox's badge, they seem to be due to him, and they may possibly have come from the cathedral itself. They do not belong to their present situation, and one of the main posts is worked with a return at a very obtuse angle, indicating some such polygonal disposition as the east end of the cathedral has. On the top of the choir-screens in the cathedral are placed six oak chests, called mortuary chests, procured by Fox, in which

20.—SCREEN ON NORTH SIDE OF CHOIR, WINCHESTER CATHEDRAL (WITH MORTUARY CHEST), 1525.

are deposited the bones of various benefactors. They are of Italian workmanship (except two which replaced the old ones in the seventeenth century), and are suggestive as being one of the sources of inspiration to native carvers. One of them is shown in Fig. 20, and just behind it can be seen the cornice of the chantry of Bishop Gardiner, who died in 1555. The portion visible is of well-developed classic character, and indicates how the use of the foreign forms had progressed during the thirty years that had elapsed since Fox's time. Even here, however, the pinnacle at the corner—the head of a heraldic animal on a

21.—CANOPY OF STALLS, HENRY VII.'S CHAPEL,
WESTMINSTER.

pedestal—shows how the designer was unwilling or unable to shake off all the trammels of his native style.

At Basing Church, in Hampshire, there is yet another example of the same limited use of Italian detail in the Paulet tombs, which are constructed in the thickness of the side-walls of the chancel (Plate VII.). The arches over the tombs and the doorway in the wall are all flat-pointed, and the spandrils are filled with Renaissance carving, which, in the case of the large arches, surrounds the arms of the founder. Except for these touches, and for the cresting along the top, which recalls that at Winchester, the detail is all Gothic. The large panel in the wall over the doorway seems to be of later date.

Another interesting piece of work of this period is found in the stalls of Henry VII.'s chapel at Westminster. The canopies (Fig. 21) are quite Gothic in character, but of a rather florid description, and although there is no actual Renaissance detail, there

PLATE VII.

PART OF SCREEN, ST. CROSS, WINCHESTER
(PROBABLY DUE TO BISHOP FOX, WHO DIED 1528.)

·PAULET TOMB, BASING CHURCH, HAMPSHIRE.

is a tendency towards it. The caps of the pilasters are also Late Gothic, while the columns are of that honeycomb pattern which is a sign of change towards the new fashion (Fig. 22). There

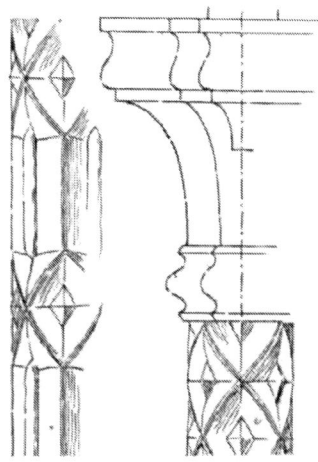

22.—DETAIL FROM STALLS, HENRY VII.'S CHAPEL, WESTMINSTER.

is woodwork of a somewhat similar character at Winchester in Langton's chapel, and in Prior Silkstede's pulpit (1520). The Spring pew in Lavenham Church, Suffolk, is another instance of the late treatment of woodwork. There are niches, canopies, fan-vaulting, and cusped tracery (Fig. 23), but a closer inspection shows that the tracery has completely departed from the simple lines of Gothic work, and has assumed fantastic forms combined of twisted strands and foliage (Fig. 24), while the columns are honeycombed or twisted into spirals.

These examples all tend to show that the old traditions died hard. The new ideas were cautiously accepted, and were utilised to help the existing methods rather than to supplant them. Hitherto it has been fittings, or chantries, or tombs which have furnished examples—comparatively small and isolated pieces of work which naturally lent themselves to experiments. But we find the same general treatment in larger and more important efforts; the native tradition still holds the field, but traces of the new manner are to be found

23.—THE SPRING PEW, LAVENHAM CHURCH, SUFFOLK.

in the spandril of an archway, the termination of a label, or the pendants of a roof. Compare the roof of the hall at Eltham Palace (Fig. 25) with that of the great hall at Hampton Court (1534—35). The roof at Eltham is still Gothic, without a touch of the Renaissance; the roof at Hampton Court is also still Gothic in conception and construction, but in the most susceptible parts—the pendants, the spandrils, and the corbels —the new influence makes itself felt (Fig. 26). These pendants are quite in the new style, and yet were carved by an Englishman, named Richard Rydge, of London.* The spandrils likewise are filled with Renaissance ornament, carved by Michael Joyner, among which the King's Arms and the "King's beasts" appear, treated in the manner customary in Late Gothic work; the Tudor badges are also carved on the pendants and

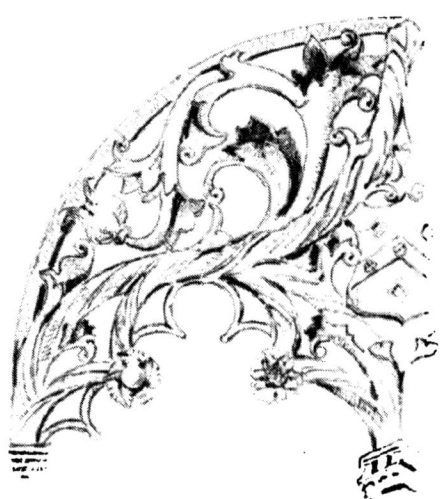

24.—DETAIL FROM THE SPRING PEW, LAVENHAM CHURCH, SUFFOLK.

corbels, amid the cherubs and balusters and foliage which go to compose the Italian ornament (Fig. 27).

Another fine piece of woodwork, which was being executed contemporaneously with the hall roof at Hampton, was the magnificent rood screen in King's College Chapel, Cambridge (Plate VIII.). There is no record as to who did this work, nor when it was done; but the evidence of the arms, initials, and badges upon it, which are those of Henry VIII. and Anne Boleyn, fixes its date between 1532 and 1536. It has been called the finest piece of woodwork this side the Alps, and its

* *History of Hampton Court Palace*, by Ernest Law, Vol. I.

PLATE VIII.

KING'S COLLEGE, CAMBRIDGE.
SCREEN IN THE CHAPEL (1532-6).

exquisite design and workmanship quite justify the description, and even incline one to omit the limiting line. It is more completely Italian in treatment than any other work of the time, and there is very little trace of Gothic influence. All the mouldings are classic, whereas in the roof at Hampton Court even the Italian pendants have a Gothic feeling in their mouldings. There is, however, a considerable similarity in feeling between the pendants in both cases, and it should be borne in mind that the work at the two places was being carried on simultaneously. Richard Rydge, of London, who

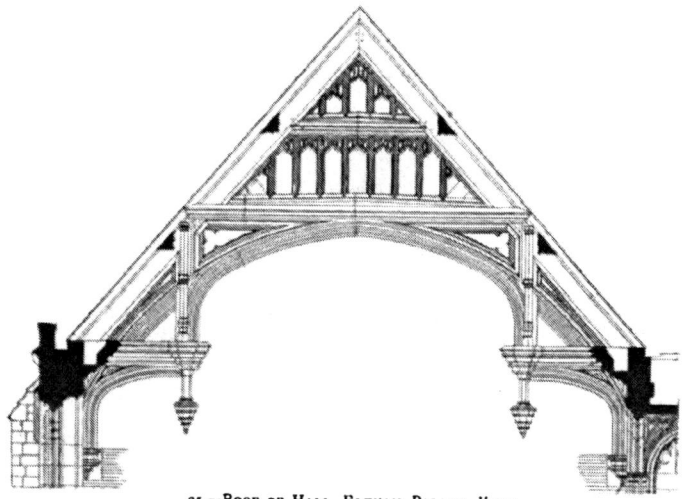

25.—ROOF OF HALL, ELTHAM PALACE, KENT.

carved the pendants at Hampton Court, may have had a hand in the King's College screen; but it is practically certain that the general design and most of the work must have been done by Italians, and the whole screen must be regarded as an isolated example, complete in itself, not growing out of anything that went before it, nor developing into anything afterwards.

The early work at Hampton Court, that is, the work of Wolsey and Henry VIII., executed between 1514 and 1540, is typical of the prevailing manner. This building was the most important one of its time. It was built by the magnificent Cardinal as his principal residence, where he could live amid

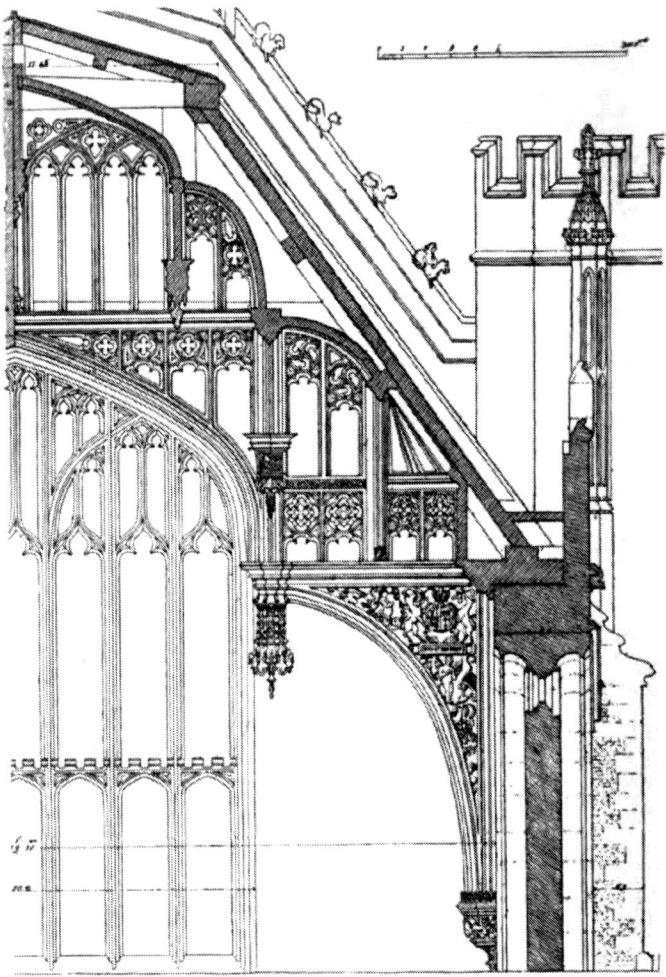

26.—Roof of the Great Hall, Hampton Court (1534—35).

quiet and healthy surroundings, and yet be in close touch with
London, which was the centre of political activity. Wolsey
lived in more than regal state, and the enormous size and
extraordinary splendour of his palace is testified to by many

27.—DETAILS FROM THE ROOF OF THE GREAT HALL, HAMPTON COURT.

foreigners of distinction who resorted to him on some of the
innumerable matters in which he was the controlling spirit.
This great palace he presented to the king some time before
his fall, and the king altered and enlarged it still further, and

made it, as was to be expected, one of his chief residences.
Here, then, we may expect to find the best work that wealth
and skill could produce ; here we may fairly look for typical
work of the time.   What is the character of the work that was
being executed between 1514 and 1540 ?   In its essentials it is
Gothic of a late type, with just such touches of Italian detail as
have been already mentioned.   The structure is of dark red brick,
with stone dressings ; the detail is of the simplest ; the windows
are generally small, and have flat-pointed heads.   Whatever
elaboration there is, is chiefly confined to central features,

28.—Hampton Court. Head of Door to Great Hall.

such as the gateways on the great axial line.   The chimneys
are of cut and moulded brick ; the archways are vaulted with
fan tracery vaulting ; the large windows of the hall are traceried
and cusped ; everything in its main outline is Gothic.   But in
certain parts the ornament is of Renaissance character.   There
are a number of terra-cotta roundels built into the walls, which
came from Italy, and were made to the Cardinal's order.   There
is a terra-cotta tablet of his arms supported by *putti* beautifully
modelled—this was also probably an importation ; it has no
essential connection with its surroundings.   The same may
also be said of the more roughly modelled panels on either side
of the doorway to the chapel, which contain the royal arms

impaling those of Henry's third queen, Jane Seymour, supported by very mundane angels. But there is also, in other
parts of the building, a little Renaissance detail, which is an
essential part of the design, and could not have been brought
from elsewhere and built in. Such is the carving in the
spandrils of doorways (Fig. 28), the pendants of the hall roof,
and the ceiling decoration of certain rooms. This must all
have been wrought on the spot, but it forms an extremely small
part of the whole. While the spandrils of three or four doorways are carved with Renaissance detail, the doorways themselves are in other respects quite Gothic. The hall roof, as
already said, is Gothic in conception, although much of its
ornament is of the newer fashion. The same may be said of the
chapel roof, which is an imitation in oak of some of the stone
vaulting and pendants of the period. The ceilings will be
referred to later, but it may here be said that most of them
are derived from the wood-ribbed ceilings of Late Gothic work,
and that only in the small room called Wolsey's Closet does
the design decidedly follow Italian models. It will thus be
seen that Hampton Court is essentially Gothic in style, and
that only in its susceptible places has it been affected by the
foreign fashion.

What happened at Hampton Court happened elsewhere,
and in all the examples which have come down to us the
same thing is to be seen—a Gothic structure with more or less
of Italian ornament: more in such places as Sutton Court and
Layer Marney Tower, less at Compton Winyates and Hengrave.

There was, however, one building, which has not come down
to us, in which the Italian manner must have been much more
in evidence, judging by such accounts as we have of the place.
This was the palace of Nonesuch, in Surrey. It was built by
Henry VIII. as a retreat, according to Paul Hentzner, the tutor
of a young German nobleman who visited England in 1598.* It
was in "a very healthful situation," he says, "chosen by King
Henry VIII. for his pleasure and retirement, and built by him
with an excess of magnificence and elegance, even to ostenta-
tion ; one would imagine that everything that architecture
can perform to have been employed in this one work ; there are
everywhere so many statues that seem to breathe, so many

* *Hentzner's Travels*, ed. by Horace Walpole

miracles of consummate art, so many casts that rival even the perfection of Roman antiquity, that it may well claim and justify its name of Nonesuch." The site was acquired by the king in 1538,* and as he died in 1547, he must have begun to build almost immediately. According to a statement in Braun's *Civitates* (1582), he " procured many excellent artificers, architects, sculptors, and statuaries, as well Italians, French, and Dutch as natives, who all applied to the ornament of this mansion the finest and most curious skill they possessed in these several arts, embellishing it within and without with many magnificent statues, some of which vividly represent the antiquities of Rome, and some surpass them."† About eight years after Henry's death the house was alienated from the Crown to the Earl of Arundel, and was thereby saved from the destruction contemplated by Queen Mary, who found it too costly to finish. The Earl, however, " for the love and honour he bare to his old master," completed the building and left it to his son-in-law, Lord Lumley, who added a second court. In 1591 it again came into possession of the Crown, and so continued until it was presented by Charles II. to his favourite, Barbara, Countess of Castlemaine, who pulled it down to help towards paying her debts. A few years before this happened Evelyn notes in his diary under date 3rd January, 1666: " I supp'd in None-such House, whither the office of the Exchequer was transferr'd during the plague, at my good friend's Mr. Packer's, and tooke an exact view of the plaster statues and bass relievos inserted 'twixt the timbers and punchions of the outside walles of the Court; which must needs have ben the work of some celebrated Italian. I much admir'd how it had lasted so well and intire since the time of Hen. VIII., expos'd as they are to the aire; and pitty it is they are not taken out and preserv'd in some drie place; a gallerie would become them. There are some mezzo-relievos as big as the life, the storie is of the Heathen Gods, emblems, compartments, etc. The Palace consists of two courts, of which the first is of stone, castle-like, by the Lo. Lumlies (of whom 'twas purchas'd), the other of timber, a Gotic fabric, but these walls incomparably beautified. I observ'd that the appearing timber punchions,

---

* *Gentleman's Magazine*, August, 1837.
† *Archæologia*, Vol. XXXIX., p. 32. Toto del Nunziata was probably one of the Italians.

entrelices, &c., were all so cover'd with scales of slate, that it seem'd carv'd in the wood and painted, the slate fastened on the timber in pretty figures, that has, like a coate of armour, preserv'd it from rotting." Some two and a half years before this visit of Evelyn's, his lively contemporary, Mr. Pepys, had gone through the park to the house and, as he says, " there viewed as much as we could of the outside, and looked through the great gates, and found a noble court." In September, 1665, he was again there, and while waiting about he examined the house, which was, he says, " on the outside filled with figures of stories, and good painting of Rubens' or Holben's doing. And one great thing is, that most of the house is covered, I mean the post and quarters in the walls, with lead, and gilded."

Of all this beautiful work nothing has survived, except a painted panel or two preserved at Loseley, in Surrey, and possibly other fragments in other houses of the district. According to a statement of John Aubrey, the antiquary, some of the materials of Nonesuch went to the building of The Durdans near Epsom. Evelyn calls it a Gothic building, and we shall probably not be far wrong in placing it in the same category as other buildings of the time—English in conception, but adorned with foreign ornament, which in this case was of greater extent and better workmanship than that on any other contemporary house. It seems clear, however, that the work, important as it was, did not have any permanent effect upon English architecture. It was the culmination of the Italian movement prevalent throughout Henry VIII.'s reign; after his death, and before the newness of Nonesuch had worn off, the Italian influence gave way to the Dutch. Nonesuch was a large building, especially after Lord Lumley had added the second court; but it would seem that Henry VIII. actually built but one court, measuring 116 feet long by 137 feet wide.* Hampton Court had four large courts besides half-a-dozen smaller ones; the largest or Base Court, measuring 167 feet by 142 feet, still remains; so also do the Clock Court, measuring 160 feet by 91 feet, and the Chapel Court; the fourth, measuring 116 feet by 108 feet, has given way to Wren's buildings. Hampton Court, therefore, stood without a rival in point of

* *Archæologia*, Vol. V., p. 429.

size, but Nonesuch was more magnificently decorated, and we can but echo Eelvyn's lament that the beautiful panels were "not taken out and preserv'd in some drie place."

Just about the time that Nonesuch was being built, Lacock Abbey in Wiltshire was being converted into a residence by William Sharington, who had bought it on the dissolution of the monasteries. He was lord of the manor in 1540, and he died in 1553,[*] so that all the work which he did must be comprised between those dates. One important part of his work is the octagonal tower at the south-east corner of the house (Fig. 29). The detail of the stonework is simple, and, except for certain brackets, does not show much foreign influence, but in the tower are two stone tables (Figs. 30 and 31), evidently made for

29.—Lacock Abbey, Wiltshire. Tower at South-East Corner (between 1540 and 1553).

their situation, which strongly display the new spirit. That one of them was expressly made for William Sharington is proved by his initials and crest being part of its ornamentation; and as a skilful mason named Chapman was working on the new buildings, it is just possible that he may have carved one or both of these tables. It is the table on the middle floor which has its base ornamented with Sharington's

* "Notes on Lacock Abbey," by C. H. Talbot, *Wilts. Archæolog. and Nat. Hist. Mag.* Vol. XXVI.

initials and crest; from this base rises a central pillar, against which squat four figures of satyrs carrying baskets of fruit and foliage upon which rests the table-top. The satyrs have that curious resemblance about their heads to North American Indians which characterises a number of such figures carved during the latter half of the sixteenth century. The second

30.—Lacock Abbey, Wiltshire. Stone Table in Tower.

table (on the top floor) has nothing about it directly connecting it with Sharington. It was evidently intended for a banqueting house, as it is adorned with figures of Apicius, the first authority on the pleasures of the table, Ceres, Bacchus, and an unnamed personage of the same hierarchy.

Sharington's work is of considerable interest, and includes, in addition to minor matters such as a chimney-piece, chimney-stacks, and panelling, a fine range of stabling

(Fig. 32), of which the detail is tolerably simple, and of a character closely resembling that which prevailed twenty years later, although here and there, in a chimney or a bracket, we get a touch more in keeping with what is usually associated with Sharington's own time. In addition to the Renaissance work in the tables there is some tile paving (Plate IX.) which displays, amid the foliage, the vases and the dolphins that form the staple of Italian ornament, the

31.—LACOCK ABBEY, WILTSHIRE. STONE TABLE IN TOWER.

initials of Sharington and his third wife, Grace, his arms (gu., between two flaunches arg. and az., two crosses formée, in pale), and his crest, a scorpion. As Sir William Sharington died in 1553, and it was during the life of his third wife that these tiles were made, they may fairly be dated about 1550.

With the close of the first half of the century we come to the end of pronounced Italian detail such as pervades the tiles at Lacock, and characterises other isolated features in different parts of the country. The nature of the detail in the second

PLATE IX.

LACOCK ABBEY, WILTSHIRE. TILE PAVING (About 1550).

SEPARATE TILES FROM THE SAME PAVEMENT.

half of the century is different; it no longer comprises the dainty cherubs, the elegant balusters, vases and candelabra, the buoyant dolphins, and delicately modelled foliage which are associated with Italian and French Renaissance work, but

it indulges freely in strap work, curled and interlaced, in fruit and foliage, in cartouches, and in caryatides, half human beings, half pedestals, such as were the delight of the Dutchman of the time. But the extreme heaviness of the Dutch work was lightened in its passage across the water, and the English workmen seem to have improved upon their later models as much as they fell short of their earlier. There is a fine carved and inlaid chest in St. Mary Overie, Southwark, which shows this change in detail (Plate X.),

32.—LACOCK ABBEY, WILTSHIRE. THE STABLES (BETWEEN 1540 AND 1553).

but it is treated with more restraint than the woodwork of later years. It was the gift of Hugh Offley, and bears his initials and marks, as well as his arms and those of his wife's family : he was Lord Mayor in 1556, and is not unlikely to have given the chest in that year.

In addition to the change in the character of the detail, we find a classic rendering of strings and cornices more prevalent ; doorways became frequently round-headed instead of flat-pointed, windows became square-headed, and all accessories parted with what remains of Gothic character they may have possessed in favour of a classic treatment.   But the general body of a building was less susceptible of change than were its particular features, and how the general body of such buildings as houses developed will be seen in the next chapter.

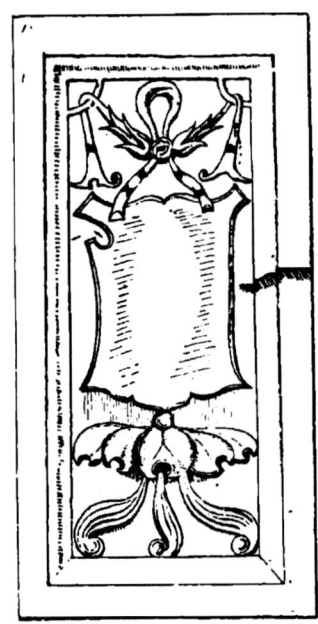

32A.—From the Sedilia, Wymondham
Church, Norfolk.

CHEST FROM ST. MARY OVERIE, SOUTHWARK (DATED 1556).

CHAPTER III.

DEVELOPMENT OF THE HOUSE-PLAN FROM ABOUT 1450 TO 1635.

NOTE.—The plans are drawn to a uniform scale of 50 feet to the inch.

THE principal buildings erected during the sixteenth and early seventeenth centuries were houses, and it is mainly in connection with domestic architecture that we must seek to trace the development of the new style. There were but few churches built after the dissolution of the monasteries, and we have no examples of sufficient importance to show how ecclesiastical architecture would have been affected. There are chapels, chantries, and fittings, such as screens, pews, pulpits, and fonts, but nothing on a large scale. We have already seen how such comparatively small and isolated features were affected. It is necessary, therefore, to look to the numerous houses that were built in order to see what progress the new ideas made.

The character of a house is largely determined by its plan, and the plan is the expression of the wants and habits of the inmates. Accordingly we find that the wants and habits of English people, being far less susceptible of change than their taste in ornament and decoration, caused the plan of their houses to follow the old lines long after the superficial decoration had taken on itself the foreign fashion. The one quality which the Italian influence gradually introduced into the plan was symmetry, and this could be obtained without sacrificing the arrangements which seemed essential to English habits. In later days an Italian feature, the open loggia, was often made use of in the form of an arcade, but even this had its English precedent in the cloisters of the monks.

What were the essential points about the plan of an English house? The most important place was the hall, which was the nucleus of the whole series of apartments. Then there was the kitchen with its adjuncts; and there were the private apartments for the family, of which the chief was the "parlour." The arrangement which naturally established

D 2

itself was that the kitchen should be located at one end of the hall and the parlour at the other. This relation of rooms had existed from a very early period, and it is in the developing of this idea with more or less elaboration and skill that house-planning consisted down to the time of Inigo Jones, when the hall gradually ceased to be the centre of household life, and became merely an entrance.

To the central group of hall, kitchen and parlour were added what other rooms were required for convenience or defence; but in regard to the latter, precautions against attack had already become less necessary in Henry VIII.'s time, and they were practically disregarded in Elizabeth's, when considerations of stateliness and display chiefly influenced the design, at any rate as far as the larger houses were concerned.

Nothing will help to show how the central idea of an English house developed, while tenaciously adhering to its essence, so much as a comparison of the plans of a number of houses built during the sixteenth century and the early part of the seventeenth. But in order to bring them into relation with what preceded them, the series commences with the plans of two houses that were built in the fifteenth century, before there was a trace of Italian influence to be found in English work. All the plans are those of fair-sized houses, chiefly of the manor-house class, and they are from examples scattered up and down the country; therefore whatever characteristics they possess may be taken to have been of fairly wide distribution.

The first example is Great Chalfield, in Wiltshire (Fig. 33), where the work is all of good Perpendicular character. The house was built towards the end of the reign of Henry VI., at a time when precautions against attack were still necessary; it was therefore surrounded by a moat. Much of the work has disappeared, and alterations have been made in what is left, but the arrangement of the hall is still plain, although the kitchen is not recognisable. The almost invariable disposition of the hall was as follows: it was an oblong apartment with one end cut off by a screen, which formed the entrance passage called "the screens." From this passage the hall was entered on one side, while from the other side access was obtained to the kitchen, the buttery, the pantry, and the rest of the servants' department. This arrangement may still be seen in use at many of the colleges in Oxford and Cambridge. The hall itself was usually lighted from both sides, and was a lofty apartment with an open roof, that is, with all the timbers showing. The effect of this disposition was that the hall divided the house into two separate portions; there was no thoroughfare above it or around it, but only through it. At the end opposite to the screens was the daïs, a platform raised some few inches above the general floor level, where the family sat at meals, in the same way as the dons sit in many colleges at the present day. The daïs was usually lighted by a bay window, which formed a convenient recess for a serving table. There are still a few houses where the daïs survives, but in most cases it has been cleared away and the floor has been lowered to the general level. That it was of

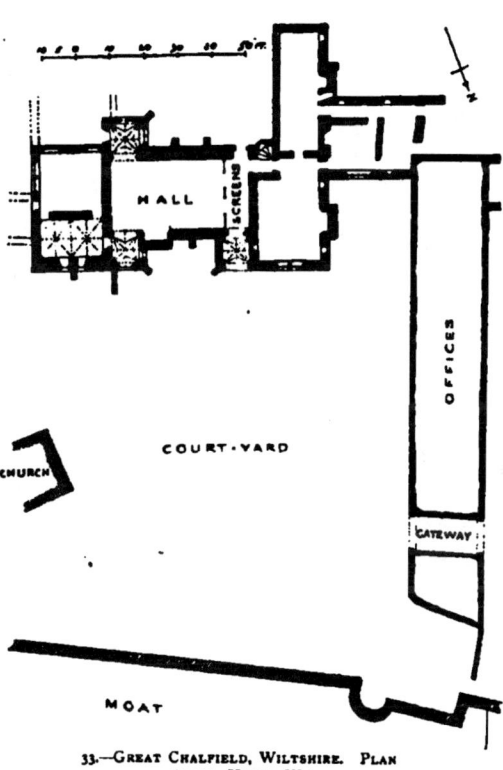

33.—GREAT CHALFIELD, WILTSHIRE. PLAN (TEMP. HENRY VI.).

universal adoption is proved by its being shown on practically all contemporary plans. The fireplace was placed in one of the side walls, and was generally somewhat nearer to the daïs end than the other. It obviously could not be placed at the screen end, because the screen itself did not go up to the roof, but was covered by a gallery, usually known as the minstrels' gallery, though it may be doubted whether in many instances it was used by the votaries of the *gaie science*. Nor could the fire-place be conveniently set in the end wall on the daïs, since it would have interfered with the table; it was necessarily placed therefore in one of the side walls.

These features, then, may be looked for in every hall of the time—the screen, the daïs, the bay window, and the fireplace—

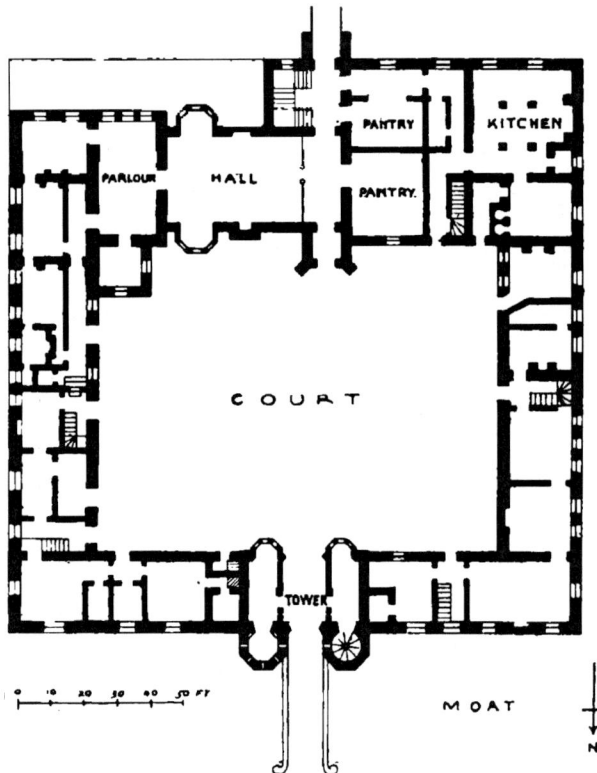

34.—OXBURGH HALL, NORFOLK. GROUND PLAN (1482).

and in some cases a good deal of ingenuity was displayed in contriving to obtain them in their due relation to each other.

From the daïs end of the hall access was obtained to the family apartments, which were few in number at first, but gradually increased with the ever-growing desire for comfort and refinement.

At Great Chalfield the hall conforms to the dispositions detailed above, but the bay windows serve rather as means of communication with other rooms than merely as windows.

At Oxburgh Hall, in Norfolk (1482), we have another type of

35.—OXBURGH HALL, NORFOLK. ENTRANCE TOWER (1482).

defensive house (Fig. 34). It was built round a court, as well as being surrounded by a moat. The entrance was through a lofty tower into the court, on the opposite side of which was the hall of the usual type. The kitchen was to the right on entering, in the extreme south-west corner of the building—not exactly the aspect we should choose in the present day. So

many changes have been made in the use to which the rooms
in these old houses have been put, and in the way of approaching them, that too much stress must not be laid upon the
details of the plan, but the relation of the hall and kitchen
at Oxburgh must have been always the same. The rest of
the building is made up of small rooms surrounding the court,
not arranged on any elaborate plan, but put to whatever use
was required. It will be seen that although there is a considerable amount of uniformity in the arrangement of Oxburgh
Hall, there is no strict symmetry. The entrance tower is in

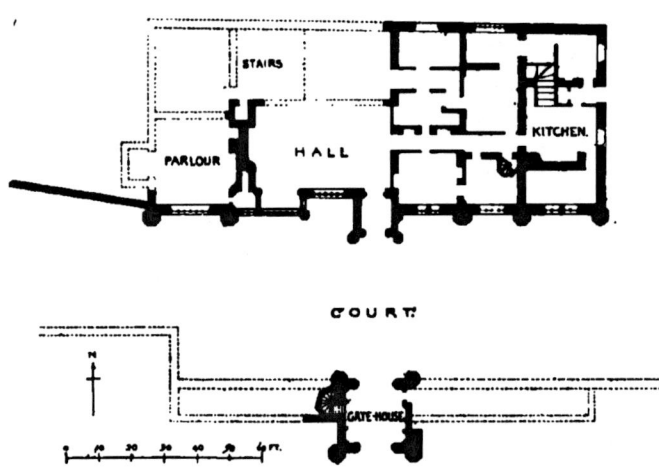

36.—EAST BARSHAM, NORFOLK. GROUND PLAN (CIR. 1500—15).

the centre of the front, but the windows on either side of it do
not tally with each other. The entrance to the hall is not on
the axial line of the tower, nor is the setting of the windows
and doors in the court by any means regular. As we advance
in time, we shall find that all these points were very carefully
attended to, especially towards the end of the sixteenth century.
The plan here illustrated was made in 1774, and a few years
subsequently the south side of the court, containing the hall
and kitchen, was pulled down. Other alterations have been
made since then, but there is still much of the original work
left. The great entrance tower (Fig. 35) shows still a certain
hankering after defensive features; there is a curtain arch

PLATE XI.

COMPTON WINYATES, WARWICKSHIRE (ABOUT 1520).

GENERAL VIEW.

thrown across between the turrets, from behind which missiles could be hurled upon unwelcome visitors, and the openings in the turrets are of the smallest. The windows generally are of few lights, the heads are pointed and cusped, the parapets are corbelled out and battlemented, and the whole work is of Late Gothic character without any trace of the new style in its decoration.

At East Barsham (about 1500—15) we get indications of the new style in the treatment of parts of the ornament. The general feeling, however, is still Gothic. There is not much of the plan to be made out, but what there is shows a large entrance tower, with the porch of the hall exactly opposite to it (Fig. 36). The hall has a bay window at the daïs end, and, contrary to custom, a fireplace in the end wall. The kitchen is to the right on entering, and is approached by a passage from the middle of the screens. The whole arrangement is in the main of the usual type, so far as it can be traced. The new feeling is indicated in one or two panels which bear a head, but most of the ornament is still of the Gothic type with cuspings, etc. At the neighbouring parsonage of Great Snoring, which resembles East Barsham in general treatment, some of the ornament is more decidedly Italian, with the characteristic balusters and foliage.

Compton Winyates, in Warwickshire (about 1520), is a very complete and charming example of its period. The plan conforms in its main features to the ordinary type (Fig. 37). A certain amount of regularity is imparted to it by reason of its being built round a rectangular court, but of symmetry in it there is hardly a trace, and there is still less in the grouping of the structure. Everything is as irregular and picturesque as the most romantic could desire; the mixture of materials— stone, brick, wood, and plaster—lends a delightful variety of texture, tone, and colour, and makes the house, next to Haddon, one of the most alluring in the country (Plate XI.). But our concern at present is more particularly with the plan. This shows a courtyard entered through a gateway which is opposite, though not exactly opposite, to the door of the screens. On the left of the screens are the buttery, the kitchen passage, and a staircase; on the right, of course, the hall, from the upper end of which access is obtained to the family rooms, the chapel, and—what previous plans have not shown—the grand staircase.

Of course, with the lofty hall cutting the building in two
halves, at least two staircases were necessary to get to the
upper rooms ; as a matter of fact there were usually more than
two, as there are here : difficulties of planning being often
removed, or at any rate lessened, by this rather costly expedient.
It will be seen that the hall has a range of rooms at the back of
it, and that its two side walls are not, as usual, both external.
The sides of the court are formed, as they were at Oxburgh, of
a number of small rooms, which originally (in all probability)

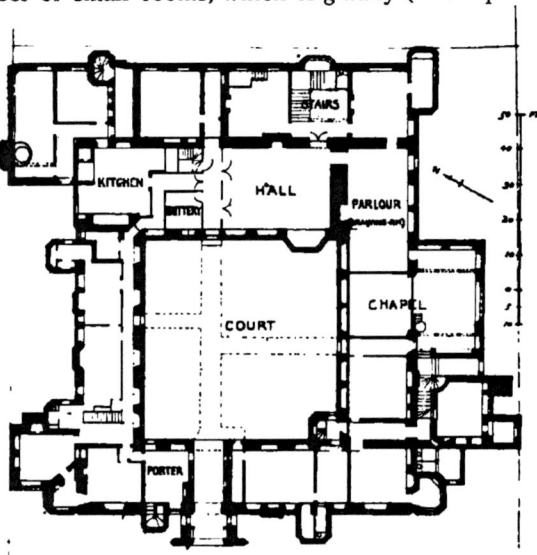

37.—Compton Winyates, Warwickshire. Ground Plan (cir. 1520).

led into one another, the passage being a later addition. The
ornament, in which the house abounds, is all of Late Gothic
character (Plate XII.). There is no actual Renaissance detail
in the external work, although much of it looks as though it
were quite ready for the change.

So far, although we have come to nearly the close of the
first quarter of the century, we have seen but little effect from
the new style. Just a suggestion in the ornament at East
Barsham, and a slight tendency towards a symmetrical treatment of the plan ; yet whatever symmetry there may have
been at East Barsham was thrown to the winds at Compton

PLATE XII.

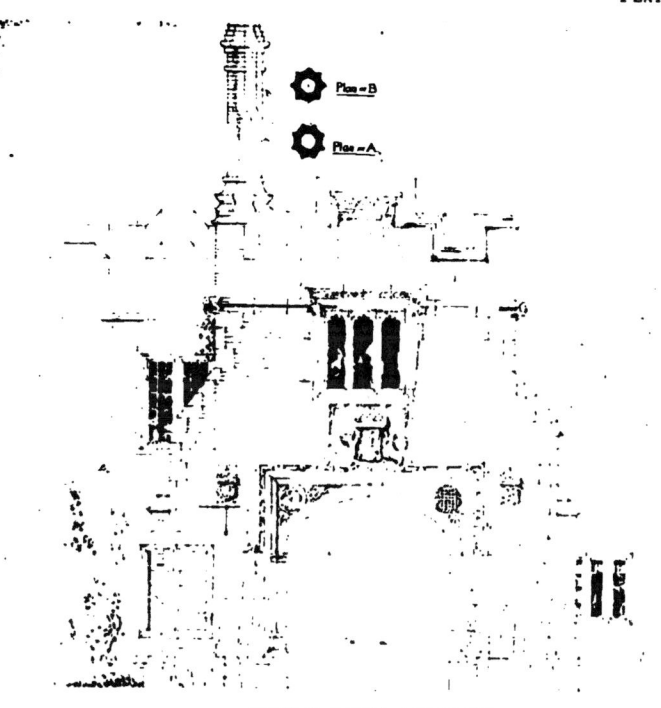

Plan B

Plan A

CENTRAL PORCH WEST FRONT
COMPTON WINYATES.

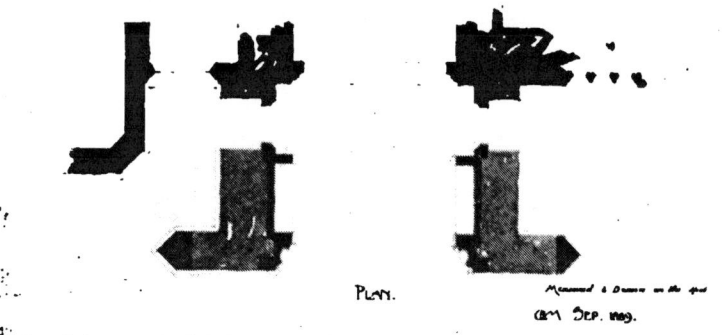

PLAN.

Measured & Drawn on the spot
C.P.M. Sep. 1889.

COMPTON WINYATES, WARWICKSHIRE
THE ENTRANCE PORCH

Winyates. In the next example, Sutton Place, near Guildford, only a few years later in date (1523—25),* we find symmetry in plan and elevation, and ornament which is strongly marked with Italian character. The entrance was as usual through a tower, and faced the hall door exactly opposite, on the axial line (Fig. 38). Such accuracy of alignment was so infrequent at this date, and it results in the hall door being placed so far

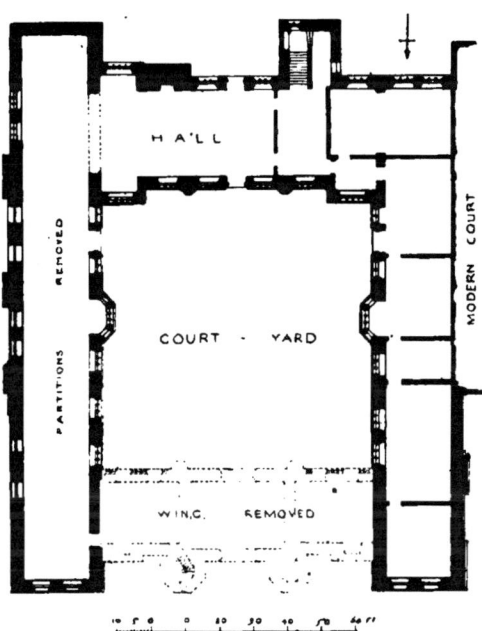

38.—SUTTON PLACE, NEAR GUILDFORD. GROUND PLAN (1523—25).

from the end wall where the screens ought to be, that a feeling of doubt creeps in as to whether we see here the original arrangement unaltered. The hall, too, is of such a height as to embrace two tiers of windows, another most unusual treatment. In the ordinary way the windows would have been made lofty in proportion to the hall. If the existing dispositions have come down unaltered, they are a striking testimony to the manner in which routine of design was broken in order to

* *Annals of an Old Manor House,* by Frederic Harrison.

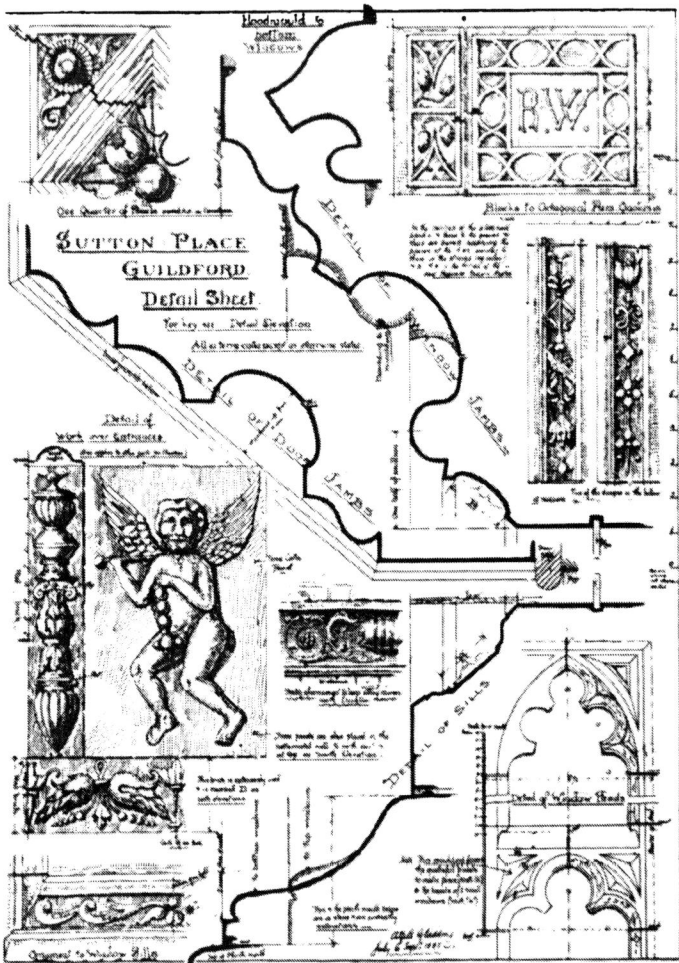

39.—SUTTON PLACE, SURREY. DETAILS (1523—25).

obtain external symmetry. Apart from this point, the plan
adheres to the usual lines. The hall connects the two wings, and
the sides of the court are formed by a series of small chambers
approached either through each other or from the outer air.
The internal walls have either been removed or altered, but the
external walls remain to show that the wings enclosing the court

were only one room thick, and not of sufficient width to allow of a corridor.

There is, however, an important point to be noticed, and that is the symmetrical treatment of the court. Not only is there a little bay window halfway along each side, but the bay window of the hall, which comes in the angle of the court, is balanced by another bay in the other angle, although there is no important room to be lighted by it. Such an arrangement was often adopted in subsequent plans, but this is the first instance which we have seen of it.

While the plan adheres in the main to the customary lines, the ornamentation has taken quite a new departure. The windows are of Perpendicular type, and

40.—SUTTON PLACE, SURREY. PART ELEVATION OF COURTYARD (1523—25).

have the old-fashioned cusping in the heads, but the hollow of the moulding is occupied with ornament drawn from Italian, or

perhaps Franco-Italian, sources (Fig. 39). The house was built
by Sir Richard Weston, and, in accordance with the custom of
the preceding half century, his rebus, or an attempt at it in the
shape of a tun, appears as a diaper in various places and in the
horizontal string-course; but instead of being shrouded in vine
leaves or other old and well-established devices, it occurs among
ornament of the new type. This is a point worth noticing, inasmuch as it shows that this ornament was made for the place,
and was not purchased out of ready-made stock. The amorini
which are introduced over the doors have not the same individuality, nor have the half-balusters which divide them into their
panels, but they were no doubt made by the same men who did
the tuns and Sir Richard's initials, which also help to form a
diaper in places. All this ornamental work is in terra-cotta, but
there is nothing to show where the patterns were cast, whether
in England or abroad. The battlemented parapet is not yet discarded (Fig. 40), and the large octagonal shafts are crowned
with a variation of the dome. Some of the panels are Gothic
quatrefoils, and in the parapet of the central block over the front
door the Italian amorini disport themselves (a little clumsily)
in panels with Gothic cusping. The whole of the ornament
is a curious and interesting mixture of the old and new forms.

Another house with many of the same characteristics is
Layer Marney Tower, in Essex (1500—25). There is not
enough left of the plan to enable us to draw any deductions
from it, but the character of the work is very similar to that
at Sutton, only a little more pronounced in its Renaissance
feeling. The lofty entrance tower recalls that at Oxburgh;
its general appearance, its pointed doorway and windows with
their mouldings, and also the cusped panels of its string-
courses are all distinctly Gothic (Fig. 41). But closely associated with the Gothic panelling is the classic egg and dart
enrichment. The large mullioned windows, though of Gothic
descent, are Renaissance in detail, while the parapets, with their
egg and dart strings, and their dolphins climbing over semicircular panels filled with radiating ornament, are thoroughly
Renaissance of the French type (Plate XIII.). In the moulded
chimneys we go back to the ordinary patterns in vogue in
nearly all houses of the time, whether touched with the foreign
influence or not. The decorative detail here, as at Sutton
Place, is in terra-cotta.

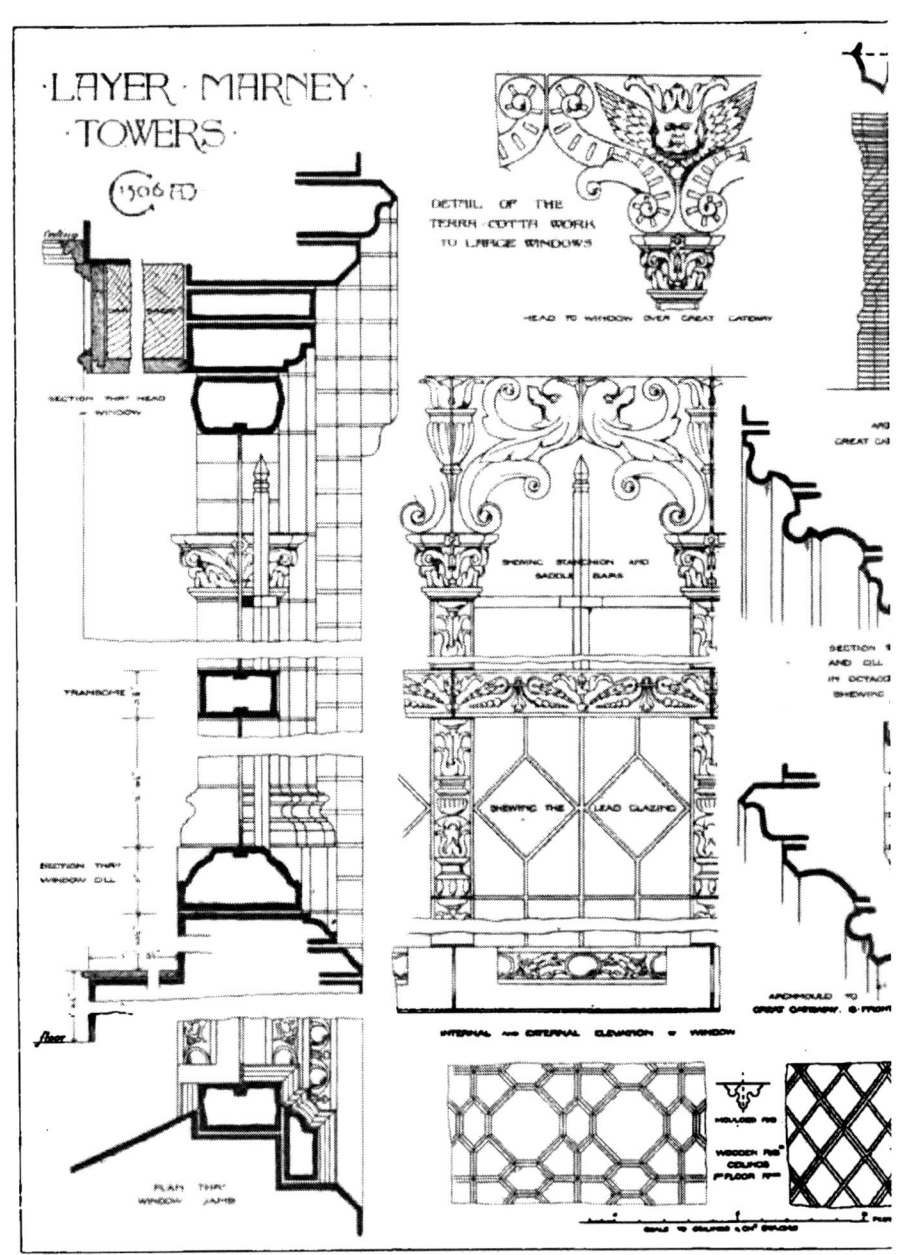

·LAYER·MARNEY·TOWERS· (1506 AD)

DETAIL OF THE TERRA·COTTA WORK TO LARGE WINDOWS

HEAD TO WINDOW OVER GREAT GATEWAY

SECTION THRO' HEAD WINDOW

TRANSOME

SECTION THRO' WINDOW CILL

PLAN THRO' WINDOW JAMB

SHEWING STANCHION AND SADDLE BARS

SHEWING THE LEAD GLAZING

INTERNAL AND EXTERNAL ELEVATION OF WINDOW

ARCH GREAT GAT

SECTION AND CILL IN OCTAG SHEWING

ARCHMOULD TO GREAT GATEWAY, S. FRONT

MOULDED RIB
WOODEN RIB CEILINGS 1ST FLOOR RM

SCALE TO CEILINGS LOW' DRAWING

DETAILS FROM LAYER

PLATE XIII.

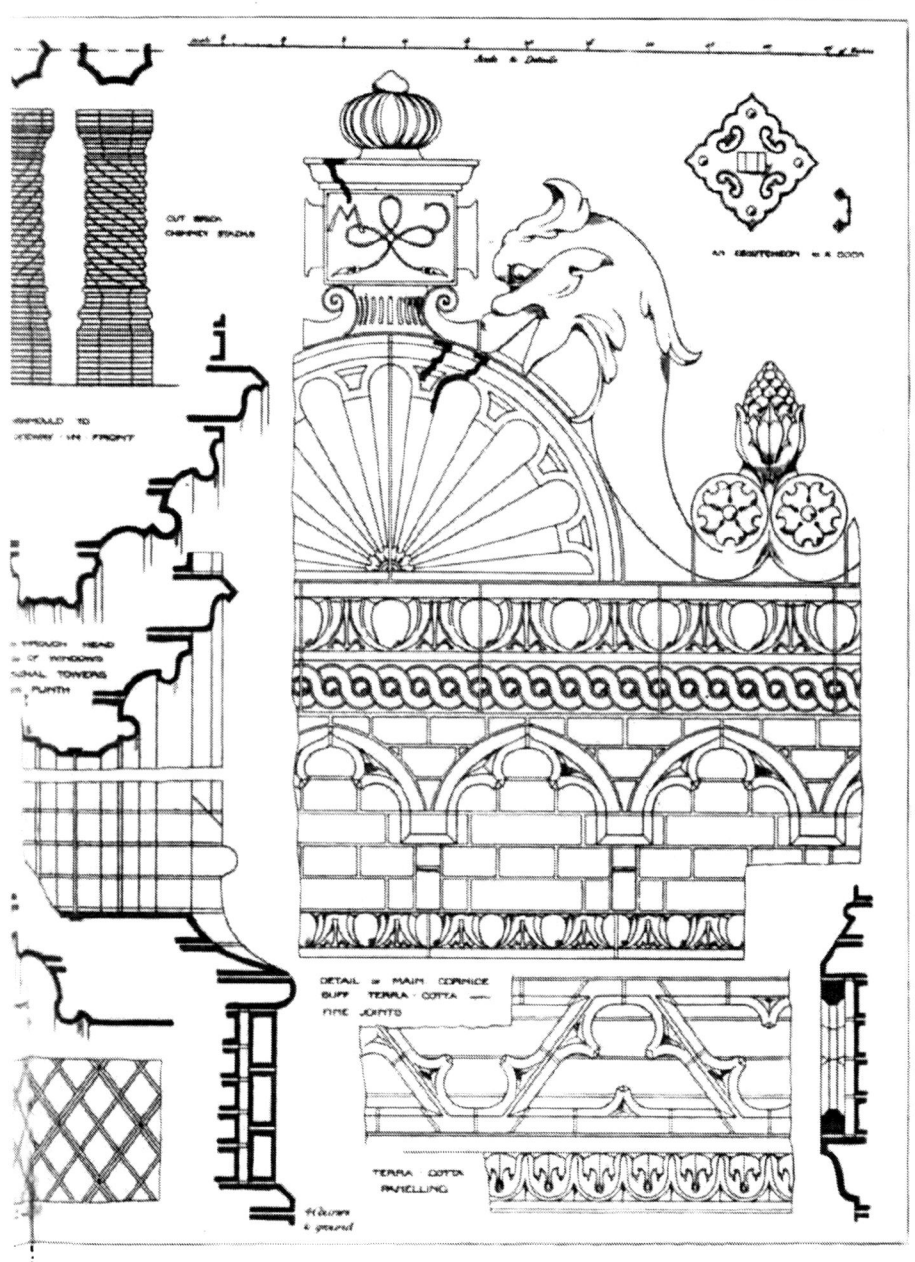

Both these houses were built by men who had spent some time in France. Sir Richard Weston was there more than once, and was among those who were present at the Field of

41.—LAYER MARNEY, ESSEX. ENTRANCE TOWER (1500—25).

the Cloth of Gold. Sir Henry Marney, who built Layer Marney Tower, was one of those attending upon Charles Brandon, Duke of Suffolk, when he took a great army to France in 1522.* But whether they took advantage of these

* "Architectural Notes on Layer Marney Hall, Essex," by C. Forster Hayward. *Trans. Essex Archæolog. Soc.* Vol. III. pt. 1.

journeys to bring back French or Italian workmen with them is not known. Unfortunately there is no documentary evidence to produce, and any opinion that may be formed can only be speculative. One thing is clear; namely, that no school was established over here of men working in the new style. The instances of its use are too few and isolated for that.

At Hengrave Hall, in Suffolk (1538), the main dispositions conform to the usual type, but without any attempt at exact

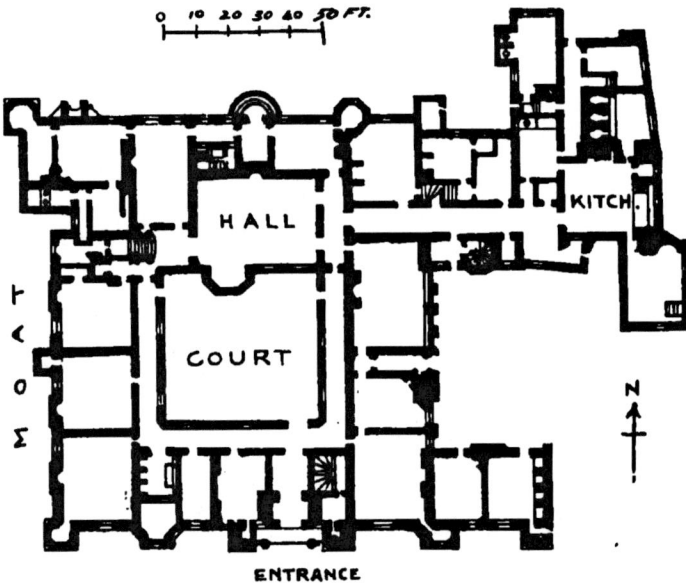

42.—HENGRAVE HALL, SUFFOLK. GROUND PLAN (1538).

symmetry (Fig. 42). The entrance leads into a court, round which a corridor is taken. This feature adds much to the comfort and convenience of the house, but it is a refinement in planning which was very seldom introduced. On the opposite side from the entrance is the hall, with the old position of the screens still preserved; to the right of the screens lies the kitchen wing. There is the usual bay window at the daïs end of the hall, and the family apartments are on the left. Owing to alterations the minutiæ of the original plan cannot now be traced; the general disposition alone can be recognised. The accompanying plan is from one made in 1775, since which time the whole of the kitchen wing has been pulled down and other alterations have been made. The general disposition shown on it may be taken as being like the original, and we see that the entrance is not in the middle of the side of the court, and that in order to obtain a symmetrical façade a wing was carried out to the right, whereby the entrance comes nearly in the centre, though not quite, and is balanced on either hand by projecting turrets corresponding one with the other.

The house was originally moated, and beyond the moat was an outer court, surrounded by low buildings, used as offices and

43.—HENGRAVE HALL, SUFFOLK. WEST FRONT (1538).

stables. It was entered through a gateway or lodge, where the keepers and falconers had their quarters. The general treatment of the architecture still follows the old lines (Fig. 43). The windows, as a rule, have few lights, they have flat-pointed heads, and their total area is relatively small in proportion to the plain surface of brick wall. The chimneys are of cut and moulded brickwork of the prevailing type; the turrets are crowned with a dome-like finish, similar to that which had been used at Henry VII.'s chapel thirty years before. The parapets are battlemented, and the strings are narrow and not of classic profile. In the entrance gateway we find the new note struck (Plate XIV.). The archway is Perpendicular in character, but above it is a triple bay window, supported on corbelling, full of

R.A.   E

Renaissance detail, while amorini in Roman armour carry long scrolls in their hands, and serve as supporters to a shield of arms (Fig. 44). The whole of the corbelling terminates at the bottom in a foliated pendant. This inextricable mixture of the old-fashioned Perpendicular detail with the new-fashioned Renaissance ornament is quite characteristic of the period, and shows that the masons, while clinging to the style with which they had been familiar since their youth, were endeavouring to make closer acquaintance with the foreign forms so much in demand. The names of the masons who did this work are on record : they were John Eastawe and John Sparke, evidently Englishmen.[*]

44.—HENGRAVE HALL, SUFFOLK. CORBELLING OF BAY WINDOW OVER ENTRANCE ARCHWAY.

Of the houses so far mentioned, Oxburgh Hall, East Barsham, Sutton Place, Layer Marney, and Hengrave are all built of brick. On the other side of the country, and in a house constructed of entirely different materials, we get—at Moreton Old Hall in Cheshire (1559)—the same kind of plan with which we have now become familiar (Fig. 45). This house is of timber and plaster, as many of the old houses in that district are. It is surrounded by a moat, and has—at any rate on the ground floor—but few windows looking out over the country ; they face into the court where possible. The relative positions of the hall, the kitchen, and the private apartments are here more clearly discernible than in some of the preceding plans, inasmuch as the family rooms have undergone but little serious alteration. The proximity of the two large bays of the hall and parlour is curious, and was the factor which caused the hall bay to be placed so far away from the daïs end.

The observations of contemporary writers are of much value when considering subjects of historical interest. It is therefore worth while to reproduce the advice of a certain Andrew Boorde,

[*] *Hist. and Antiq. of Hengrave,* by John Gage.

PLATE **XIV**.

HENGRAVE HALL, SUFFOLK (1538).
ENTRANCE GATEWAY.

Doctor of Physicke, in regard to the arrangements of a house, which he offers in the fourth chapter of his *Compendyous Regyment, or a Dyetary of Helth*, published in 1542. In this chapter he proceeds to "shewe under what maner and fasshon a man shulde buylde his howse or mansyon in exchewyng thynges the whiche shulde shorten the lyfe of man." He dwells upon the necessity of a good soil and good prospect, which latter advice was frequently neglected, a great number of houses in those times being built in a hole. The air, he says, must be pure, frisky, and clean, the foundations on gravel mixed with clay, or else on rock or on a hill. The chief prospects are to be east and west, especially north-east, south-east, and south-west; never south, for the south wind "doth corrupte and doth make evyll vapoures." He holds it better that the windows should open plain north than plain south, in spite, he says, of Jeremiah's saying that "from the north dependeth all evil."

He then enters upon particulars of the plan, and it will be observed how exactly his suggestions, so far as they go, agree with the plans we are examining. "Make the hall,"

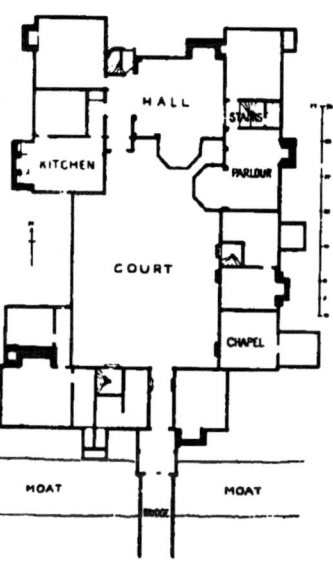

45.—MORETON OLD HALL, CHESHIRE. GROUND PLAN (1559).

he says, "under such a fashion that the parlour be annexed to the head of the hall, and the buttery and pantry be at the lower end of the hall; the cellar under the pantry, set somewhat abase from the buttery and pantry, coming with an entry by the wall of the buttery; the pastry-house and the larder-house annexed to the kitchen. Then divide the lodgings by the circuit of the quadrivial court, and let the gatehouse be opposite or against the hall door (not directly), but the hall door standing abase, and the gatehouse in the middle of the front entering into the place. Let the privy chamber be annexed to the great chamber of

estate, with other chambers necessary for the building, so that
many of the chambers may have a prospect into the chapel."
The necessity for these particular arrangements, so far as health
is concerned, does not seem quite obvious, especially the direc-
tions not to have the hall door exactly opposite to the entrance
gateway; and it may be supposed that this particular passage in
his treatise was suggested by what he had frequently seen rather
than by what science led him to prescribe. When he goes on
to dwell upon the necessity for removing "fylth," he was
probably taking a more original attitude, as also when he
recommended the stables, slaughter-house, and dairy to be kept
a quarter of a mile away from the house. The bakehouse and
brewhouse should also be isolated, he thinks; but in all these
respects his advice was not universally followed, for the whole of
these particular places are to be found attached to the house on
one or other of contemporary house plans. His next advice is
applicable to Moreton Old Hall. "When all the mansion is
edified and built, if there be a moat made about it, there should
be some fresh spring come to it, and divers times the moat
ought to be scoured and kept clean from mud and weeds. And
in no wise let not the filth of the kitchen descend into the
moat." Most of Dr. Andrew Boorde's advice is practical and
to the point, and he is not so much in bondage to ancient
authorities as many of his contemporaries were, in spite of his
reference to Jeremiah. The rest of his chapter refers to the
gardens and other surroundings of the house, which need not
now be dealt with.

The prevailing treatment of the ornament at Moreton is still
Gothic (Plates XV., XVI.), in spite of its date being beyond the
middle of the century. Nevertheless the influence of the new
style is seen here and there, especially in the carved pendants
of the overhanging work. The fine bay windows were made,
as an inscription tells us, by Richard Dale, carpenter, in 1559,
a further testimony to the fact that it was English workmen who
did most of the work of the time, even when it shows signs of
foreign ornament. Although the bulk of the house was built
in 1559, considerable alterations were made nearly half a century
later, in 1602; and to this date may be assigned the long gallery,
with its continuous row of mullioned windows reaching from
end to end almost without a break. The effect is very quaint,
but the room must always have been uncomfortable, whether

PLATE XV.

MORETON OLD HALL, CHESHIRE.
ELEVATION OF ENTRANCE GABLE.

PLATE XVI.

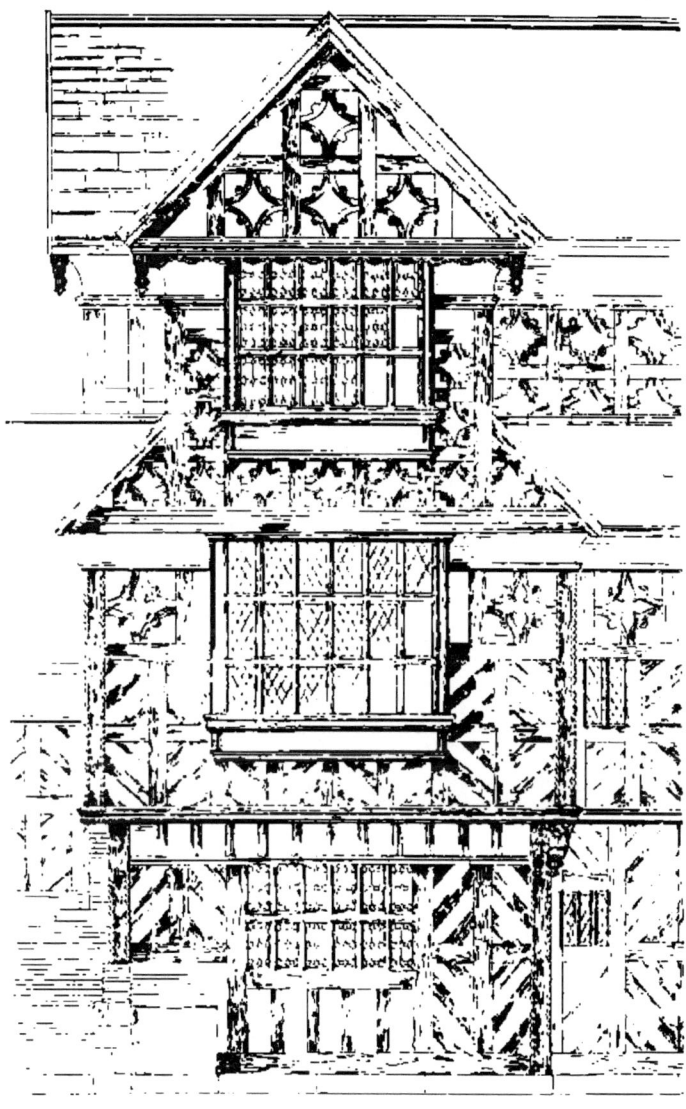

MORETON OLD HALL, CHESHIRE.
ELEVATION OF GABLE ON FRONT.

in summer by reason of the heat, or in winter by reason of the cold ; and as a comment upon the effect of time on the stability of these timber houses, nothing can be more striking than an attempt to walk quickly down the seventy feet of billowy floor which the gallery presents.

With our next plan we enter upon the Elizabethan era, an era marked by an extraordinary amount of house-building, which led to a great degree of attention being bestowed upon the planning. This attention, it is true, does not seem to have been directed so much towards comfort or economy as towards magnificence and display. No doubt comfort of a kind was aimed at, but people did not then require comfort as we understand it, and designers were not likely to be much in advance of their clients. The sacrifices of common sense to architectural effect were nevertheless few. The relative positions of the principal apartments were settled by considerations of convenience, not of external grouping. The kitchens, for instance, were always fairly in touch with the hall, not, as in later days, when Palladian architecture was in vogue, located some hundreds of feet away in a detached wing, connected by a curved colonnade, and balanced on the other extremity by the stables or the remainder of the servants' rooms, in a similar wing. Nor were the servants' bedrooms hidden away in the roof with windows looking out on to the back of a solid pediment, or even looking inwards and only lighted by borrowed light. It was the architects of a more strict Italian school who were reduced to such expedients in the early part of the eighteenth century; but in the late sixteenth the prevalent style was sufficiently elastic to enable the dictates of common sense to be obeyed. No doubt bay windows were placed in useless situations in order to balance others that were useful. Lofty windows were sometimes divided by floors half-way up their height in order that the uniformity of the front should not be interrupted; but the rooms themselves were cheerful enough and had good prospects. The features which the Elizabethan designer had to marshal were smaller and more manageable than those which fell to the lot of his successor in the days of Anne and the Georges ; and this was particularly the case with his windows. In a mullioned window an additional row of lights in the width, or even the height, can be managed without attracting undue attention, but the sash window has to conform to the size and situation of its brethren.

Economy of planning, in the sense of avoiding waste spaces, or saving the footsteps of the inmates, was not much studied. The only evidence we have of its consideration lies in the occasional lopping off of extravagant features, or the substitution of a reduced set of plans for one of more extensive area.

The real aim of the designers seems to have been magnificence and display—sometimes on a large scale, sometimes on a small. The principal means used for this end was symmetry—not so much a symmetry of detail as a symmetry of parts, of large features rather than of small. We shall find this quality in almost every kind of plan, and an extremely valuable quality it is if not carried to excess. The symmetry of the Elizabethans was generally under control. It was sometimes wasteful and its results were occasionally amusing, but they were never ridiculous or fatal to the comfort of the house.

Up to the present the plans we have examined have not—with the exception of Sutton Place—shown any determined attempt at a symmetrical treatment, only a certain hankering after it. With Kirby Hall (1570—75) we get a more resolute effort in this direction (Fig. 46). The entrance gateway and the screens are on an axial line running through the house and its green court. The inner court is quite symmetrically treated, door answering to door, and window to window; but the exterior façades were left to take care of themselves, and no attempt was made to balance one mass by another.

The symmetry of plan was carried out in the elevations too, at least so far as the courtyard is concerned. The south side, in which the projecting porch stands, is quite symmetrical, the great windows of the hall on the right being exactly balanced by similar windows on the left (Plate XVII.). The hall reaches from floor to roof, but the left wing had two storeys, and the floor of the upper one occupied one row of the glazed lights This expedient cannot be justified on the principle of causing the exterior treatment to indicate the internal arrangement; but it can hardly be denied that the general effect would be marred were the left-hand windows divided into two tiers. The door below the windows to the left is a later insertion. A curious fact about this front is that the two outside gables, which contain much delicate detail, are partly blocked by the roofs of the side wings, which abut against them; yet it is quite

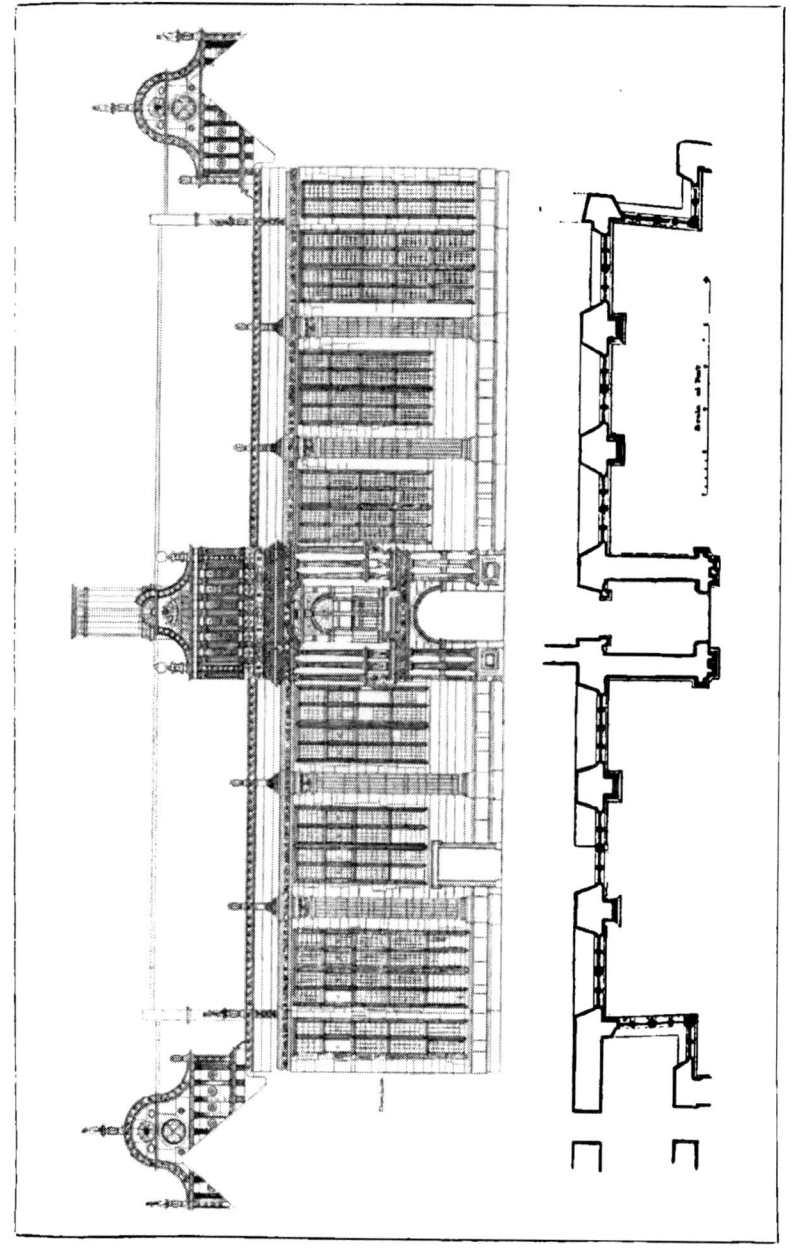

KIRBY HALL, NORTHANTS.

ELEVATION OF SOUTH SIDE OF COURTYARD (1570—75).

certain, from the character of the detail, and from the badges

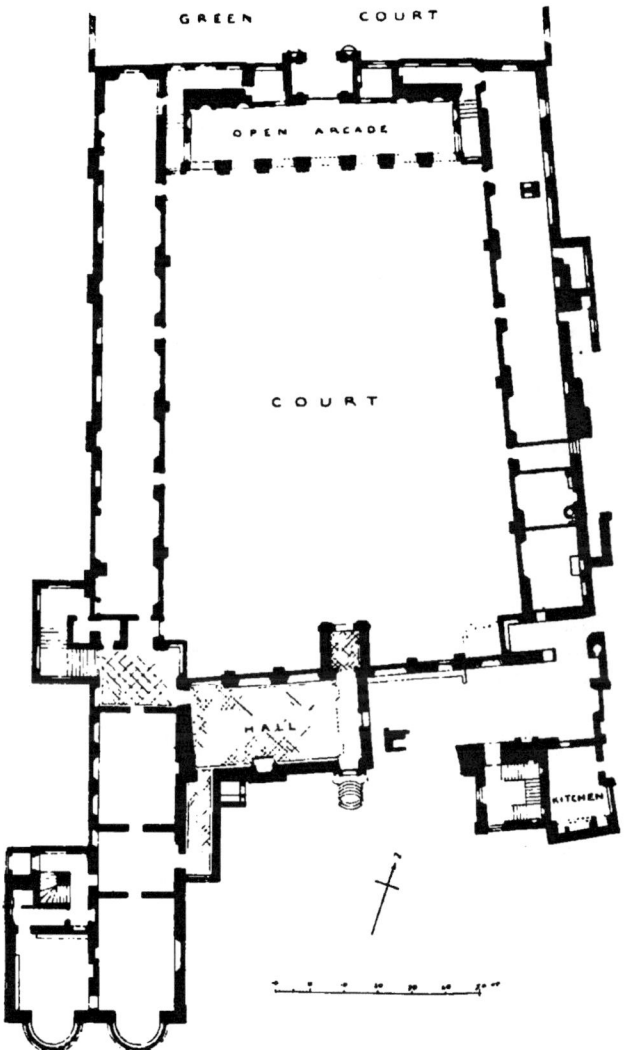

46.—KIRBY HALL, NORTHAMPTONSHIRE. GROUND PLAN (1570—75).

which are used as ornaments in the wings, that the whole court
was built at the same time, ends and sides, and it is equally

certain that the whole building operations were comprised within the five years 1570 to 1575.

Although no attempt seems to have been actually made to carry symmetry of treatment into the external façades, yet an examination of the plan made by John Thorpe, the surveyor, at the time that Kirby was built, shows that such a treatment was contemplated on each of the four faces (Plate XVIII.). There are other points of interest which Thorpe's plan elucidates. Having entered through the principal doorway, in the north or upper side of the plan, and having traversed the length of the court, we find a projecting porch through which the screens are reached. The arrangement is the typical one which we have seen in all the plans yet examined, and which tallies almost exactly with Dr. Andrew Boorde's advice, already quoted (see page 57), with the exception that he was opposed to the hall porch being exactly opposite the entrance gateway. On the right (as the plan lies) are the buttery and pantry, and the passage leading to the kitchen department; on the left is the hall. The details of the kitchen department are shown more clearly than in any of the foregoing houses, which have all undergone alterations. They comprise the kitchen, with its large fireplace; "the pastry," where the ovens are; the dry larder under it; the surveying place; and the wet larder. Close to these, and approached by the kitchen passage, is the winter parlour, a room which occurs on many plans of the time in close proximity to the kitchen. This endeavour to get a living room conveniently situated for winter use is one of the refinements which were now creeping in. Returning to the screens, and passing into the hall, we find the daïs marked on the plan, the fireplace in the side wall, but no bay window: there is one indicated, but it was not carried out. From the daïs the family apartments are reached, together with a great staircase. Next to the head of the hall, as Dr. Andrew Boorde has it, is the parlour (pler); the other rooms are not named. The division of " the lodgings by the circuit of the quadrivial court " is shown on Thorpe's plan, but most of the cross walls are now gone. It will be seen that these lodgings consist of a number of groups of two or three rooms (which were called "lodgings"), each group being entered from the court by a door, and each room communicating with its neighbour, so that the complete circuit of the building could be made through

PLATE XVIII.

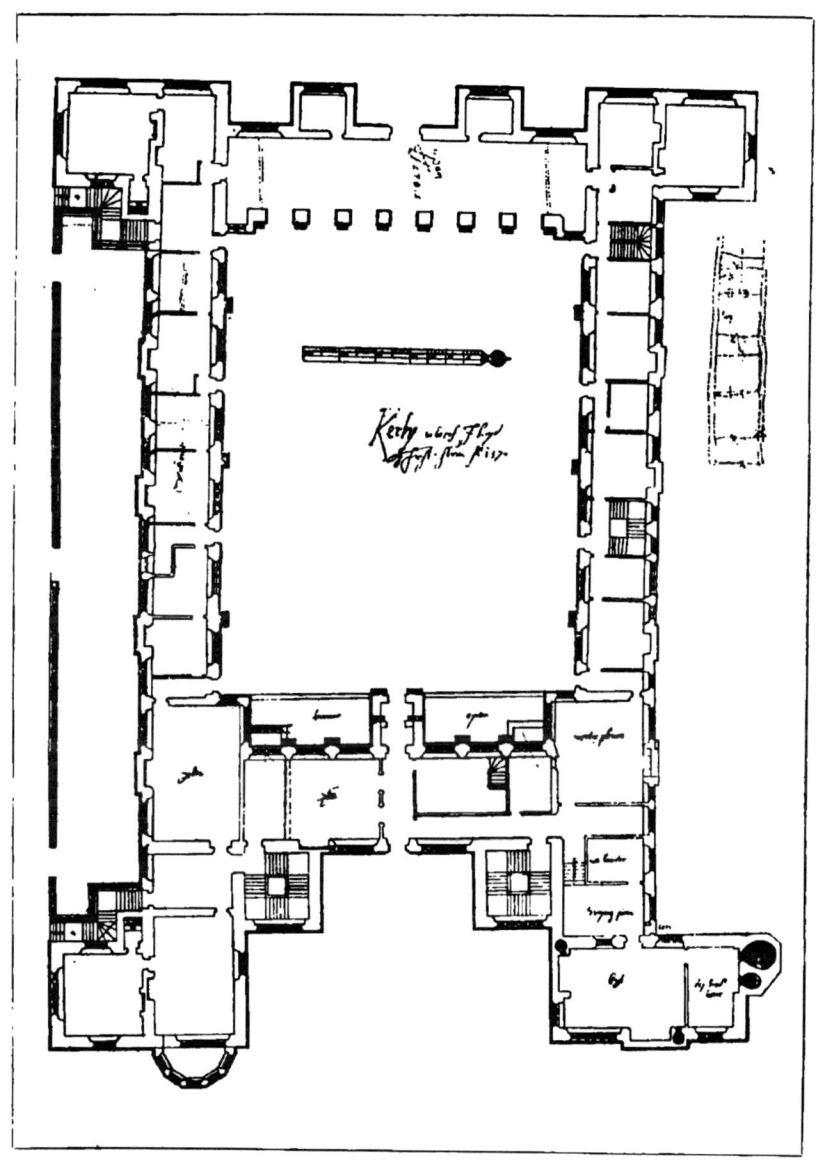

KIRBY HALL. JOHN THORPE'S GROUND PLAN.

From the Soane Museum Collection.

them. The object of this grouping was to give a small suite of rooms to every guest, in which he could establish himself with his principal attendants; in the case of a large retinue it could overflow into the next group. It was necessary to traverse the open court to reach the places of general resort, such as the hall, the "great chamber of estate," and the gallery; but it is evident that this was not felt to be a drawback, since the practice was widespread. The next point to notice is that here we have the first instance of the open terrace, or arcade, or loggia. It occupies the north side of the court, thus being open to the full midday sun. The long gallery, which was one of the principal features of an Elizabethan house, and frequently affected the planning, inasmuch as endeavours were made to obtain a gallery of the greatest possible length, was over the western or left-hand side of the court: it was 150 feet long by 16 feet wide. The upper floor was to be reached, according to Thorpe's plan, by four large internal staircases, and two external ones on the west front. As a matter of fact, indications actually remain of five principal staircases, besides a subordinate one, and they are more conveniently placed than those shown on the old plan. The great extent of the rooms, and their being placed round a court, necessitated several means of access, and it must not be forgotten that the upper part of the hall interposed an impassable barrier between the two sides of the house on the upper floor. The time was soon to come when the height of the hall was to be restricted to that of other rooms on the same floor, but at Kirby the traditional lofty hall was still retained.

The detail at Kirby is thoroughly Elizabethan, but there are a few windows, dated 1638, 1640, which were inserted by Inigo Jones, and he remodelled the north wing. His work, however, is easily distinguished from that of earlier date. The house was built by a Sir Humphrey Stafford, the head of a family seated at Blatherwyck in the immediate vicinity. It was begun in 1570, and it bears on the parapet of the courtyard the dates 1572, 1575; in the latter year Sir Humphrey died, having practically completed his house, which was then sold by his heir to Sir Christopher Hatton. Not only are the parapets dated, but amid the ornament of the various bands which make the circuit of the courtyard, and in the gable over the porch, occur the Stafford cognizances. Their presence indicates the extent of the work of Stafford, and proves that practically the whole place was built between the years 1570—75, though the Hattons probably made some trifling alterations during the last ten years of the century, and subsequently employed Inigo Jones to partly modernise the house fifty years later. The detail is unusually free and fresh, and has more variety than Elizabethan masons generally bestowed upon their work. The gable over the porch in the courtyard has no counterpart in England; the coping of the parapet round the whole court has an unusual but effective wave ornament (Plate XIX.).

There are, of course, the usual classic columns applied with a liberal hand, and all the horizontal string-courses have classic profiles. The carving of the friezes is interesting, inasmuch as it is somewhat out of the common in detail, and its component parts were evidently carved in large numbers, and used as occasion required, for in many places where the length of a carved stone was too great for its intended position it was ruthlessly shortened to fit, and the carving was mutilated. .

So far all the plans have shown a courtyard round which the house was built, first adopted, no doubt, from reasons of defence, and afterwards retained because it had become customary. We now come to another type of very frequent occurrence, in which two narrow parallel wings are connected by a narrow body, thus forming a figure like the letter H. It is in effect a curtailment of the older plan by leaving out the "lodgings" which enclosed the court; but there is no change in the old idea of placing the hall in a central situation and flanking it at one end by the family apartments and at the other by the kitchen and servants' rooms. At Montacute, in Somerset (1580), the original relation of hall and kitchen is preserved, but the intermediate rooms have been allotted to modern uses (Fig. 47). It should be observed that the passage at the back of the hall was formed by inserting between the wings the porch and part of the walls from an earlier house at Clifton Maubank in the year 1760. This passage, which is a great convenience to the house, must therefore not be looked upon as part of the original plan. The detail of the part thus inserted is of Late Tudor character. The profiles of the mouldings are Gothic, the carving inclines towards Italian, the parapets have cusped panels, the pinnacles have the spiral twist so dear to the Tudor mason, and a battlemented moulding beneath the heraldic

PLATE XIX.

· KIRBY · HALL ·
NORTHANTS.

Porch in Courtyard.

Plan of do

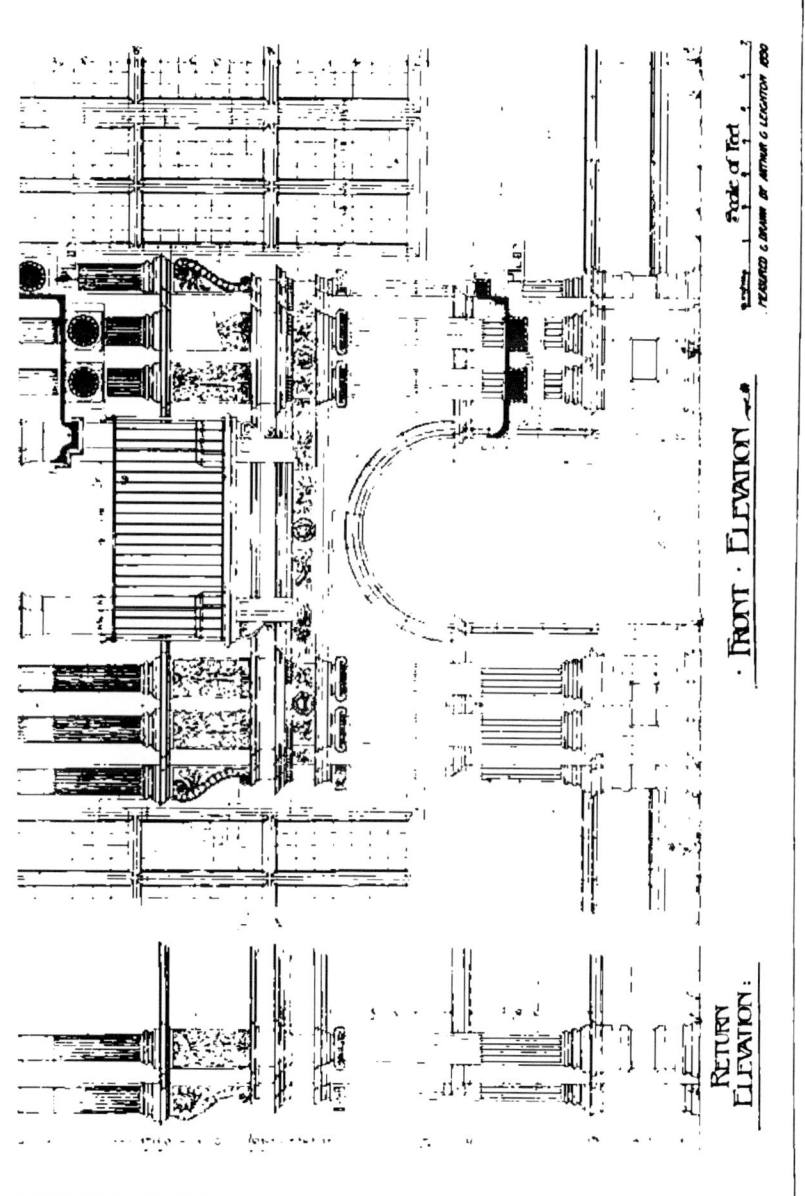

KIRBY HALL, NORTHANTS. DETAIL OF PORCH.

animals which they support (Plate XX.). The treatment is quite different from that of the house itself. Another point to remark

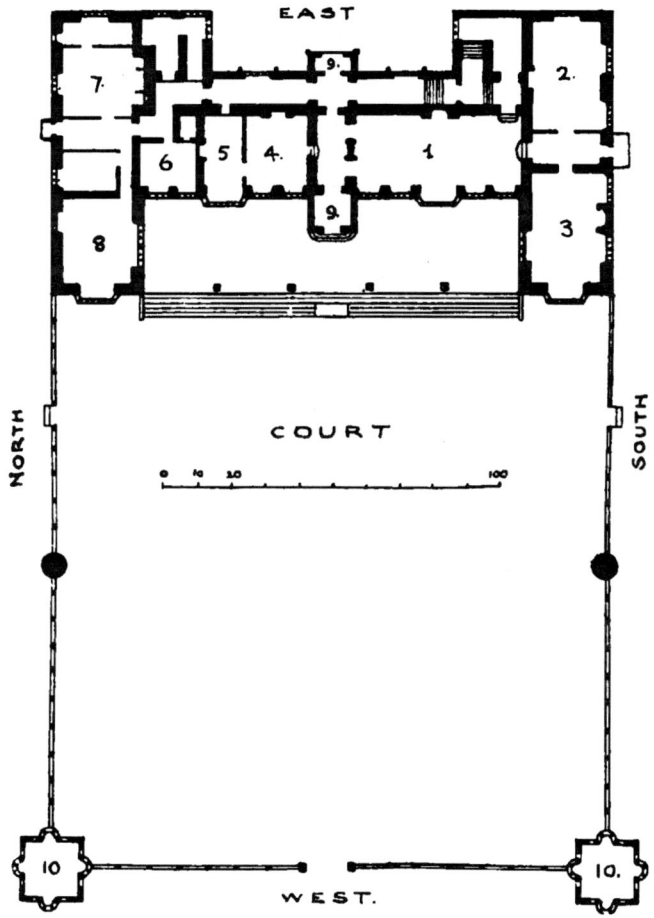

47.—Montacute House, Somerset. Ground Plan (1580).

1. Hall. 2. Drawing-room. 3. Large Dining-room. 4. Small Dining-room. 5. Smoking-room.
6. Pantry. 7. Kitchen. 8. Servants' Hall. 9. Porch. 10. Garden-house.

about the plan is that all thoughts of defence are here abandoned, and the windows look freely out on all sides. Indeed, far from desiring to exclude people, the builder, Sir Edward Phelips, wrote up over his door, " *Through this wide-opening gate, none come too early, none return too late.*" It will also be noticed that in order to get a truly symmetrical disposition of windows, the bay is removed from the end to the middle of the hall, which is another indication of a tendency to depart from the ancient arrangements.

It is true that there is a court at Montacute, but it is enclosed by an open balustrade and not by solid buildings; it is there for delight and not for defence, and everything in the planning shows that the builder considered he could occupy his house in security.

On the top floor, over the hall and running from end to end

48.—MONTACUTE HOUSE, SOMERSET. WEST FRONT, WITH COURT AND GARDEN-HOUSES (1580).

of the building, is the gallery; it is lighted at each end and down so much of the side as is not blocked by the wings of the house, which of course it cuts off from the staircases and the other rooms. The treatment of the elevations is as symmetrical as that of the plan (Fig. 48). The area of window space is in excess of that of wall space, the strings are of some depth and of classic profile, and the whole appearance contrasts strongly with that of Hengrave. Along the topmost floor in the spaces between the windows are eight statues, which, with a ninth in the central gable, are said to represent those Nine Worthies whom Holofernes and his companions tried to represent in a more dramatic manner before the Princess of France and her lively attendants.

It has already been observed that the plan of Montacute is

PLATE XX.

MONTACUTE HOUSE, SOMERSET
PART OF ENTRANCE FRONT SEEN FROM WING.

shaped roughly like the letter H. This type of plan is very frequent, and is the same in its essence as the E plan, of which many writers have made more than is needful. The m plan is in fact the same as the H with the side strokes curtailed. To make a just comparison, either the centre stroke of the m should be omitted or it should be added to the cross of the H, inasmuch as it represents the projecting porch, which was present equally in each arrangement. The fact that the m plan resembles the first letter of Elizabeth is probably a coincidence merely, and not a compliment to the queen. At the same time it would have been quite in accordance with the spirit of the time to have taken such a way of expressing loyalty, only in that case we should have expected to find fewer plans of the H variety, and more of the other; but as a matter of fact there are few, if any, houses with a perfectly straight front such as the back of the m demands.

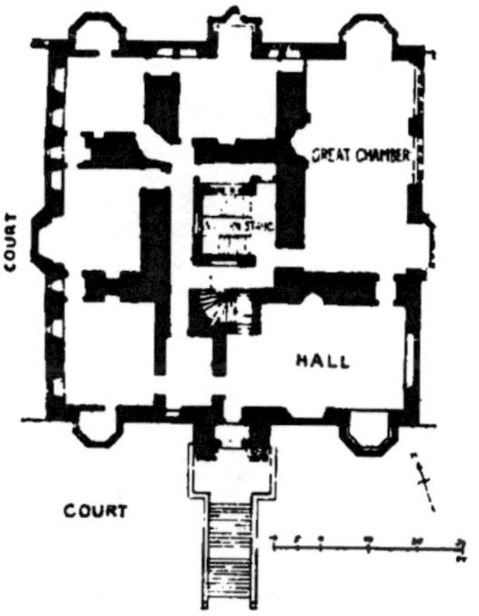

49.—Barlborough Hall, Derbyshire. Plan of Principal Floor (1583).

At Barlborough, in Derbyshire (1583), we get again a different type. The house is built round a court, but an extremely small one, now filled with a modern staircase (Fig. 49). All the windows look out into the open country. Instead of extending itself along the ground, the house provides its accommodation by extending itself vertically, and the kitchen and servants' rooms are placed in the basement. This was an idea introduced, it is said, from Italy, but it is one which, though sometimes met with, did not commend itself to Elizabethan builders when space was plentiful. The hall is on the principal floor, and is approached from outside up a long flight of steps. The screens led to the staircase which penetrated to the kitchen in the basement. The hall had its bay window at the daïs end, from which the great chamber was approached. We have still, therefore, the old idea of the hall as a living room, and part of a series of rooms communicating with each other; not yet as an entrance from which the living rooms are approached.

The detail at Barlborough is of a simple kind; the house was not of a large size and did not require much elaboration (Fig. 50). The actual classic treatment is confined to the front door, which is flanked with columns. The parapet is

50.—BARLBOROUGH HALL, DERBYSHIRE. ENTRANCE FRONT (1583).

battlemented, the strings are narrow, and the windows are not overwhelming in size. The roof is flat, and there are none of the gables which are so marked a feature of the time. Picturesqueness of outline, however, which was always sought for, is here obtained by carrying up the bay windows as turrets, a treatment which lends much distinction to an otherwise simple exterior.

PLATE XXI.

DODDINGTON HALL, LINCOLNSHIRE.

ENTRANCE FRONT WITH GATE-HOUSE (1595).

Twelve years later than Barlborough we get at Doddington, in Lincolnshire (1595), a plan which reverts to the type of Montacute (Fig. 51). It has the usual characteristics of the simplest kind—wings one room thick; the entrance at the end of the hall, leading on the left to the buttery, pantry, and kitchens; the parlour at the head of the hall, and the principal staircase adjacent. Here, however, as at Montacute, the hall is only one storey in height; it has a room above it—the great chamber: and on the top floor the gallery extends over the whole central part from wing to wing.

There is an entrance court in front of the house enclosed by a wall. It is approached through one of the quaint gate-houses

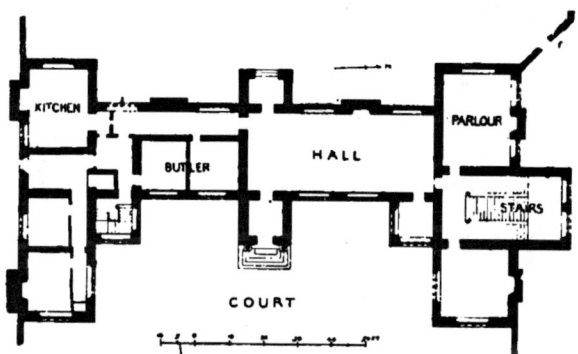

51.—DODDINGTON HALL, LINCOLNSHIRE. GROUND PLAN (1595).

of the time, which were a reminiscence of a more turbulent state of society, when it was necessary for all who went to the house to do so under the eye of the porter, but which in the calmer times of Elizabeth were occupied by some of the numerous functionaries who ministered to the pleasures of the rich. The detail at Doddington is of the plainest, the only attempt at richness being round the front door. The windows are of reasonable size, the strings are narrow, and are all of the same quasi-classic profile. The parapet is perfectly plain, and the roof is without gables, the sky-line being broken, as at Barlborough, with turrets, formed by carrying up the porch and the two projections in the internal angles of the front (Plate XXI.). The house is an example of a plain and business-like type, which may be accounted for by the fact that it was

built for a business man, one Thomas Tailor, registrar to the
Bishop of Lincoln.

With the opening of the new century we get at Burton
Agnes, in Yorkshire (1602—10), a repetition of the same leading
idea which we have been following for a hundred and fifty years
(Fig. 52). We have the screens at the end of the hall, the
kitchens on the left, and the bay window, the family rooms and
grand staircase at the head of the hall. The family apartments
have increased in number. The tendency was towards having
separate apartments for various uses, and on plans of the time
we not infrequently find a "dining parlour" specially named.

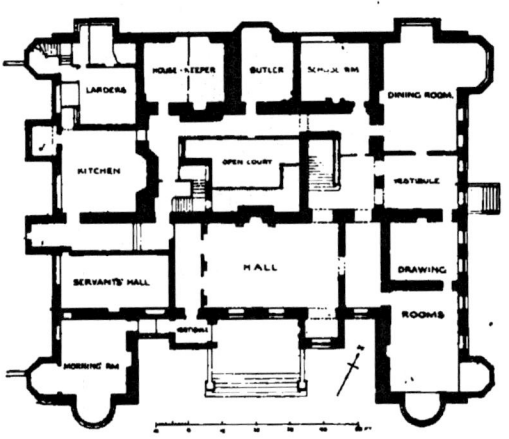

The intro-
duction of this
refinement
marks the
dwindling im-
portance of
the hall. The
latter is ceas-
ing to be the
centre of
family life,
and becoming
merely an en-
trance. The
daïs end is no
longer the
comfortable
place it was,

52.—BURTON AGNES, YORKSHIRE. GROUND PLAN (1602—10).

with its bay window and the fireplace close by: it is becoming
pierced with doors, and draughty. The family find it more
comfortable to have a separate room for their meals, and the
servants' quarters are becoming more self-contained. The old
usages of the hall are being discontinued.

This change is quite apparent in the last plan of the series,
that of Aston Hall, in Warwickshire (1618—35). The hall is
still central, the kitchen is in one wing, the family rooms in
the other, supplemented by a row at the back of the hall
(Fig. 53). But the hall itself is now merely an entrance—it has
ceased to be a living-room; it is entered from the middle of
the side, no longer at the end, where indeed the fireplace now

finds itself: there is no daïs and no bay window. This is a
revolution which it has taken more than a century to produce,

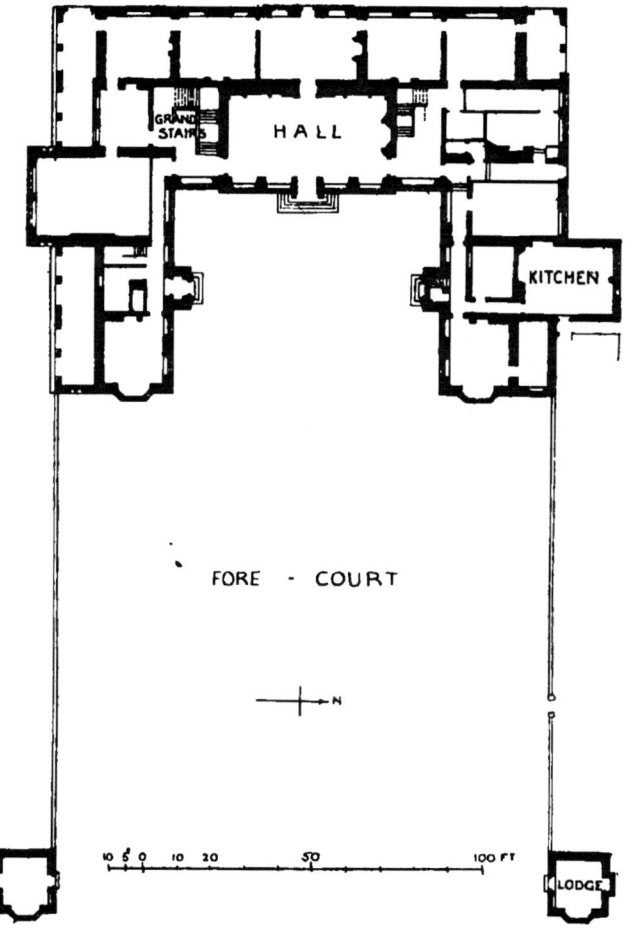

53.—Aston Hall, near Birmingham. Ground Plan (1618—35).

counting from the first appearance of the Italian influence.
The change no doubt was effected from the inside more than
the out: from the gradual alteration of habits, rather than
from the wish to Italianize our English plans. But the two

tendencies co-operated with each other and combined to lead English designers further and further away from the old traditions.

Although the hall shows a departure from the old lines of planning, the general arrangement adheres to them. The symmetrical wings, the mullioned windows, the turrets (Fig. 54), the fore-court with its lodges at the corners, and the open arcade on the south front, are all in keeping with Elizabethan and Jacobean methods, and offer a striking contrast to the work at Rainham Hall, in Norfolk, which was built by Inigo Jones in 1630, five years before Aston was finished.

54.—Aston Hall, Warwickshire. North Wing.

The disappearance of the hall as a living-room, and its adoption as a vestibule, mark a great change in our domestic architecture. The tie with the mediæval past is loosened, and with the almost contemporaneous departure of the mullioned window it is severed altogether; there is nothing now to prevent English designers from assimilating their buildings ever more and more to the models which they sought direct in Italy, without being diverted from their purpose by what they passed in intermediate countries.

CHAPTER IV.

EXTERIOR FEATURES.

LAY-OUT OF HOUSES, LODGES AND GATEWAYS, DOORWAYS AND PORCHES.

THERE was a very remarkable amount of building done in the last quarter of the sixteenth century. Plenty of money was available, much of it acquired from the lands of the dissolved monasteries; the country was at peace, and the strong rule of Elizabeth gradually produced a state of prosperity hitherto unknown. Defensive precautions, save such as seemed necessary against vagrants, were abandoned in all kinds of houses. The outer courts, the inner courts, and the gate-houses, which formerly were built for the sake of security, were now retained chiefly for the sake of appearance, and because they added to the privacy of the house. The porter at the gate exercised a certain amount of control over those who wished to enter, and on occasion he closed his gates against the populace, although sometimes without complete success, as we learn from a scene in Shakespeare's play of " Henry VIII.," where the people, in their anxiety to see something of the christening of the infant Princess Elizabeth, managed to crowd in, in spite of " as much as one sound cudgel of four foot could distribute " at the hands of the porter's man.

Everyone who could afford it seems to have built in the time of Elizabeth and James. The great nobles erected vast palaces like Theobalds and Holdenby, like Audley End, and Knole and Buckhurst. Men of smaller wealth built mansions like Kirby and Montacute, Wollaton and Blickling. Squires built their manor houses in the villages, merchants their homes in the towns, not infrequently, indeed, leaving the city for some neighbouring parish, and there ending their days as lords of the manor. When the condition of an existing house did not warrant its actual removal, additions in the new style were made; something had to be done to keep in the fashion.

Throughout the length and breadth of the land the same activity was displayed. From Yorkshire and Westmoreland in the north, to Cornwall and Kent in the south ; from Shropshire in the west to Suffolk in the east, we find work of this period scattered up and down the country in mansion, manor house, cottage and church.

A good deal of building was done in Henry VIII.'s time, but vastly more in Elizabeth's. The examples left to us of the former period are few compared with those of the latter ; but in both cases it must be remembered that the old gave way to the new. The builders of Elizabeth's days removed the work of their grandfathers to make room for their own, only to have this in its turn replaced in the times of Anne and the Georges. Many as are the houses of the sixteenth century which remain, we know that many others, of equal interest and beauty, have been pulled down.

LAY-OUT.

It is not always easy in the present day to grasp the system upon which the larger houses of Elizabeth's time were laid out. Modern methods of locomotion, and modern ideas of convenience, have in many cases caused the approach to the houses to be altered. It is the same with regard to most of our ancient cities. The railway now brings us to a spot which has no relation to the old landmarks of the place, and instead of approaching our destination through the ancient arteries, which were the growth of many years, we slip in through by-ways and slums, or along a new street made expressly for the purpose. The approach to one of the larger Elizabethan houses was an affair of time. Roads were then of a very primitive description, and depended for their condition upon the nature of the soil. "There is good land where there is foul way," was a saying of the time ; and conversely, where there was a hard road there was likely to be stony land. From the main road a similar rough track led, perhaps through an avenue of newly planted trees, in a straight line towards the house. There was no gate-keeper's lodge at the end of a finely gravelled road winding through a park. The lodge was part of the out-buildings of the house, and until you arrived there the road was generally left to take care of itself. After passing through the lodge, there were often two courts to traverse before the hall

was reached. The lodge was on the great axial line of the
house, so that as you stood waiting, if all the doors happened
to be open, you could see right through the courts and the
screens and get a glimpse of the garden beyond.

The accompanying plan of the lay-out of Holdenby (Fig. 55), from a survey made in 1587, gives a good idea of the surroundings of the larger Elizabethan houses. The road between two villages ran along the north side of the park, and from this road branched another one which led up to the house. While it traversed the park it was allowed to wind according to the undulations of the ground, but when it came to within a quarter of a mile of the lodge it was

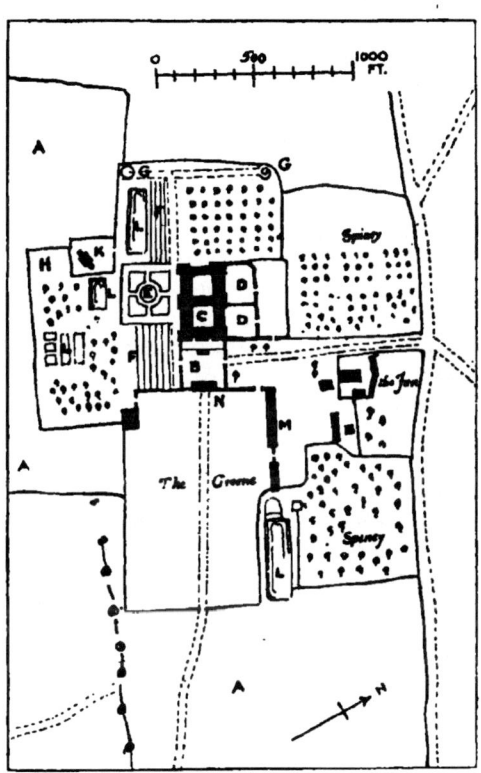

55.—HOLDENBY HOUSE, NORTHAMPTONSHIRE. PLAN OF LAY-OUT.
FROM A SURVEY MADE IN 1587.

A A.	The Park.	G G.	Mounts.
B.	Base-court.	H.	Site of Old House.
C.	First Court of House.	K.	Church.
D D.	Gardens.	L L.	Ponds.
E.	Rosery.	M.	Stables.
F F.	Terraces.	N.	Porter's Lodge.

made perfectly straight, and so ran through the midst of "the
green"—"a large, long, straight, fair way," as Lord Burghley
called it. It led directly to the porter's lodge, which was a
building separate from the house, and self-contained, and it

passed the long range of stabling on the right. The porter's lodge opened into the first court, the "base-court," as it was called, walled round, and entered on its two sides by large gateways. At the further end of the base-court stood the house, raised a few steps above the general level, where Lord Burghley "found a great magnificence in the front or front pieces of the house, and so every part answerable to other, to allure liking." The house was built round two great courts, the first 128 feet by 104 feet, the second 140 feet by 110 feet, comparable in point of size to those at Hampton Court, and a good deal more intricate in detail. To the north of the house itself were two walled gardens, of nearly an acre each, and beyond these were spinneys, or small woods, and the little village with its inn. The ground on the south side of the house sloped pretty steeply away, and was laid out in a series of terraces. At the top of these, and flanking the whole length of the base-court, the house, and the orchard beyond, ran a broad straight path. In the midst of the terraces a great platform was run out at the level of this long path, containing a rosery laid out with paths in a simple geometrical pattern. At the extreme end of the long path was a cross-path leading each way to a prospect mount, up at least one of which wound a spiral path, ending (in all probability) in a banqueting house, such as Lord Bacon describes in his essay "Of Gardens," and such as the Parliamentary Commissioners describe as being at Nonesuch in the year 1650. At the foot of the terraces lay fishponds amid orchard-trees, and, in a small enclosure of its own, the church. Close to the church was the site of the old manor house, the home of Sir Christopher Hatton's fathers, but which he found far too insignificant a dwelling for the Lord Chancellor.

Such were the surroundings of one of the most splendid palaces of Elizabeth's splendid courtiers, and an examination of the contemporary survey shows upon what a large scale the house and its appurtenances were laid out. The house covered nearly two acres; the base-court more than one acre; the green more than seventeen. In comparison with the house the village is a mere collection of outhouses, not so extensive as the range of stabling. The garden has not acquired all the architectural adjuncts in the way of stone terraces, and garden-houses, lead vases, statuary and *jets d'eau*, which became fashionable a hundred years later; but it has a fine simplicity about it and a largeness of scale which are in keeping with the house it belongs to.

Theobalds, in Hertfordshire, was the model upon which Sir Christopher Hatton professed to have founded his own more magnificent house at Holdenby, and there is an interesting account, written by John Savile, of King James's visit to Theobalds on his first coming to London in 1603.* It is an early example of descriptive reporting which would do credit to one of our great daily papers. Theobalds was the house of Sir Robert Cecil, afterwards Lord Salisbury, and had been built and embellished by his father, the great Lord Treasurer. The writer particularly mentions the approach to the house, which stood back from the highway, unlike the "manie sumptuous buildings" in the neighbourhood, most of which belonged "to the cittie marchants." It was reached by a most stately walk raised above the general level, and beset about either side with young elm and ash trees extending from the common street way to the first court belonging to the house. In order to obtain full particulars of the proceedings, Savile stationed one of his party

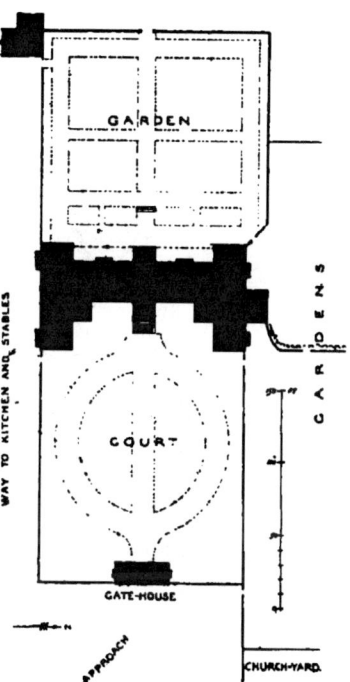

56.—DODDINGTON HALL, LINCOLNSHIRE.
BLOCK PLAN.

at the upper end of the walk, another at the upper end of the first court, while a third stood at the second court door, and he also arranged with "a gentleman of good sort" to stand in the court that led into the hall, and furnish particulars of the ceremonies invisible to the others. After the king had at length entered the house, the crowd of sightseers

* *Nichols' Progresses of King James I.*, Vol. I. 135.

surged even into the uppermost court, apparently without protest from the porter, and to their view the monarch graciously displayed himself at his windows for the space of half an hour, previous to going into the " laberinth-like garden to walke."

Lodges and Gateways.

Sometimes the lodge formed part of the buildings enclosing the first court, in which case one or two rooms or " lodgings " of the wing on either side of the gateway would be devoted to the porter, in the same way as the entrance to most of the colleges at Oxford and Cambridge is still arranged. But very frequently it was separated from the house by a court enclosed by a wall, as it was at Holdenby, and again at the much smaller house at Doddington (Fig. 56). This wall was sometimes high and solid, and sometimes coped " leaning height," as John Thorpe has it on one of his plans, or sometimes pierced with ornamental patterns.

57—Stokesay Castle, Shropshire. The Gatehouse.

The lodge itself was generally large enough to accommodate

STANWAY, GLOUCESTERSHIRE (ABOUT 1630).

THE GATE-HOUSE.

PLATE XXIII.

WESTWOOD, WORCESTERSHIRE.

THE GATEHOUSE.

the porter and his family, having two rooms downstairs and perhaps three above, but occasionally there were even three floors, as at Stanway in Gloucestershire (Plate XXII.), while at Hamstall Ridware, in Staffordshire, the lodge was merely a gateway between two flanking turrets only seven feet across inside. At Stokesay Castle, in Shropshire, is a charming lodge or gate-house of timber and plaster, added in Elizabeth's time to the ancient castle (Fig. 57); and at Westwood in Worcestershire the lodge is formed of two separate brick buildings connected by an open timber

58.—COLD ASHTON HALL, GLOUCESTERSHIRE. ENTRANCE GATEWAY.

roof and some pierced stonework, displaying the mullet or five-pointed star of the owner (Plate XXIII.).

The smaller houses had merely a gateway of more or less. pretensions, such as may be seen at Cold Ashton, near Bath (Fig. 58), a charming little entrance on the roadside leading straight up by a paved walk to the front door of the house; or at Winwick, in Northamptonshire (Fig. 59), the stately

59.—WINWICK, NORTHAMPTONSHIRE. GATEWAY TO MANOR HOUSE.

60.—Gateway to Almshouses, Oundle, Northamptonshire.

remnant of a house now much curtailed in size. This example is treated in a more important manner than usual, the masonry flanking the archway on either side being of considerable width, and elaborately ornamented with sunk patterns and carving. The well-proportioned columns are disengaged from the wall behind them, and the whole treatment of the lower part as far as the top of the cornice calls to mind some of the Roman arches to be met with in Italy. The pediments above the cornice are hardly equal to the structure upon which they stand, but they give that variety and piquancy of outline which was considered indispensable in work of the time; moreover, the circular gable over the archway affords room for a panel containing the owner's arms, although, by an irony of fate which would have annoyed him deeply, the bearings are now indistinguishable. This gateway vies in importance with those at Holdenby

61.—Holdenby, Northamptonshire. Gateways to Base-court (1585).

(Fig. 61), but the house at Warwick could never have been more than a good-sized manor house. At Cold Ashton the gateway is more in scale with the house, and although the central feature above the cornice is mutilated, the arms still remain. The effect of this roadside gateway is heightened by the circular steps and the mounting-block. At Oundle, in Northamptonshire, there is an example of a small gateway in the front wall of some almshouses (Fig. 60) which, in spite of its insignificant size, imparts considerable interest and even dignity to the group of which it is the central feature. In large houses the entrance courts not infrequently had archways in their side walls to afford access to the gardens or the orchard. The base-court at Holdenby has already been mentioned as having a gateway in each of its sides, apart altogether from the gate-house or porter's lodge. These two gateways still remain (Fig. 61), although most of the house and its adjuncts have dis-

62.—KENYON PEEL, LANCASHIRE. GATEWAY AT SIDE OF COURT (1631).

appeared, leaving them stranded in a position that is hardly intelligible without the aid of a plan showing the original arrangement. They bear the date 1585, and a shield of arms containing fourteen quarterings of the owner, Sir Christopher Hatton. In general treatment they resemble the similar gateways in the forecourt at Kirby, which also belonged to Sir Christopher, and they are more remarkable for their size and stateliness than for the beauty of their detail: but it should not be forgotten that the walls which supported them on either side, and which connected them with the great house, are gone, and that, denuded of their original surroundings, they appear much more heavy and cumbrous than when they

were a small part of a large scheme. Much smaller than the
base-court at Holdenby was the forecourt at Kenyon Peel, in
Lancashire, a half-timber house with a symmetrical ⋔ front,
and approached through a two-storey stone gate-house, joined to

63.—Doddington Hall, Lincolnshire. Entrance Doorway (1595).

the house itself by stone walls. The gate-house is rather gaunt,
like many of the stone buildings in that district, but in the little
gateways in the side of the court (Fig. 62) an effort has been
made to produce something less severe. The mixture of the
stonework and the black-and-white work of the house is effective,
and the small court, with its formal paved walks leading from
the gate-house to the porch, and from one side doorway to the

other, is full of interest ; especially as the house lies amid the chimneys of a busy part of Lancashire, and is surrounded by the abomination of desolation which accompanies the spread of populous places. The initials G. R. occur in the topmost step of the coping, and the date 1631 on the lintel of the doorway.

ENTRANCE DOORWAYS AND PORCHES.

The lodge or the gateway, as the case might be, was generally adorned in some conspicuous place with the arms of the family, the squires of the time being as proud of their various cogni-zances as Justice Shallow was of his twelve luces. Five out of the eight examples already illustrated are so adorned. The same shield that appears on the gateway is also fre-quently to be seen over the door of the house itself, which is reached after crossing the court. The door-way generally formed part of a somewhat elabo-rate piece of orna-

64.—PORCH AT CHELVEY COURT, SOMERSET (CIR. 1640).

ment, for, however simple (and sometimes even monotonous) the general treatment of the house was, the front door was made handsome. At Doddington, in Lincolnshire, while the bulk of the house is of plain brickwork, including the parapet, the doorway is treated with a considerable amount of elaboration (Fig. 63).

The door stood more often than not in a projecting porch,

which, although sometimes only one storey in height, as at Chelvey Court, in Somerset (Fig. 64), was usually higher, and was frequently carried up the full height of the building. It is round these doors that we find pronounced classic features employed in the shape of pillars and pilasters, friezes and cornices, and pediments. But it was seldom that the English mason did not introduce into his design some departure from strict classic treatment, suggested by his native traditions.

65.—DOORWAY AT NAILSEA COURT, SOMERSET.

At Chelvey the doorway has a flat-pointed head resting on an impost, such as usually accompanies a semicircular arch: there is also a keystone which protrudes from the straight lintel instead of crowning the arch, which in the ordinary way would be there. The twisted columns support pilasters of a different scale, which in their turn, however, are relieved of anything to carry. The broken pediment encloses a shield of arms, which rests in the usual fashion upon a base carried by the keystone. Over all is a pierced parapet divided into square panels by shallow pilasters. The spirit of the whole composition is Jacobean, but the treatment betokens a late date, with its twisted columns and broken pediment; and the arms confirm the conjecture prompted by the character of the work, though the exact date is not recorded. It is evident, however, that even in Somerset, the home of good masons, the lesson of making appropriate use of classic features had not yet been mastered. The treatment of the doorway at the neighbouring

PLATE XXIV.

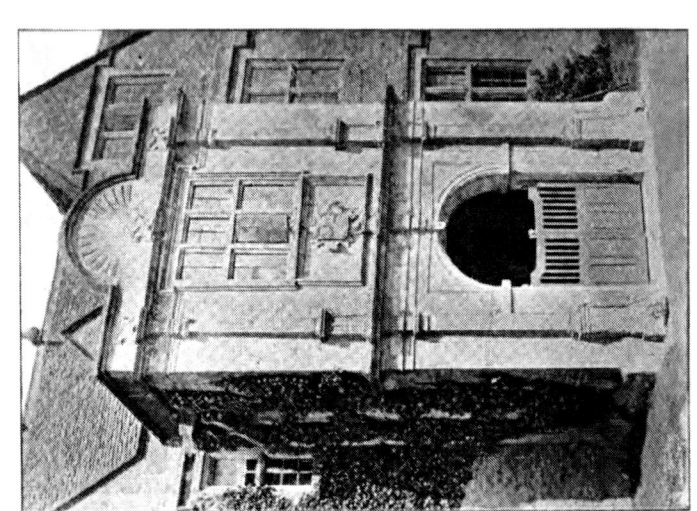

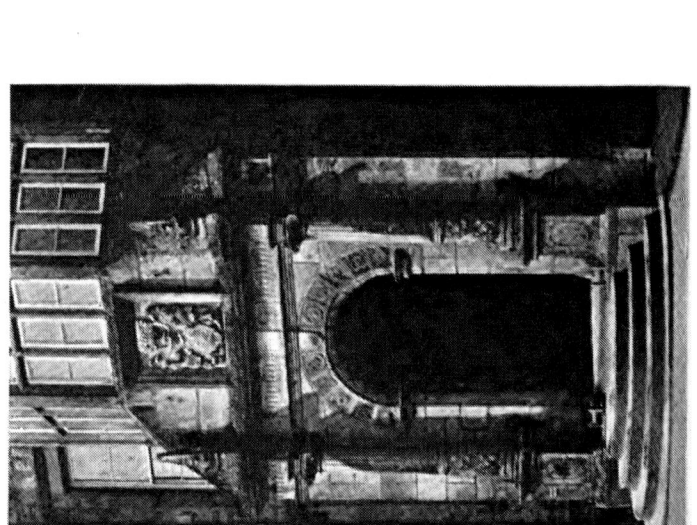

house of Nailsea Court (Fig. 65) is more logical and pleasing. There is a quaint mixture of pointed arch and classic cornice and corbelled bay-window; and the manner in which the central projection in the cornice is made the starting-point of the corbelling to the bay is a happy illustration of the freedom with which the new features were handled.

At Chipchase Castle, in Northumberland (Plate XXIV.), a square porch is combined with a canted bay above it. The doorway follows the more usual pattern; it has the circular arch resting on imposts, a project-ing keystone carried up to break the lines of the cornice, and is flanked on either side by a circular column, which endeavours to justify its presence by carrying an obelisk. The obelisks serve the useful purpose of breaking the severe line of the splay which joins the octagonal bay to the square porch below it, and they, together with the shield of arms and the carving on the columns and the voussoirs of the

66.—DOORWAY AT GAYHURST, BUCKINGHAMSHIRE.

arch, impart considerable richness to the whole composition. At Gayhurst, in Buckinghamshire, the columns, which are primarily introduced for the sake of ornament, are made to do actual duty by supporting a slight projection of the storey above them (Fig. 66); and there are two tiers of them, a fact which helps to increase the importance of the entrance. In this, as in similar cases, the cornices are continued along the sides of the projecting porch, and are stopped against the face of the main building. At Upper Slaughter, in Gloucestershire (Plate XXIV.), the porch has more of the appearance of being an excrescence, the only connecting member being the string over the upper windows of the house, which is returned along

the sides of the porch.
The cornices of the porch
are in this instance only
just returned round its
outer angles, and not carried back to the main
building. The pilasters
are merely ornamental
adjuncts : there is no pre-
tence about them of doing
any work ; the head of the
upper window breaks un-
ceremoniously into the
frieze of the cornice, the
keystone of the arch is
carried up so that the
lines of the lower cornice

67.—Doorway at Cold Ashton, Somerset.   may break round it, and

the whole treatment shows that the designer was free from
any morbid craving after
correctness. In the door-
way at Hatfield, in the side
of the court (Plate XXV.),
the work is handled in
a more formal manner.
There is the semicircular
arch, with its impost, and
the two flanking pilasters
carried up in order to
break the cornice, while a
central projection follows
up from the keystone.
There is no crowning
pediment, but in its place
is a strapwork pattern
terminating at the top
with a point which finds
itself in the centre of one
of the triglyphs in the

68.—Doorway at Cheney Court, Somerset.

entablature which makes the circuit of the whole house at the

HATFIELD HOUSE, HERTFORDSHIRE. DOORWAY
IN COURT (1611).

WARDOUR CASTLE, WILTSHIRE. THE GRAND
STAIRCASE.

first floor level. The archway at the foot of the grand staircase at Wardour Castle (Plate XXV.) is treated with still greater propriety; the designer has allowed himself to take no liberties with his copy, but the severity is relieved by the informal manner in which the steps wind away to the left. This is an accident arising from the fact that the staircase is of an older date; it is covered with Gothic vaulting, and at its upper end the original pointed arch has been made semicircular, and the stone round it has been recessed so as to surround it with a square moulded frame in the manner prevalent at the beginning of the seventeenth century. At Cold Ashton we have a simple pedimented doorway in a shallow projection between the two wings of the house

69.—WOOLLAS HALL, WORCESTERSHIRE. PART OF ENTRANCE FRONT (1611).

(Fig. 67), and at Cheney Court there is another simple form of doorway; it has no pilasters, but a curved pediment, supported on corbels, forms a hood (Fig. 68)—a mode of treatment adopted towards the close of the Jacobean period, and handled here with a pleasant freedom, a panel being contrived in the middle of the frieze to contain the family arms. At Woollas Hall (Fig. 69) there is a boldly projecting porch, thrusting itself out beyond the main face of the house, and giving from its oriel on the top floor a wide view over the surrounding country.

The ruins at Gorhambury, near St. Albans, a house built

70.— PORCH AT GORHAMBURY, HERTFORDSHIRE (1568).

by Sir Nicholas Bacon, the father of Lord Bacon, present another treatment, which can still be made out in spite of the modern brick buttresses, and the brick arch which has been inserted below the original one of stone (Fig. 70). There is a projecting porch of two storeys, with all its three external faces carefully treated, the front being made rather more elaborate by the introduction of niches with statues. The employment of statues and busts as decorative features was a favourite device of the time. They were almost invariably of classic origin, and attired in classic garb, the most modern personages usually admitted to this distinction being those three of the Nine Worthies who were of Christian extraction. In the spandrils of the arch are circular medallions with busts, and in the parapet are the royal arms. There was also over the arch (we are told) a grey marble panel with four Latin verses, stating that the house was finished in the tenth year of Elizabeth's reign by Nicholas Bacon, whom she made a knight, and Keeper of her Seal. Below these verses was the aphorism " Mediocria firma," that is, " Firm is the middle state."

71.—HAMBLETON HALL, RUTLAND.

Statues, busts, and inscriptions are all characteristic of the taste of the period, and will be more particularly dealt with later on in connection with the design of chimney-pieces. The house which was thus finished in the tenth year of Elizabeth, that is in 1568, was begun (according to an account in the possession of a local antiquary) on the 1st day of March, 1563, thus taking five years to build. It was not of vast extent, but it comprised two courts, one for the house, the other for the kitchens. The porch illustrated was approached in a direct line across the larger of these courts, and led into the screens in the usual way; the windows visible to the left of the porch lighted the great hall at the daïs end. There is very little left of the old walls, but the extent of the hall can be made out, as well as the position of a clock tower; and at some little distance there remains another niche with a headless statue in it, no doubt that of Henry VIII., which we are told was put up on the occasion of the Queen's second visit to Gorhambury. Her first visit was paid in 1572, four years after the completion of the house, on which occasion the Queen told the Lord Keeper that he had made his house too little for him, whereupon he replied, "Not so, madam, but your Majesty has made me too big for my house." He was, however, resolved not to be open to such a reproach again, and on receiving an intimation that the Queen would visit him a second time (in 1577) he is said to have built a gallery of lath and plaster 120 feet long by 18 feet wide, beneath which were cloisters, and in the middle of their length the statue of King Henry in gilt armour. This enlarging of the house for the express purpose of receiving the Queen was only one of numerous instances, which will be referred to in a subsequent chapter, as also will the proportion of the long galleries so distinctive of the period.

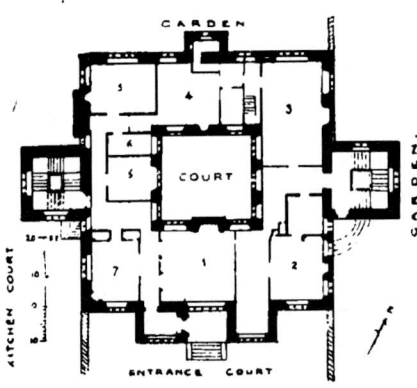

72.—CHASTLETON, OXFORDSHIRE. GROUND PLAN (CIR. 1603).

1. Hall.	4. Nursery.
2. Little Parlour.	5. Chamber over Kitchen.
3. Great Parlour.	6. Pantry.
	7. Parlour.

The gallery was panelled with oak gilt, and on the panelling were Latin inscriptions, so aptly selected that it was considered worth while to collect them in a small volume. illuminated with much beauty. In the orchard was a banqueting-house, which in its turn was adorned with busts and inscriptions. These all related to specific subjects—grammar, arithmetic, logic, music, rhetoric, geometry, and astrology; and each subject was not only depicted on the walls, but was further illustrated by appropriate verses and the pictures of such learned men as had excelled in it.* Although most of them were selected from the ancients, yet Sir Nicholas Bacon was

* *Nichols' Progresses of Queen Elizabeth*, Vol. II.

Plate XXVI.

CRANBORNE MANOR HOUSE, DORSETSHIRE

THE PORCH (ABOUT 1612).

sufficiently catholic in his taste to admit such modern names as Lilly, the grammarian, and Copernicus, the "astrologer," the latter of whom had only been dead some thirty years.

Another kind of entrance is afforded by the arcaded porch, of which a simple example is to be seen at Hambleton, in Rutland (Fig. 71), and a more elaborate one at Cranborne, in Dorset (Plate XXVI.), where it was added, along with other "modern" features, to an old manor house dating from the thirteenth century, in order to bring the house into the prevailing fashion.

So far all the entrances which have been mentioned were in the main face of the building, the front doors being in the centre of the façade. As the front door almost always led into the screens at the end of the hall, it followed as a matter of course that the hall itself occupied only a little more than half the length of the façade. In some instances, however, the hall was made to occupy

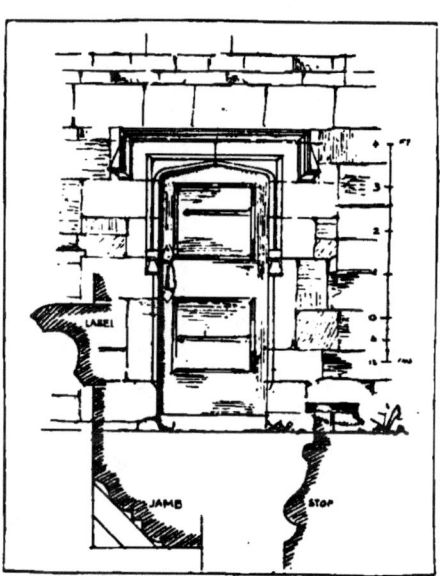

73.—DOORWAY AT LYDDINGTON, RUTLAND.

the centre of it, and in such cases the porch could no longer be central, but was moved to one side, and made to balance a corresponding projection which served as the bay window of the hall: the doorway was then placed, not in the front face but the side face of the porch, as may be seen at Chastleton, in Oxfordshire (Fig. 72), and Burton Agnes, in Yorkshire (Fig. 52). The main approach was therefore still on the axial line, but on mounting the final steps, instead of going straight forward into the porch, you turned either to the right or left (in the two instances illustrated it

was to the left) and so through the porch to the screens. At
Chastleton the old arrangement remains perfect; the screen is
there, and also the dais with the bay window at the end of it.
At Fountains Hall, in Yorkshire, the same idea is carried out,
but as the ground slopes very steeply, the principal floor is
some feet above the ground at the entrance. The doorway
is central, and immediately on entering, a straight flight of
steps leads off to
the right up to the
main floor, which it
gains just in time
for a turn to the
left to lead into the
screens.

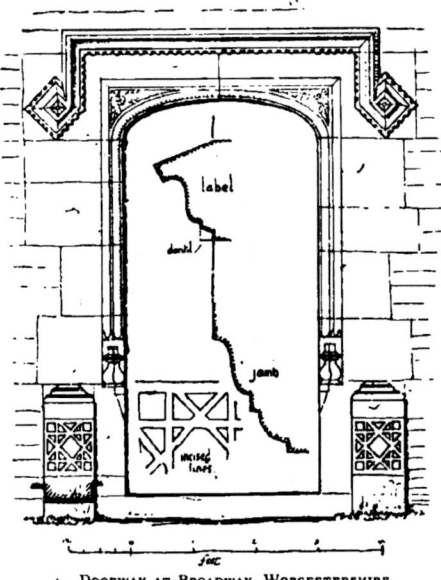

4.—Doorway at Broadway, Worcestershire.

In situations re-
quiring less orna-
mental treatment,
a very pleasing type
of doorway came
into use, and lin-
gered on in remote
places far into the
days of regular
classic architecture.
Such doors abound
in the stone villages
of Somerset and
thence northwards
through the Cots-
wolds and Oxfordshire, up to Northamptonshire and Rutland.
They are usually flat-pointed, and the jambs have two moulded
orders, the inner one going round the flat-pointed head, while
the outer one forms a square frame round it, as in the example
from Lyddington (Fig. 73). There is not much of the classic
manner about such a door, especially when, as in this instance,
the label is returned down the ends of the head. But the
section of the jamb-mould is an adaptation of the contours
found in classic work, and the label not infrequently was treated
in the manner of a cornice, instead of being returned, as it is
in this example and that from Broadway in Fig. 74. There
is a small doorway of this kind at Aylesford Hall, in Kent

(Fig. 75), which shows a curious mixture, for the head has a fairly high-pointed Gothic arch, while the label is of classic profile, and is ornamented with dentils : the spandrils are filled with shields of late design, one of which bears the date 1590, thus showing how long the old traditional forms lingered in places. The masons of the time made use of a type of door which was chiefly of Gothic descent, but they varied its features at will. The head was either high-pointed, flat-pointed, or elliptical, as their fancy dictated ; and the label was either moulded after the fashion of their youth, or in accordance with the newer forms which they saw in use around them. It is in such unimportant matters as these, where no one was particularly concerned about the result, that we see how the workmen availed themselves indifferently of the old forms or the new.

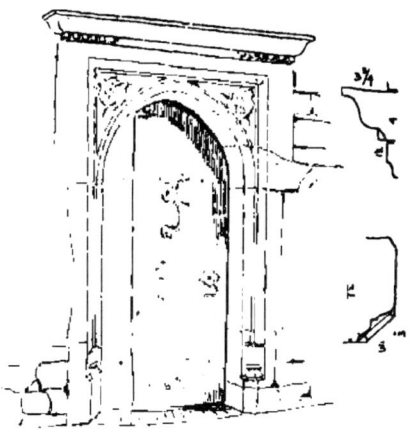

75.—Doorway at Aylesford Hall, Kent (1590).

CHAPTER V.

EXTERIOR FEATURES (*continued*).

GENERAL ASPECT, EXTERNAL APPEARANCE, WINDOWS, &c.

BEFORE proceeding to enter one of these doorways and to
examine the interior treatment of an Elizabethan house, it will
be well to look at the exterior more closely. We find that the
effect, although often elaborate and striking, is produced by
very simple means. The picturesque appearance of Haddon
and Compton Winyates is chiefly due to the irregularity of the
plan, which in the case of the former was largely the result of
a gradual growth, extending over some centuries. The stately
effect of the Elizabethan house is the result of regularity and
symmetry in the plan, and its picturesqueness springs from its
windows, gables and chimneys. The English designer avoided,
as a rule, very large plain surfaces and long unbroken façades,
differing in the latter respect from his Italian contemporaries.
He diversified his long fronts by throwing out bay-windows;
he broke up the skyline with gables; he grouped his chimneys
so as to add emphasis to the design; and there were always
the mullioned windows, of which the relatively small divisions
gave scale and life to the whole. There are many houses which
have no further attempt at ornament than these features, and
these are felt to be quite sufficient; but occasionally, when a
great effort was demanded, the Elizabethan designer borrowed
his ornament from abroad, and added a multiplicity of pilasters
and niches to his walls. extravagant and fantastic curves to his
gables, while, in order to avail himself of classic forms to the
full, he turned his chimneys into the semblance of columns.
His zeal was not always accompanied by knowledge; he sometimes misapplied his borrowed features; he too frequently
regarded a pilaster as in itself an agreeable ornament, without
troubling to bring it into scale with the building or with his
other pilasters used elsewhere, and without providing for it

even a semblance of anything to support. The more ignorant masons evolved designs which bore but a distant resemblance to the originals which inspired them. All this is true, and it is so manifest that one cannot be surprised at the opprobrious epithets bestowed upon work of this period by purists of other

76.—KIRBY HALL, NORTHAMPTONSHIRE. SOUTH SIDE OF COURT (1570-75).

schools. Still, in spite of errors and ignorance in the application of ornament, there is an exuberant vitality about the buildings of the time which accords with the vitality of its literature. Moreover, their character is essentially English: an Elizabethan house could no more have been designed by Palladio or Du Cerceau or Vriese than a play like those which Shakespeare gave us could have been written by one of the novelists, essayists, or dramatists of Italy, France and Germany, from whom the Englishman, however, did not hesitate to borrow some of his material.

EXTERNAL APPEARANCE.

The courtyard of Kirby Hall is one of the finest examples that is left of the period (Fig. 76), and although pilasters of different scale are employed as ornamental features rather

than as constructional, the whole effect is both dignified and
picturesque. The mullioned windows have a lively simplicity,
the large pilasters prevent monotony, and the small detail
about the central porch contrasts happily with the plainer

77.—KIRBY HALL, NORTHAMPTONSHIRE. WEST FRONT (1570-75, PARTS POSSIBLY 1595).

78.—LONGLEAT, WILTSHIRE (1567).

treatment of the main walls. The external façade on the west,
though not symmetrical, is kept in subjection; the strong
horizontal lines of the strings and cornices bind it together,
and the great chimney stacks are so ordered at regular intervals
that they alone would give dignity and rhythm to the front
(Fig. 77). The work on this front is not all of one time,
though the various parts cannot be separated by many years,
and it is quite possible that the curved gables were added by
a somewhat later hand. Sir Christopher Hatton's successor

PLATE XXVII.

WOLLATON HALL, NOTTINGHAMSHIRE.

may have modified this façade towards the end of the century, when he built the stables, which have now disappeared.

Kirby is freer in its treatment than Longleat, in Wiltshire, which has to submit to a more severe symmetry (Fig. 78). The windows here are rather overpowering, but the whole effect is restful, owing to the strong horizontal lines, while the projecting bays entirely relieve it from monotony. There are no gables, and apparently never were, which is a somewhat unusual circumstance, considering the date of its erection, 1567. Wollaton, near Nottingham (Plate XXVII.) bears some resemblance to Longleat in its detail, but it is far more fantastic in its treatment, and its plan places it in a category almost by itself. It cannot be called a typical house either in

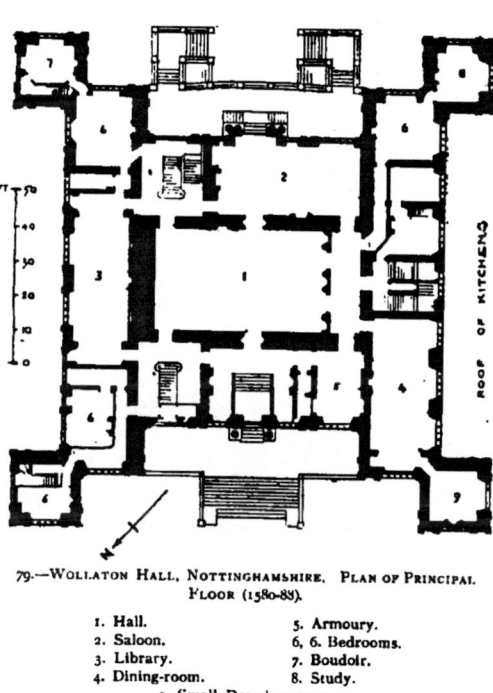

79.—WOLLATON HALL, NOTTINGHAMSHIRE. PLAN OF PRINCIPAL FLOOR (1580-88).

1. Hall.	5. Armoury.
2. Saloon.	6, 6. Bedrooms.
3. Library.	7. Boudoir.
4. Dining-room.	8. Study.
9. Small Drawing-room.	

its arrangement or its design, although from its striking appearance and excellent state of preservation it is frequently quoted as such. Its plan shows a central hall, surrounded by a range of rooms, with a projecting pavilion or tower at each of the four corners (Fig. 79). The general effect is undoubtedly impressive, but the ornament is overloaded, and shows a too careful study of extravagant Dutch models. The work, however, and the design are those of well-instructed masons, familiar with the features they were handling. Wollaton is another instance of combining a central hall with a central doorway. The present flight of steps inside the front door, together with the doors in the long sides of the hall immediately opposite, is comparatively modern. The original approach, after entering the front door, was up a flight of steps to the right, at the top of which, by turning to the left (as at Fountains Hall), the screens were gained, and the hall was entered in the usual way.

At Burghley House we revert to a simpler treatment. The main walls are of plain masonry pierced with windows, and divided by the usual horizontal cornices (Plate XXVIII.).

80.—CHARLTON HOUSE, WILTSHIRE (1607).

Diversity is obtained by projecting turrets, lofty bay windows, and the boldly-curved entrance porch on the north front. There are no gables, the skyline being broken by the turrets, the chimneys, and the ornamental parapet. It is, perhaps, an exaggeration to say there are no gables, but there are none in the later part built between 1575 and 1587. The great hall has gables, but that was built some years earlier.

At Charlton, in Wiltshire (Fig. 80), there is an example of the open arcade, which became rather fashionable, but which later generations have, in many houses, found unsuitable to our climate, and of which the arches have in consequence been filled up. The gables here are ornamented with a kind of filigree, which is more curious than beautiful. At Aston Hall,

PLATE XXVIII.

BURGHLEY HOUSE, NORTHAMPTONSHIRE.
GENERAL VIEW.

near Birmingham, the south front presents another instance of an open arcade (Fig. 81), and a good deal of picturesqueness is imparted by the broken outline of the gables. Corsham Court, in Wiltshire, shows a more restrained treatment (Fig. 82). The animated effect is obtained by a number of plain gables, and by square projecting windows crowned with flat pediments, the whole bound together with conspicuous horizontal strings. At Kentwell Hall, in Suffolk, the digni-fied effect is produced by the combination of two turrets

81.—Aston Hall, Warwickshire. South Front (1618-35).

with the front gables, by projecting windows carried up the whole height of the building, and by massive chimney-stacks (Fig. 83). The approach is still on the axial line, although the present low wall is but a poor substitute for the usual enclosure ; but in many of the examples cited the general effect is decidedly impoverished by the disappearance of the outer courts.

Coming now to somewhat smaller houses, we find the same simple materials relied upon, and producing equally good effects. In the ruins of the old Hall at Exton, in Rutland (Plate XXIX.), the front façade shows curved gables separated by a length of

82.—CORSHAM COURT, WILTSHIRE (1582).

pierced parapet, and the side has three straight gables close together, with a huge stack of chimneys placed irregularly against them. The Manor House at Glinton, in Northampton-shire (Plate XXIX.), is even simpler ; nevertheless, its curved gables, carefully wrought chimneys, and projecting porch give it a considerable amount of character. It is not on record when either of these houses was built, but Exton Hall was

83.—KENTWELL HALL, SUFFOLK.

probably the work of John, Lord Harrington of Exton, the tutor of the Princess Elizabeth, only daughter of James I. There is nothing left inside the house, which was burnt down in 1810, but enough of the exterior remains to show that, like most manor houses in the district, it must have been a fine place in its palmy days. In the church at Exton are a number

PLATE XXIX.

EXTON OLD HALL, RUTLAND.

THE MANOR HOUSE, GLINTON, NORTHAMPTONSHIRE.

of exceptionally good monuments of the sixteenth and seventeenth centuries, commemorating the Harringtons and their
descendants (see Fig. 6).   The manor of Glinton was granted
to the Dean and Chapter of Peterborough at the dissolution of
the monasteries, and so remained till long after the house was
built, which may therefore have been used as a country residence
for the Dean.   At Cheney Court, near Bath (Fig. 84), another
house without a history, the treatment is quite simple, consisting of nothing more than three evenly placed gables along
the side, and two others, in combination with large chimney-

84.—CHENEY COURT, SOMERSET.

stacks, along the end.   The reason for the sudden jumping up
of the strings in the right-hand gable of the side is not apparent ;
but as a matter of fact, at the present time that part of the
house is occupied by one tenant, while the remainder is let to
another.   This type of manor house, with its extremely quiet
handling of gables, chimneys, and mullioned windows, is common
all over the country, and so far as its exterior is concerned, it
owes little besides its symmetrical disposition to the Italian
spirit.   An extra touch is given to the doorway here (Fig. 68),
and the internal fittings show the foreign influence, but otherwise it is entirely a native production.   The same may be said

of Cold Ashton (Fig. 85), another house in the neighbourhood

85.—MANOR HOUSE, COLD ASHTON, GLOUCESTERSHIRE.

of Bath, but here the symmetrical treatment is more marked, as will be seen by looking at the plan (Fig. 86), and the chimneys are gathered into two groups which serve the whole house. This is an interesting example of the smaller kind of manor house, and it has been subjected to very few alterations. Its history is not recorded, but it was evidently built by one of the numerous squires of the time, who put his arms over the gateway on the road side (see Fig. 58). Judging by the two doorways remaining in the screen on the left of the central passage, one of which now leads into a pantry, the hall has been shortened by the space required for the pantry, but except for this alteration the plan seems to indicate the original arrangement, including that of the front garden, with its gateway and circular steps, its paved walk, and the flight of steps

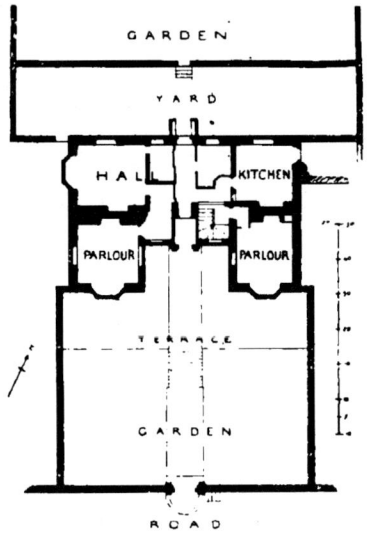

86.—MANOR HOUSE, COLD ASHTON, GLOUCESTERSHIRE. GROUND PLAN.

leading to the terrace in front of the house. The external detail throughout is of the simplest, but there is a good ceiling in one of the parlours, and some of the woodwork is of unusual elaboration. The character of the work points to the early part of the seventeenth century as the date of erection. In these simpler examples the windows do not occupy nearly so large a proportion of the wall space as they do in the more ambitious houses.

An interesting adaptation of the symmetrical arrangement of the forecourt and lodges is to be seen at Bolsover Castle (Figs. 87, 88), where the square house has been built on

87.—BOLSOVER CASTLE, DERBYSHIRE (1613).

the site of the ancient keep, which no doubt largely controlled its size. There are no gables, all the roofs being flat; that over the house itself is approached by a staircase in a domed turret, and was intended as a place of resort. The usual picturesqueness of outline is obtained by various turrets and chimneys. In the illustration the two chambers in the sides of the courtyard are hidden behind those which form the entrance to it. It is not easy to say to what use these chambers were to be put. They are all furnished with fireplaces, most of which are carefully wrought, as though for the delight of the owner rather than of his retainers. The house itself is full of

R.A.   H interest; all the rooms on the basement and principal floor are vaulted, and the vaulting ribs and corbels are managed with such care as was seldom bestowed upon those features even in the days of stone vaulting. This method of construction was rapidly going out of fashion, most of the houses of the sixteenth century having floors of joists and boards, the underside being ceiled in the early part of the century with wood, and in the latter with plaster. But at Bolsover, as late as 1613, we have stone vaulting beautifully wrought. There is a large amount of good panelling also left, and the chimney-pieces are unrivalled in any house of the time for their beauty and variety. Some of these will be illustrated when that subject comes to be dealt with. This part of Bolsover Castle, although so carefully built and embellished, is but a small portion of the whole scheme. There was an immense gallery in close proximity, which, however, has fallen to ruin. It is in a style somewhat later than its smaller neighbour, with gigantic doorways and unwieldy mouldings, and forms a link between Jacobean work and the more fully developed classic treatment of the close of the seventeenth century.

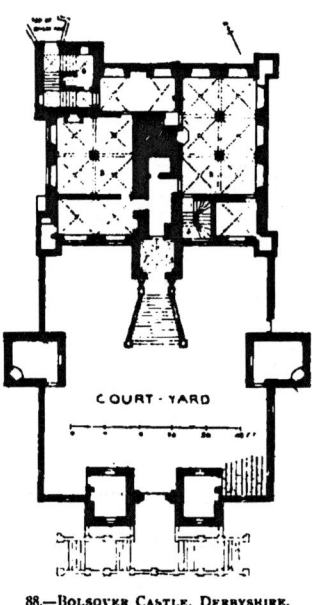

88.—BOLSOVER CASTLE, DERBYSHIRE. GROUND PLAN (1613).

1. Porch. 3. Pillar-room.
2. Hall.   4. Main Staircase.
   5. Small Staircase.

At Condover, in Shropshire (Fig. 89), an agreeable variety of treatment is introduced on the garden front by contriving to get a range of low rooms over the open arcade, the heads of the windows being at the same level as those of the principal rooms. The central gable on the same face is occupied by a bay window, which starts from corbels over the centre arch of the arcade and is carried up to the topmost storey. Variations like these serve to relieve the monotony which is sometimes to be found in the symmetrical houses of the period.

The amount of detail bestowed upon these houses varied according to their locality and the materials at hand. In Yorkshire, Lancashire, and Derbyshire, where the stone is hard, great simplicity is the rule. The entrance doorway usually received some attention, and the gables often had finials, but otherwise the work was of the plainest description. The roofs were generally of flatter pitch than in less boisterous districts, and the whole house gives the impression of rough sturdiness quite in keeping with the character of the owners. Compared with the work in Northamptonshire, as exemplified at Kirby, Rushton, or Apethorpe; in Hampshire at Bramshill; in Sussex at Cowdray; or in Somerset at Montacute, the work in the north is severe and wanting in detail. But it has its own charm, just as the rocky "edges" of Derbyshire, and its wild, boulder-strewn

89.—CONDOVER HALL, SHROPSHIRE. THE GARDEN FRONT (1598).

tors, with their memories of prehistoric tribes perched upon their bleak summits, have a grim fascination not less powerful than that which hangs over the forest districts further south, where ancient oaks, so old as to retain little beyond their huge trunks, call to mind the curious and cruel laws which once protected the animals that lived beneath their shade. Haddon Hall is a large house, and was the home of one of the first families of the county, but its stonework is comparatively plain. Hoghton Tower, in Lancashire, is another large house, but the detail is even simpler than at Haddon. Clegg Hall, near Rochdale (Fig. 90), is a good example of a Lancashire house of medium size, except that, compared with others to be found on the wolds and in the dales of that part of the country, it is unusually lofty. Mount Grace Priory, in Yorkshire (Plate XXX.), is of a more usual type, but even here there is rather greater liveliness than generally distinguishes the Yorkshire manor house ; the windows are larger, and the dormers are of steeper pitch than is common. Oakwell Hall, East Ardsley and Swinsty Old Halls are good examples

90.—CLEGG HALL, LANCASHIRE.

of their kind, with flat-pitched roofs, plain gables, and windows of many small lights. The courtyard at Ingelby Manor (Fig. 91) has an open arcade with some amount of detail about it, but the effect is grim and chilly, and serves to illustrate the mistake of transferring a child of the Italian sun to the bleak regions of Yorkshire. In some parts of Lancashire, in Cheshire, Staffordshire and Worcestershire, and generally in the west, timber was much employed. The " black-and-white," or " magpie," or " post-and-pan " work, as it is variously called, has much charm about it, and appeals keenly to lovers of the picturesque. The contrast between the dark framework

MOUNT GRACE PRIORY, YORKSHIRE.

Plate XXXI.

SPEKE HALL, LANCASHIRE

and the light-coloured plaster, together with the variety of line consequent upon the constructional necessities of the framework itself, insure a lively result; and when the straight lines of the greater part of the framing are relieved by the introduction of curved braces or more fanciful panels in the gables, the combination is very attractive. The effect is often enhanced by dainty little bits of detail in the wood finials and pendants and verge-boards, but even without these aids the texture of the wood becomes so beautiful through age and weather as hardly

91.—COURTYARD, INGELBY MANOR, YORKSHIRE.

to require the help of a chisel. One example, Moreton Old Hall, has already been mentioned (Plates XV., XVI.); Speke Hall, in Lancashire, near the banks of the Irwell, is another (Plate XXXI.), and it has at the entrance a certain amount of stonework which adds considerably to the interest of the house. There is a fine example at Bramall Hall, near Stockport; a plainer one at Pitchford Hall, in Shropshire; while, among others, may be mentioned the Market-house at Ledbury and the Grange at Leominster, both in Herefordshire. Some examples, although not so many, are to be found in the southern counties; but all through Kent, Surrey, Sussex and Hampshire the usual treatment of cottages and small houses was to hang them with weather-tiling. The ground floor was generally of brick, the upper one was tile-hung: there was nearly always a good chimney, sometimes rising out of the roof, but often carried on a massive base which was continued down to the ground. The rich colours which come to these bricks and tiles with age tend to spoil those who live in their midst, and to make them look with a somewhat dull eye upon the quieter tones prevalent in stone districts. Examples of half-timber or "magpie" work,

92.—House at Mayfield, Sussex.

however, are not wanting amid the tile and brick, and one of the most elaborate is to be seen at Mayfield, in Sussex (Fig. 92), but it is far behind similar work in Cheshire and Lancashire in richness of detail. In the eastern counties, as in the southern, brick is the chief material, but here, too, plaster played an important part in clothing the construction. In the west all the detail was put into the wood; in the east it was put into the plaster, and there are many examples still left of elaborate modelling in plaster to be found upon houses and cottages in Essex and Suffolk. Cut flint was also largely employed for walls, and was used in combination with stone to produce highly-ornamental designs; but its employment seems to have largely died out with the Gothic forms in which it was so successfully manipulated. The brickwork, which in the early part of the century was very rich and elaborate, became much plainer towards its close, and indeed the terra-cotta and the

wonderful chimney-shafts of Henry VIII.'s time are hardly to
be found in the work of succeeding reigns. It is not in brickwork that we must look for Elizabethan detail, but rather in
the easily-worked stone which underlies the central district of
England from Devon and Somerset in a north-easterly direction
to Rutland and Lincoln.

WINDOWS.

It has already been said that an Elizabethan house depends
for its picturesqueness chiefly upon its windows, gables, and

93.—COWDRAY HOUSE, SUSSEX. PART OF COURT.

chimneys. The mullioned and transomed window is indeed
one of the characteristic features of the Elizabethan style, the
openings being all rectangular. Already during the prevalence of
Gothic forms the vertical spaces formed by the mullions of the
windows had been divided horizontally by transoms, but this
treatment was rather the exception than the rule. In Tudor times
the windows were usually small, sometimes consisting only of
one light, but often of two or even three, and occasionally being
two tiers in height. The lights almost always had flat-pointed
heads. The small size resulted from the old wish to have a

defensible house, but as the need for such precaution lessened, the lights increased in number; the desire for well-lighted rooms led to still further extension and to doing away with the pointed heads in favour of straight ones. The gradual changes in the form of windows is well seen in the courtyard at Cowdray (Fig. 93). The window on the extreme right of the illustration, with its pointed arch and traceried lights, is Gothic; next to it comes a Tudor bay window, made up of a number of flat-pointed lights, which there was no need to restrict in this case, because the window looked into the court. To the left are two bays of Elizabeth's time, with rectangular lights three rows in height and many in width. At Barrington Court (Plate XXXII.) may be seen a more usual example of Tudor windows, as well as the twisted

94.—Hoghton Tower, Lancashire. Bay of Hall.

finials of which the early sixteenth century was so fond. Another kind of treatment is occasionally to be found, in which brackets are introduced in the upper lights, springing from the mullions and supporting the horizontal head. One version of this method is to be seen at Layer Marney in the windows over the archway (Plate XIII.), and another at Lacock Abbey (Plate XXXVI.). In the latter window should also be noticed the circle introduced at the crossing of the centre mullion and transom, which resembles the treatment adopted

PLATE XXXII.

BARRINGTON COURT, SOMERSET. (TUDOR.)

in the screen at King's College Chapel (Plate VIII.). The date of Layer Marney may be put at 1520, Lacock Abbey at about 1540, and the screen at 1535. The greatest development of windows was, however, to be found in the bay. The bay window is one of the most important features in the architecture of the time. English designers had always been fond of bay windows: they put them to the daïs of their halls in quite early times, and there are many examples

of small bays being corbelled out on an upper floor, where the exigencies of the ground plan did not permit of their starting from the ground. But as a rule these early bays were only one storey in height: as time went on, however, they grew to two storeys, and then to as many as the main building itself had. From being an adjunct they became a dominating feature, and most of the large houses of

95.—BURTON AGNES, YORKSHIRE (1602—10).

the time derive variety of outline and rhythm of composition from their bay windows. Hoghton Tower, in Lancashire (Fig. 94), has a fine bay at the end of the hall. It is only one storey high, but that storey is the full height of the building in that part. The sill is brought down lower than those of the other windows in order to enable the occupants of the daïs to look out into the court. At Astley Hall, also in Lancashire (Plate XXXIII.), the two bays are the dominating feature of the front; indeed, the whole architectural interest of this side of the house lies in the management of the windows, for the doorway, flanked by double columns which lend their united strength to supporting a peaceable lion, is hardly worth attention. The long range of windows which reaches continuously from one end of the building to the other forms a striking feature, but must be a matter of much concern to the housewife who has to drape them on the inside, and to consider the claims of her carpet on sunny days.

At Burton Agnes the grouping of a circular bay in the gable with an octagonal one just round the corner (Fig. 95) is very effective pictorially, and makes an interesting plan. The circular bays at Lilford, in Northamptonshire, set within the curved gables, produce a pleasing combination (Plate XXXIV.); but of all circular bays the palm must be assigned to the great twin bays at Kirby (Plate XXXIII.). It was not only in important houses that these striking features were introduced; they are to be found in all kinds of dwellings, and frequently impart interest to small and insignificant cottages, whether of stone, as at Bourton-on-the-Water (Fig. 96), or of wood and stucco, as at Steventon, in Berkshire (Fig. 97). In both these examples much of the pleasant effect is derived from the small size of the windows and the proportionately large space of plain wall between them; but the same effect can hardly be obtained in the present day, because the rooms have to be higher, and toleration is seldom accorded, either by private taste or

96.—House at Bourton-on-the-Water, Gloucestershire.

PLATE XXXIII.

ASTLEY HALL, LANCASHIRE.

KIRBY HALL, NORTHAMPTONSHIRE. THE BAY WINDOWS.

PLATE XXXIV

LILFORD HALL. NORTHAMPTONSHIRE (1635)

public regulations, to windows which start a long way from the floor and end a long way from the ceiling.

There was no great variety in the mouldings of the stone-work. Several sections of jambs and mullions are shown on Fig. 98, of which No. 1 was most frequently used in Elizabethan and Jacobean work. The jambs and principal mullions had an outer member, slightly splayed. which formed a frame within which the subsidiary mullions and the transoms were enclosed, as may be seen by referring to Figs. 71, 96, and 103. Sometimes this outer member was moulded instead of splayed, as shown in No. 2 (Fig. 98), and occasionally an extra member was introduced close to the glazing line, as shown in No. 3. These three examples are all varieties of the same type. No. 4 shows a type with a hollow moulding, which was prevalent in Tudor

97.—Cottage at Steventon, Berkshire.

work, as it had been previously in Gothic; and it remained in use, along with the plain splayed mullion, up to the time of the sash-window. Although it preceded the type No. 1, and might therefore be considered to indicate an earlier date, it is not by any means a safe guide, inasmuch as both forms were in use at the same time. No. 1, however, was not used before the middle of the sixteenth century, and may be taken as a fairly safe indication of a date subsequent to that time. No. 5 shows a sunk splay, and was occasionally

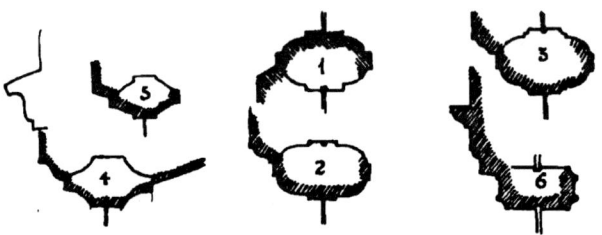

98.—Section of Window Jambs and Mullions.

used, but it is not frequently met with. The label shown on No. 4 was used in late Gothic work, and survived in some instances as long as the mullioned windows themselves; but in the more ambitious designs its place was taken by the lower member of a cornice founded on classic models. No. 6 is

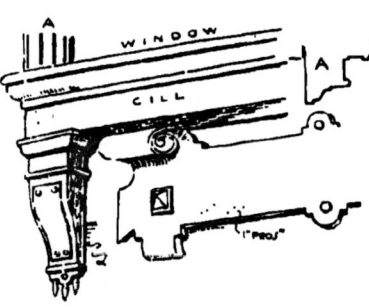

99.—Window-sill at Wollaton Hall.

an example of a quite different type. In all the others, the windows were of the ordinary mullioned type, with a label (or cornice) over them. In No. 6 not only does the shape of the mullion follow a new idea, but the whole of the mouldings outside of it are carried round the head and jambs of the window to form a regular architrave: the effect can be seen in the windows at Wollaton, in Fig. 106. As this architrave projected beyond the face of the wall, the window-sill was brought forward to receive it, as shown on Fig. 99. The projecting sill is supported at each end by a quaint corbel, and the space between the corbels is filled by a projecting panel fashioned like a piece of fancifully-shaped leather nailed on to the wall, and having some of its cut ends curled up.

This treatment of windows involved a considerable amount of labour and expense, and accordingly was not often adopted; but the use of the architrave became general during the seventeenth century, after the mullioned window had given way to sashes.

99A.—HEAD OF A WINDOW AT HATFIELD HOUSE.

CHAPTER VI.

EXTERIOR FEATURES (*continued*).

GABLES, PARAPETS, FINIALS, CHIMNEYS, RAIN-WATER HEADS, GARDENS.

GABLES.

THE gable is one of the characteristic features of the period. As a rule it was of steep pitch—indeed, in many thatched barns and cottages the apex is very acute (Fig. 100). In such cases the cottages generally had attic-rooms in the roof, which were lighted by dormer windows, over which the thatch was worked in such a way that they appeared to be a growth out the main roof rather than an extraneous window applied to it. In stone and brick houses the gable wall rose above the roof, and was coped with stone to prevent the wet penetrating into it. The coping rested at the bottom on a

100.—A NORTHAMPTONSHIRE COTTAGE.

kneeler, which projected sufficiently to accommodate itself to the projection of the eaves, and at the apex it was usually crowned by a finial. A considerable amount of variety was introduced into the design of the kneelers and finials, and many a small house and cottage is redeemed from insignificance by the possession of one or two of these features (Fig. 101). Even where there was no finial, the mere fact of the apex of the coping projecting above the line of the ridge produced a point that showed against the sky,

101.—STONE FINIALS AND KNEELERS.

and helped towards the general picturesqueness of effect. In some of the more important houses the finials were worked

102.—MANOR HOUSE, FINSTOCK, OXFORDSHIRE.

with greater elaboration, and were placed not only on the apex of the gable but on the kneelers at its foot (see Fig. 108, and the dormer on Fig. 113; also Plate XXX.). The effect of plain gables contrasted with those having simple finials is shown on Plate XXXV., while examples of larger and more important finials may be seen at Kirby and Rushton (Figs. 107,

103.—Cottage at Rothwell, Northamptonshire. (1660.)

113), the prevailing forms being some variety of the obelisk.

The use of simple gables or their combination with dormer windows and chimneys, all without elaborate detail, is quite sufficient to impart interest to a building, which otherwise would have little claim to attention. Examples of these unpretentious houses are to be met with in every county; one or two are illustrated here from Finstock, in Oxfordshire (Fig. 102), Broadway, in Worcestershire (Plate XXXV.), and Holmshurst, in Sussex (Plate XXXV.). There is very little conscious effort about the design of either of these, beyond the introduction of a certain amount of symmetry. At Finstock Manor House there is a range of three equal gables occupying most of the front, and the door is in the centre. At Tudor House, Broadway, there are three gables, but they are detached from each other, and the middle one is rather larger than its neighbours; a bay window of two storeys occupies the centre of the front, and the very plainly treated door is

TUDOR HOUSE, BROADWAY, WORCESTERSHIRE.

HOLMSHURST, BURWASH, SUSSEX.

at one end. The house at Holmshurst is, like most of those in the Weald, built of brick: it has stone windows, but very little detail, its effect depending upon the two [gables, each flanked with a large chimney-stack.

The style which was prevalent at the end of the sixteenth century lingered on far into the seventeenth in buildings that were not subject to the passing fashion: indeed, the treatment was hardly adopted consciously, but was rather the obvious and natural way of building, otherwise it would not have

104.—COTTAGE AT TREETON, NEAR SHEFFIELD.

been applied to such cottages as that at Rothwell (Fig. 103) and Treeton, near Sheffield (Fig. 104).

In houses which were constructed of timber and plaster it was impossible to carry up the gables above the roof; the method of building did not admit of it, and there would have been no adequate means of covering them from the weather. They were finished, therefore, with projecting verge-boards, which served to protect the surface of the walls, and which were often carved or cut and moulded. A simple instance applied to a cottage is to be found at Steventon (Fig. 105), but there are plenty to be seen in different parts of the country, particularly in the west.

In the more important houses the gables were not infrequently curved, especially in later times, that is to say, the curved gable is more frequent in Jacobean work than in Elizabethan. This idea no doubt came from the Low Countries, where it was very extensively adopted, but the extravagant and fantastic curves which the Dutchman loved were much simplified by his English imitator. Some of the more ambitious efforts, such as Wollaton, went near in their elaborate strap-work to rival the original models. A study of one of the corner pavilions

105.—COTTAGE AT STEVENTON, BERKSHIRE.

(Fig. 106) will show how, not only in the gables but in the whole treatment, the foreign influence is predominant. The simplicity of the native type is entirely wanting. There are no plain surfaces of any extent; the columns are broken by a projecting band; the pedestals on which they stand are adorned with panels of double projection; not only are the corner piers of the parapet crowned with an obelisk, but the pediment at the top of each gable carries a small statue on a pedestal: everything is done to add to the picturesqueness and richness of effect. Nevertheless, through all the ornament with which the design is overloaded, its main ideas are plainly visible: the large and simple windows, the emphasizing of the angles, the gables of studiously irregular outline. In some Dutch and German work the designers seemed to lose sight of their purpose in the exuberance of their ornament, but here it is not so. It will be seen that the circular niches on the side faces are filled with busts, although the vertical niches between the pilasters are empty. The busts, so far as they are named or can be identified, are those of classic personages—Plato, Aristoteles, Vergilius—and are said to have been brought over from Italy.

The west front of Kirby (Fig. 107) offers a great contrast to Wollaton. Here everything up as high as the parapet is as simple as it can well be; there are no pilasters, no niches, no strapwork panels. The windows and the cornices which make the circuit of the building are the only architectural features. The gables have the strap-work, but it is of a simpler form than that at Wollaton: the irregularity of their outline, combined with the tapering obelisks, some of which have open stone bows at the bottom, something after the fashion of a jug handle, imparts the necessary picturesqueness, without

106.—WOLLATON HALL, NOTTINGHAMSHIRE.
ONE OF CORNER TOWERS (1588).

I 2

having recourse to the expensive devices employed at Wollaton.
The latter house was built between the years 1580 and 1588,
and the gables may therefore be taken as dating from 1588 :
the date of the west front of Kirby is not recorded, but
from the character of the work it may very well have been
subsequent to the main building operations in 1570—75, and,
as already stated, these gables were not improbably added
towards the close of the sixteenth century. One curious point
about this front is the care which was taken to make the quoins
perfectly regular in size : in some cases where the quoin stone

107.—Kirby Hall, Northamptonshire. Part of West Front (possibly 1595).

was larger than the regulation size, the overplus was slightly
sunk, and then scored with false joint-lines to match those of
the adjacent rubble.

There was a simpler type of curved gable which was freely
used, as in the courtyard at Rushton (Fig. 108), and it was
sometimes combined with steps, as at Apethorpe (Fig. 109),
the result being picturesque without being fussy. The date
of the example at Apethorpe is 1623—24, and that at Rushton
1627. The curve, instead of being ogee-shaped as in these
instances, was sometimes composed of two curves of similar
form, with a square shoulder between them, like those at
Blickling (Plate XXXVII.), or the sweep of the ogee was broken

by the introduction of a vertical line, such as may be seen in the gables at Lilford (Plate XXXIV.). Further varieties occur at Montacute (Fig. 48), Stanway (Plate XXII.), and Westwood (Plate XXIII.).

PARAPETS.

The gables and the dormer windows in the larger houses were often connected by a parapet, broken at intervals by a shallow pilaster carried up to form the base of a finial or the seat for some heraldic animal. Sometimes the parapet was solid, as at Apethorpe (Fig. 109), Doddington (Plate XXI.), and the courtyard at Kirby (Fig. 76); sometimes it was formed of a series of arches, as at Exton (Fig. 110, and Plate XXIX.), and at Hambleton (Fig. 71); sometimes of stone panels pierced with a pattern, as at Bramshill (Fig. 111) and Audley End (Fig. 112); and sometimes of stone balusters, of which Rushton Hall offers one example (Fig. 113) and Wollaton Hall (Plate XXVII.) another. There was a considerable amount of variety, according to the ability of the mason to design and of the owner to pay.

108.—GABLE IN COURT, RUSHTON, NORTHAMPTONSHIRE (1627).

109.—GABLE IN COURT, APETHORPE, NORTHAMPTONSHIRE (1623—24).

The effect of the pierced panels carried along a considerable length of parapet is very rich and lace-like. The stone balusters were occasionally of very meagre proportion, and

110.—EXTON OLD HALL, RUTLAND. STONE PARAPET.

used with too sparing a hand, but at Rushton this is not felt to be the case. The parapet to the main roofs here is more satisfactory than the rather confused ornament which serves a similar purpose for the bay. This gable also affords a good example of the manner in which the lights of the mullioned windows were stepped up

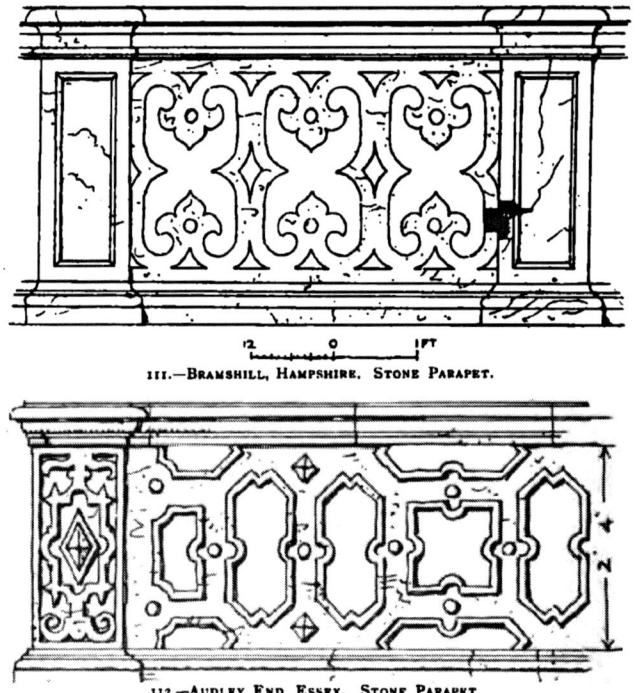

111.—BRAMSHILL, HAMPSHIRE. STONE PARAPET.

112.—AUDLEY END, ESSEX. STONE PARAPET.

so as to follow roughly the slope of the roof. In one or two houses (Castle Ashby in Northamptonshire, and Temple

Newsam in Yorkshire) the parapets are formed of stone letters forming a series of legends which make, more or less, the circuit of the house.

CHIMNEYS.

The chimneys were always dealt with boldly. In many cases, as already said, they were massed into great stacks at intervals along the walls, and made the dominating features of the whole design. Wherever they occurred their presence was frankly accepted, and, as a rule, much skill and ingenuity were bestowed upon them. In later centuries chimneys appear to have become a source of considerable annoyance to architectural designers, and a great deal of misapplied ingenuity was expended in trying to conceal their existence, owing to the idea that they interfered with the purity of classic façades.

113.—RUSHTON HALL, NORTHAMPTONSHIRE.
GABLE ON EAST FRONT (1627).

But in the early days of the introduction of classic features, the problem of making chimneys harmonize with the rest of the building seems to have been a source of delight instead of annoyance.

The general use of chimneys was at this time rather a novelty. So late as the time of Henry VII., in the new palace called Richmond Court, built to replace an older structure destroyed by fire in 1498, the great hall was warmed by a fire in the middle of the floor with a lantern in the roof over it.

114.—CHIMNEY AT DROITWICH,
WORCESTERSHIRE.

There is a description of the Court in the return of the Commissioners of Parliament made in 1649, which is interesting not only as mentioning the fire, but as bearing out what has already been said of the hall of a large house. The higher storey, they say,* "contains one fayr and large room 100 feet in length and 40 in breadth, called the Great Hall. This room hath a screen at the lower end thereof, over which is a little gallery, and a fayr foot-pace in the higher end thereof [the daïs]; the pavement is square tile, and it is very well lighted and seeled [*i.e.*, panelled with wood], and adorned with eleven statues in the sides thereof; in the midst a brick hearth for a charcoal fire, having a large lanthorn in the roof of the hall fitted for that purpose, turreted and covered with lead." But early in the sixteenth century chimneys came into general use, and they are one of the most characteristic features of a Tudor house. They were generally built of moulded brick, and were fashioned in elaborate and complicated ways. An illustration from Droitwich is given in Fig. 114, in which the moulded bases stand on panelled

* *Nichols' Progresses of Queen Elizabeth,* Vol. I. (1566).

pedestals; the shafts also are moulded, each after a different

115.—Brick Chimney from
Huddington Court
House, Worcestershire.

117.—Chimney at Toller Fratrum,
Dorset.

116.—Brick Chimney from
Bardwell Manor House, Suffolk.

118.—Chimney at Kirby Hall,
Northamptonshire.

manner, and the caps are crowned with a battlemented
ornament. Some of the simpler forms are illustrated among

the details from Layer Marney (Plate XIII.), also from Huddington Court House, in Worcestershire (Fig. 115), Bardwell, in Suffolk (Fig. 116), and a stone example from Toller Fratrum, in Dorset (Fig. 117). But far richer specimens are to be seen at Compton Winyates (Plate XI.) or at Hengrave (Fig. 43), besides many other places. With the death of Henry VIII. this elaboration disappeared, and a plainer treatment prevailed. In some of the more pretentious edifices the chimneys were cast into the form of columns, as they were at Wollaton (Plate XXVII.) and Burghley (Plate XXVIII.), and at Montacute also, where the column carries a kind of stone cowl. The columnar form had occasionally been used in earlier days; there is a well-proportioned and excellently wrought example at Lacock Abbey (Plate XXXVI.), where the shafts are fashioned into fluted columns, and the cap takes the shape of a short length of classic entablature with architrave, frieze, and cornice complete. The columns stand upon a pedestal, the face of which is occupied with a panel surrounded by strap-work; and as there seems every reason to suppose the work to be part of Sharington's prior to his death in 1553, the whole idea and its mode of execution is unusually early, strap-work being associated as a rule with a period fifteen or twenty years later. The consoles carrying the projection of the base are an additional feature, and the whole group is carefully designed. The notion, however, of making the chimney-flue into a column and taking a short length of entablature as a cap is hardly satisfactory, and a more reasonable type was employed at Kirby (Fig. 118), while throughout the stone district of the Midlands the usual form is that in Fig. 119, a form which, with modifications, has lingered on even down to the present day. A somewhat ornamental variety of the same idea is to be seen at Chipping Campden (Fig. 120), and another variation at Drayton House, in Northamptonshire (Fig. 121). The quaint triangular chimney of the Triangular Lodge at Rushton (Fig. 122) is really the same in principle, but its unusual apex and carved panels place it in a class by itself. The brick chimneys of Elizabeth's time have straight stalks and an oversailing cap of thin bricks, occasionally varied with still thinner courses of tiles. The profile is nearly always the same, but considerable variety is imparted by varying the plan, and by adding square or

PLATE XXXVI.

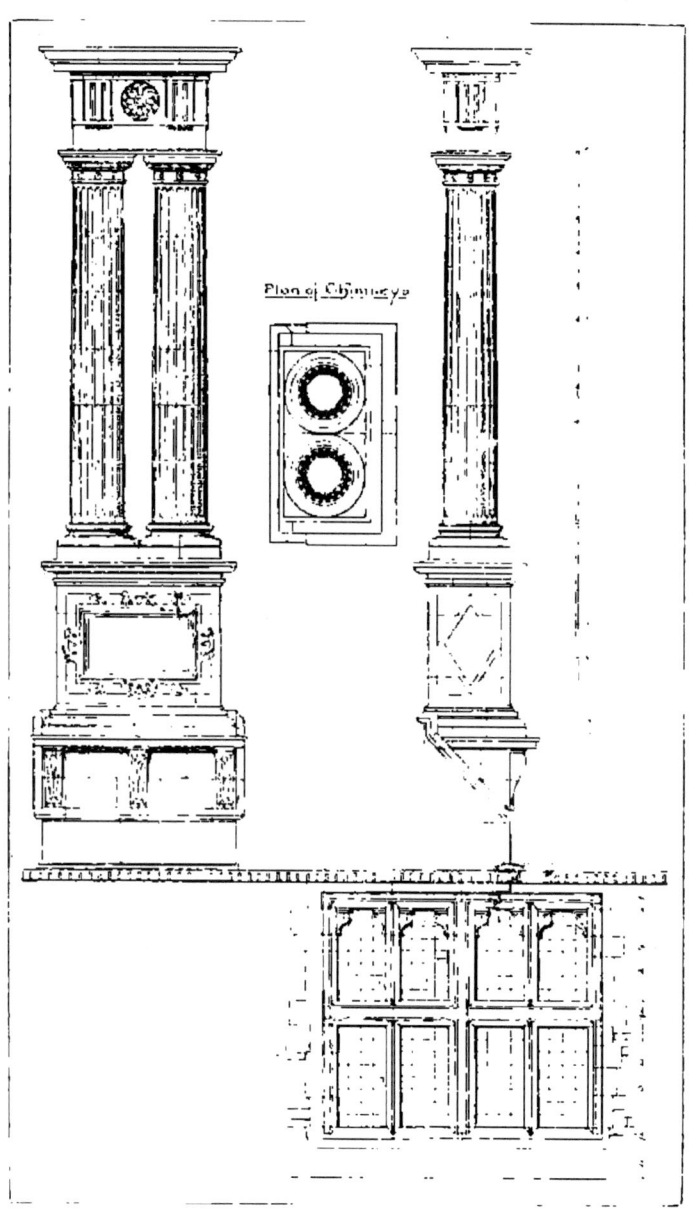

Plan of Chimneys

LACOCK ABBEY, WILTSHIRE.
CHIMNEY-STACK AND WINDOW.

119.—TYPICAL CHIMNEY IN THE
MIDLANDS.

120.—CHIMNEY AT CHIPPING CAMPDEN,
GLOUCESTERSHIRE.

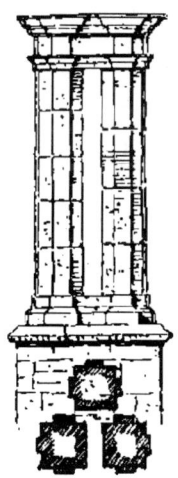

121.—CHIMNEY AT DRAYTON
HOUSE, NORTHAMPTONSHIRE
(1584.)

122.—CHIMNEY AT TRIANGULAR LODGE,
RUSHTON, NORTHAMPTONSHIRE (1595).

triangular projections to the plain faces of the flues. A simple but effective example may be seen at Bean Lodge, near Petworth (Fig. 123). More elaborate specimens are found at Knole House and Cobham Hall, in Kent; Blickling Hall, in Norfolk (Plate XXXVII.); at Moyns Park, in Essex, and indeed on almost every brick house of the time.

Blickling Hall affords examples of many of the features which have been described. It has fine stacks of chimneys, curved gables, and pierced parapets over the windows; on each gable is a dainty little statue. The front doorway is richly embellished, and over it are the owner's arms set forth with much heraldic display. Classic features are used with moderation and restraint ; a cornice marks the level of the first floor; other cornices crown the bay windows ; and columns flank the archway. But they are all used because they answered the designer's purpose, and not because he hoped by loading his building with classic features to give it a character which, without such help, he was powerless to impart.

123.—BEAN LODGE, PETWORTH, SUSSEX.

RAIN-WATER HEADS.

Attention should be drawn to another feature of which nothing hitherto has been said, but which was one of the recognized means of obtaining effect—namely, the rain-water pipes. These

PLATE XXXVII.

BLICKLING HALL, NORFOLK (1619-20).

PART OF ENTRANCE FRONT

necessary adjuncts to a building have ceased to play the important part which once they did; they are still tolerated, because they cannot be abolished, but they are only admitted grudgingly and of necessity. In the sixteenth and seventeenth centuries a large amount of care was bestowed upon their design, and being made of lead they were susceptible of interesting treatment. Their use was in the nature of a novelty, since up to this time the water from the roofs had been allowed to splash on to the ground from projecting gargoyles. They very frequently carried either the date or the family crest upon them, and were often ornamented with pierced work. The examples shown in Figs. 124—126 are from Haddon Hall; two of them bear the cognizance of the Vernon family (the boar's head), and one that of the Manners family in addition (the peacock). Haddon passed into the possession of Sir John Manners, by his marriage with Dorothy Vernon, in the year 1567, and these lead heads must be ascribed to a date subsequent to the marriage, otherwise they would not bear the peacock of the Manners family. They still retain in their ornament some trace of Gothic feeling, but the topmost moulding, with the dentils beneath it, is clearly of classic derivation. The third head with the cresting of fleur-de-lys may well be of rather earlier date, and the work of Sir George Vernon, the father of Dorothy. Allied to the last example from Haddon is the rain-water head from Sherborne, Dorset (Fig. 127), dated 1579, also with a battlemented cresting. At Knole, in Kent, is another good example (Fig. 128) with a pierced front and two triangular projections ending in a pendant; the top is ornamented with a battlemented cresting, now mutilated. Another specimen, of somewhat plainer character, comes from Bramshill (Fig. 129); it is dated 1612, and has its outlet towards one end, so as to bring the water horizontally along the wall for a short distance in order that the pipe may not interfere with some feature in the wall below. At Rushton there are some lead heads bearing the date 1627, which depend for their effect upon their shape rather than upon their decoration, which is practically limited to a very simple treatment of the cresting. These are two or three examples out of a great many that still remain, some of them being even more ornamental; the greater number, however, were more nearly allied to the plainer than the richer examples.

124.—Lead Rain-water Head from
Haddon Hall, Derbyshire.

125.—Lead Rain-water Head from
Haddon Hall, Derbyshire.

126.—Lead Rain-water Head from
Haddon Hall, Derbyshire.

127.—Pipe Head from Sherborne,
Dorset.

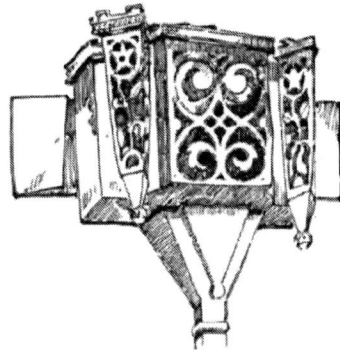

128.—Lead Pipe Head from Knole, Kent.

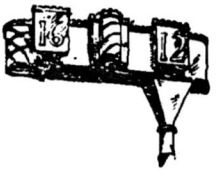

129.—Lead Pipe Head from
Bramshill.

PLATE XXXVIII.

HADDON HALL, DERBYSHIRE. STEPS TO TERRACE.

CLAVERTON, SOMERSET. TERRACE WALL.

GARDENS.

This is not the place to enter into an elaborate account of gardens, but they touch the subject under discussion so far as this—that there was a certain amount of architectural design bestowed upon them in the shape of terraces, flights of steps, balustrades and garden-houses. The view of Montacute shown in Fig. 48 gives a good idea of the manner in which the house was set off by a formal garden enclosed by stone walls and balustrades, which were emphasized at the angles by garden-houses, and along their lengths either by gateways or some kind of special object, such as the quaint kind of temple, which serves no purpose but to vary the monotony of the balustrade. The well-known terrace at Haddon is as good an example as can be found of the fine effect of a raised walk approached by a broad flight of steps, and protected by an arcaded balustrade (Plate XXXVIII.). The detail is quite simple, there is no particular effort visible, every thing seems to be there because it is wanted, but the whole effect is extremely picturesque. At Claverton, near Bath, are the remains of a fine house and garden, of which a long terrace wall is also illustrated on Plate XXXVIII. Here the straight length is broken by the large gate-piers, which rise some twelve feet high before tapering off into the universal obelisk. Claverton must have been a splendid example of Jacobean work, judging by the illustrations in Richardson's *Elizabethan Architecture*, but unhappily little of it now remains. At Gayhurst, in Buckinghamshire, there are a number of quaint stone piers flanking the main approach, set a few yards apart (Fig. 130), the space between them being filled in with cut yew hedges. Hedges do not enter into the scope of the present work, but they were

130.—GAYHURST, BUCKINGHAMSHIRE. STONE PILLAR IN GARDEN.

much in vogue, as were also pleached alleys and the green
shaded walks so much desired by the Noble Gentleman in
Beaumont and Fletcher's play of that name. With arches in
walls we have more concern, and have already dealt with them
in dealing with the approaches to the house ; but an additional

example from a
garden at Ling-
field, in Sussex, is
illustrated in Fig.
131 ; and another
from Highlow
Hall, in Derby-
shire, on Plate
XXXIX.

The lay-out of a
late sixteenth cen-
tury garden was
tolerably simple,
the whole being
treated on a defi-
nite system, and
with straight lines.
The bowling-green
was an important
adjunct, and the
larger houses had
mounts for pro-
spect, and also a
"wilderness" of
considerable ex-
tent. The de-
scription of the
gardens at None-
such, given by the
Parliamentary

131 —GATEWAY IN GARDEN, LINGFIELD, SUSSEX (1617).

Commissioners in their survey of April, 1650* (already quoted),
gives a good idea of the gardens attached to the larger sort of
houses. The "frontispiece," or approach, was railed with handsome rails and balusters of stone ; at a distance of eight yards
from the house was the bowling-green, from which a fair and

* *Archæologia*, Vol. V. p. 429.

straight path led along an avenue to the park gate, which (they
say) being very high, well-built, and placed in a direct line
opposite to the house, was, in consequence, a good ornament to
it.   On three outward sides of the inner court lay the " Privy
Garden," surrounded with a brick wall 14 feet high, and cut
out and divided into various alleys, quarters, and rounds, set
about with thorn hedges.   Adjoining this garden was the
kitchen garden, also enclosed by a 14 feet wall: on the west
of this lay the wilderness.   In the privy garden was a spiral
pyramid of marble, set upon a base of similar material,
" grounded upon a rise of freestone;" and near this there was
a large marble wash basin, over which stood a marble pelican,
fed with water through a lead pipe.   There were also two
other marble obelisks, and between them a fountain of white
marble, set round with six lilac trees, "which trees bear no
fruit, but only a very pleasant flower."   In the highest part
of the park stood the banqueting-house, a three-storey timber
building of quadrangular form, enclosed within a brick wall.
The ground floor was occupied by the hall, the upper storeys
had respectively three and five rooms, and they were all
panelled with oak.   In each of the four corners of the whole
house there was a balcony placed for prospect.   This is worth
remembering, for the desire to obtain a prospect is generally
considered to be of modern growth; and no doubt until quite
recently it was necessary to a beautiful view that it should be
obtained in ease and comfort.   The notion of climbing a wild
mountain for the sake of the view was probably never entertained
before the beginning of this century.

There is a good example of the lay-out of a forecourt to a
small house at Eyam Hall, in Derbyshire, and although tradition
and the only date to be found about the building (on a spout-
head) place the erection of the house in the latter part of
the seventeenth century, it looks much earlier, and is characteristic of the beginning of the century rather than of the end.
There is very little detail about it; but the formal disposition
and the broad and simple treatment combine (with the assist-
ance of time) to impart a fine and dignified effect.   It will be
seen from the plan (Fig. 133) that the court is nearly square.
It is entered from the road through a pillared gateway up a
short flight of semicircular steps ; a broad paved walk leads to
another flight which lands on to a wide paved terrace extending

along the whole front of the house (Plate XXXIX.).   Exactly
opposite the steps is the front door, placed centrally in the main
face of the house, which is recessed from the faces of the projecting wings.   At either end of the terrace is a doorway, one
leading to the kitchen approach, the other to the garden, which
is reached down another flight of semicircular steps.   The paths
in the vicinity of the house are straight, and the rise of the
ground necessitates still more steps, which give access eventually

132.—Chipping Campden, Gloucestershire.   Garden-house.

to a long, straight walk beneath a south-west wall.   Away from
the house the treatment has lapsed into less formality ; but the
house itself, together with the court, the terraces, and the flights
of steps, the whole gay with flowers, makes a very attractive
picture.

The banqueting-house at Nonesuch was, like the other part
of the house itself, built of timber.   So, also, in all probability,
was the "goodly banqueting-house" which the Lord Admiral
built for the Queen when she went to his place in the year
1559 from Hampton Court.   It was richly gilded and painted

PLATE XXXIX.

GATEWAY AT HIGHLOW HALL, NEAR HATHERSAGE, DERBYSHIRE.

EYAM HALL, DERBYSHIRE   TERRACE STEPS.

(we are told), "that lord having for that end kept a great
many painters for a good while there in the country." But
the more usual material was brick or stone, and a fair number
of examples of such buildings still survive. One of the most
elaborate is to be seen at Chipping Campden (Fig. 132), in
Gloucestershire, where the fall of the site enables an under-
storey to be obtained without being buried in the ground.
The illustration shows the ground floor only, but there is a
storey below it approached by a substantial staircase. The
work is elaborate, and has lasted well in spite of its rather
unworkmanlike treatment, as for instance in the jointing of
the stone parapets. The detail is too fanciful, and the building
is illustrated not so much for the sake of its design, as to show
how much trouble and expense were lavished upon a structure
which could only have been used a few times during the year.
It and its fellow on the opposite side were, however, important
features in the general lay-out.

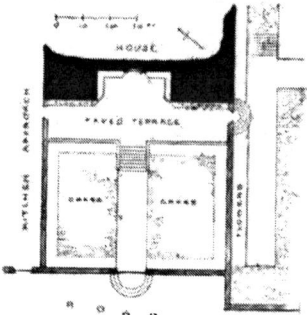

133.—Eyam Hall. Plan of Lay-out.

K 2

CHAPTER VII.

INTERIOR FEATURES.

THE chief points in the internal arrangement of houses of
the period have already been explained in the third chapter.
The hall was the central feature, entered at one end; next to
this end was the kitchen; next to the other, or daïs end, was
the parlour. The kitchen and the parlour respectively were
amplified according to the accommodation required, and in the
larger houses the amplification entailed one or more courts,
but the hall remained the centre of the system. The need for
such great amplification as we find in the larger houses arose
from the fact that large retinues accompanied great personages
on their visits to each other, and that there was always the
chance that the sovereign might have to be entertained upon
one of the progresses which were undertaken three or four
times every year. Both Elizabeth and James adopted this
method of keeping in touch with their subjects, and they must
have become tolerably familiar with their dominions, except,
perhaps, the extreme outlying parts in the north and west;
and so far as James was concerned, he made the acquaintance
of a good many houses in the north, on his journey from
Scotland when he came to take possession of the crown.

ROYAL PROGRESSES.

When Queen Elizabeth made her progresses, she was frequently entertained with elaborate shows, which, presumably,
must have pleased her, since they occurred so often, but which
afford tedious reading to the modern inquirer. They were
usually cast in an allegorical form, and had more or less
dramatic action. They took place in the daytime and in the
open air: it can hardly be said that they were performed, for
the thread of the plot was so thin, and the stage of operations
so large, that the whole effect must have appeared rather

fortuitous, and wanting in cohesion. At night time and in one of the great halls, either of a city, a college, or a great house, there were other performances, in which the interest was more concentrated, and the characters more varied; these were called plays, of which a great number were performed, written by all sorts of people, and all affording (apparently) equal pleasure to the onlookers. The majority of these pieces have faded into oblivion, but a certain number have survived, and go to form much of what we know as the Elizabethan drama.

But it is with the entertainments provided in the daytime that we are more particularly concerned: they were of an ephemeral nature, and have not, like many of the plays, passed into the literature of the country: and our concern with them lies in the form in which they were cast and the spirit which animated them. When Elizabeth made her passage through the city of London to Westminster the day before her coronation—that is, on January 13th, 1558—the whole journey was interspersed with "pageants," as they were called.* These consisted of triumphal arches of various designs, upon which living allegorical figures were placed: one represented the Queen's immediate ancestors: another four virtues treading down four contrary vices; another the eight beatitudes; on another were Time and Truth his daughter; and so forth. Each of these personages, says the account, according to their proper names and properties, had not only their names in plain and perfect writing set upon their breasts easily to be read of all, but also each of them was aptly and properly apparelled, so that his apparel and name did agree to express the same person that in title he represented. As each pageant was reached, there stepped forth a "child" on to some prominent part of it, who recited a number of verses explanatory of the device, and a copy of these verses was affixed in a tablet upon the pageant, balanced by another bearing a Latin version of the same lines. Besides these, it says, every void place in the pageant was furnished with sentences touching the matter and ground of the said pageant. We have here, therefore, on a large scale, the same kind of treatment which was applied on a small scale to chimney-pieces—allegorical figures and various inscriptions more or less pithy. It is a matter for speculation

* *Nichols' Progresses of Queen Elizabeth.*

whether either the Queen or the populace at large thoroughly
grasped the full meaning of the several devices upon which
so much ingenuity had been lavished; but certainly to the
monarch, who stopped at every pageant, and received an
explanation of it, the journey must have been extremely tiring,
seeing how great were the number and ingenuity of the
pageants. To preserve so much good work from oblivion,
within the next ten days an account of the whole " passage "
was printed, which towards its close gives much credit to the
city, forasmuch as without any foreign person, of itself, it
beautified itself. This casual reference to the foreign person,
and to the city being able to manage without his help, shows
that he was a recognized factor in the production of design.

When King James made his " memorable Passage from the
Tower to Whitehall," on the 15th March, 1603—4, there were
seven triumphal arches erected, of such importance that they
were considered worthy of being engraved and published.
They were designed by an Englishman, Stephen Harrison,
" Joyner and Architect," and their architectural treatment
followed the lines of the more pronounced Anglo-Italian work
of the time, in which classic feeling has superseded Gothic.
They are interesting as showing how completely the English
craftsman had familiarized himself with the foreign methods of
design. They were published by Harrison in 1604, the engrav-
ings being by William Kip.* They were built in a substantial
manner, nearly six months being spent upon their erection.
Two of them were called respectively " The Italians' Pegme "
and " The Pegme of the Dutchmen," residents of these two
nationalities being responsible for their erection; but it is
curious to see that the Dutchmen's arch is not more Dutch in
treatment than the Italians'. It evidently did not occur to
Harrison to emphasize the character of his designs to suit the
two nations, even if he were aware of the points in which
their architecture differed.

It was perhaps natural in those days that when Queen
Elizabeth visited the great seats of learning she should be

---

* The title of the book, which is well worth inspection, is " *The Archs of
Triumph, erected in honor of the High and Mighty Prince James, the First of that
Name King of England, and the Sixt of Scotland, at his Maiestie's Entrance and Passage
through his Honorable Citty and Chamber of London, upon the 15th day of March*, 1603.
Invented and published by Stephen Harrison, Joyner and Architect; and graven
by William Kip."

greeted with a shower of Latin verses and orations. Pages after pages of these have been preserved, but it seems extremely doubtful whether the recipient of them could have found time to master their contents. The orations she listened to and understood, for the expression of her face is said to have changed with the subject-matter of the speeches, and some of them she answered in the same tongue. But it was by no means to Eton or to Oxford and Cambridge that Latin verses and orations were confined : obscure parsons in small towns seized their opportunities, and were often handsomely praised by the Queen for their skill. As to verses, when she visited Sandwich in 1573, "upon every post and corner, from her first entry to her lodging, were fixed certain verses, and against the court gate all these verses put into a table (*i.e.*, a frame) and there hanged up."

The Queen's visit to Kenilworth Castle in July, 1575, is one of the best known episodes of her Progresses, and the " Princely Pleasures at Kenilworth Castle," recorded (and largely devised) by George Gascoigne, consisted of the same kind of entertainments as greeted her at her coronation. They are too long to quote extensively, but a few of the principal efforts will serve to show the kind of spirit that was abroad at the time.

As the Queen approached the castle, Sybilla met her and prophesied prosperity in a number of verses. On entering the gate Hercules, who acted as porter, seemed inclined to dispute her entry, but being overcome by the " rare beauty and princely countenance" of her Majesty, he gave up his keys, and burst into poetry. In the base-court there came a lady, attended by two nymphs, and the lady welcomed her Majesty in another set of verses. A few steps further on came an actor clad like a poet, who pronounced a number of Latin verses, which were also fixed over the gate in a frame. After leaving the poet, she was received into the inner court with sweet music, and then escaped to her own "lodgings." A day or two after her arrival there met her in the forest, as she came from hunting, one clad like a Savage man, all in ivy, who was so much over-come with wonder at the Queen's presence that he fell to quarrelling with Jupiter, and called upon Echo to explain who the resplendent personage might be, incidentally contriving to lavish a number of compliments in the course of the inquiry.

Then Triton came, and the Lady of the Lake, and Proteus sitting on a dolphin's back, who all delivered themselves of further compliments in lengthy verses. It is just conceivable that her Majesty grew a little weary of these pedantic interludes, for one long show was prepared by Master Gascoigne, in which Diana and her nymphs, Mercury, Iris, and others were to have acted; but in spite of every actor being ready in his garment for two or three days together, it never came to execution, being prevented (its author thought) by lack of opportunity and seasonable weather. At the Queen's departure, being commanded by the Earl of Leicester to devise some worthy farewell entertainment, Master Gascoigne clothed himself as Sylvanus, the god of the woods, and meeting the Queen as she went hunting, broke out into a long extempore oration, which her Majesty at length interrupted by proceeding on her way. Sylvanus, however, kept pace with her, and continued his speech running at her side, until in very pity for his breathless condition, the Queen stopped her horse. At Sylvanus's humble request, however, she continued her ride, and he continued the ceaseless stream of his oration, until coming to an arbour, a second actor in the tedious drama, by name Deep Desire, took up his part, spake some verses, and sang a song. A few more lines from Sylvanus released the Queen from this very diverting farewell show.

Many other entertainments might be cited to illustrate the direction which popular taste took in these matters; but to multiply instances would be as tedious to the reader as (one cannot help thinking) the shows themselves were to the Queen and her attendants. This, at any rate, becomes clear—that the favourite themes, personages, and allusions were of classic origin; the thoughts were clothed in pedantic language; verses were freely written and hung up for passers-by to read, and the Latin tongue was employed in preference to the English, where it was not absolutely necessary that the points should be understanded of the people. The accounts that have been handed down of these interludes are, it is true, somewhat tedious reading, but under the genial satire of Shakespeare they lose their dulness and become amusing. We do not tire of Holofernes and his party in their presentation of the Nine Worthies, nor of Bottom and his company in their great classical interlude of " the tedious brief scene of young Pyramus and his love Thisbe," nor of Orlando and his verses, which he hung on every tree.

It was no small matter to entertain royalty in those days. Even in the present day, when facilities for moving about and for obtaining provisions are so vastly greater, and when the mode of life in the Court is so much simpler, it requires a large house and a well-filled purse. But in the sixteenth century the undertaking was more like providing for a small army, and it is not surprising to find that outside the wealthier owners of great mansions, there was a disposition to evade the honour. Lady Anne Askewe wrote to Sir Christopher Hatton, about the year 1581, to know if she might be excused on account of the shortness of the notice and her " unfurnished house."* The officials of the Court so far sympathized with this feeling that we find one of them writing to a friend who was threatened with the honour, Mr. More, of Loseley, to say what a " great trouble and hindrance " it would be, and to advise him to " come and declare unto my lord of Leicester your estate that majesty might not come unto your house."† It is not clear whether these representations were actually made, and if made whether they were successful or not; but, however that may be, the same gentleman (he was now knighted) received an intimation in August, 1583, from Sir Christopher Hatton that the Queen intended in about ten or twelve days to visit Loseley, and to remain there some four or five days, and that he had better see everything well ordered and the " house kept sweet and clean to receive her highness." Three weeks later Sir William More had another letter from Sir Christopher to say that on the third day thence the Queen intended to go to bed at Loseley for one night only, and that he should see that the house was " sweet and meet to receive her majesty," and should send his family away. These involuntary hosts were not always consulted beforehand, for one of them wrote to Sir William More in July, 1577, to say that he found the lists were issued for a progress into his county, and his house was one of those to be visited; accordingly he wrote to his loving friend, Sir William, to beg him, for the sake of old acquaintance and friendship, to say what order was taken by the Queen's officers in respect of provisions when her Majesty visited Loseley, as

* Sir Nicholas Harris's *Memorials of Sir Ch. Hatton,* p. 223.
† *Loseley MSS.,* p. 266.

the writer was altogether unacquainted with the order of pro-
cedure. The lists of places to be visited, or "gests," as they were
called, were carefully prepared beforehand, and gave the names
of the houses and their owners, the number of nights the Court
intended to stay, and the distance between one stopping-place
and the next: this distance was on the average about ten miles,
but it varied, according to circumstances, from five to fourteen,
the latter being the longest journey attempted.

To entertain the Sovereign and the Court the houses were
necessarily large, indeed we shall not be far wrong in attributing
the enormous size of the largest—such places as Holdenby,
Theobalds, and Audley End—to the express intention of providing suitable accommodation for Elizabeth and James. Sir
Christopher Hatton, in a letter to Sir Thomas Heneage, in
1580, talks of Holdenby being dedicated to "that holy Saint,"
meaning the Queen; and Lord Burghley, in writing to Hatton
about Holdenby and Theobalds, says "God send us both long
to enjoy Her, for whom we both meant to exceed our purses
in these."* In another letter (August 14th, 1585) he says, "My
house at Theobalds was begun by me with a mean measure,
but increased by occasions of her Majesty's often coming."†
These mansions may be regarded almost in the light of large
hotels, with certain common apartments for the guests, a large
kitchen department, and a vast number of rooms arranged in
groups of two or three.

Although notice of the sovereign's intended visit was usually
given, it was not considered necessary for less exalted people
to send word. When James's queen was journeying towards
London from Scotland, a certain Lady Anne Clifford hurried
with her mother to meet her. The lady describes her journey,
and how they went without notice to a large house in Bed-
fordshire.‡ She says that having killed three horses that day
—it was midsummer—with extreme heat, they came to Wrest,
my Lord of Kent's house, "where we found the doors shut,
and none in the house but one servant, who only had the keys
of the hall, so that we were enforced to lie in the hall all
night, till towards morning, at which time came a man and

---

* *Memorials of Holdenby*, by Miss Hartshorne, p. 16.
† *England as seen by Foreigners in the days of Elizabeth and James I.*, by W. B.
Rye, p. 213.
‡ *Nichols' Progresses of King James I.*, Vol. I., p. 174.

let us into the higher rooms, where we slept three or four
hours." This artless account quite casually illustrates the
relation of the hall to the rest of the house. It was the room
first entered from the outside, and was shut off by doors from
all the rest of the house. The servant who let the travellers
in probably slept either in the buttery or a "lodging" attached
to it, and beyond those two apartments and the hall neither
he nor they could go until the "man" came who had the keys
which gave access to the stairs and the higher rooms.

The Manner of Decorating Rooms.

Some idea of what the rooms were like which surrounded a
courtyard of the time may be gathered from the description of
the suite allotted to the Earl of Lincoln when he went to
Cassell, in 1596, on an embassage to the Landgrave of Hesse;
and although they were in a German castle the description
would apply almost equally well to those in a large English
house. The rooms were five in number, and they occupied
the end of a goodly quadrangle, like the Louvre at Paris, high
and stately.* They consisted of two dining chambers, two
drawing chambers, and between the two latter a bed chamber,
so placed "for his more quiet and private being." His lordship's own dining chamber was panelled with wood and marble,
"with crestings, indentments, and Italian pillar work;" there
were escutcheons with the blazoned arms of the Landgrave's
"friends and allies of the Protestant part," and on the four
sides of the room next the ceiling were carved four stories of
the Creation, the Passion, the Resurrection, and the Judgment;
the ceiling was wrought with knot-work. The next room,
where the ambassador's gentlemen dined, was hung with
tapestry. The next "was a fair drawing chamber, seated
round about, and covered with scarlet; above the seats hung
round with a rich small wrought tapestry of an ell broad, of
emblem work, and verses written underneath; over this, upon
a ledge of wainscot, were divers tables [pictures] of sundry
devices, well painted, with their posies to garnish the chamber,
and, among all, that was the best which had this motto : ' Major
autem horum est caritas,' for it waxed cold. The roof was

* *Nichols' Progresses of Queen Elizabeth*, Vol. II.

likewise flourished with painting and devices. These rooms had the through light of four fair windows." The bedroom was decorated with a painted tree that grew up at the door, the branches spreading all over the ceiling, full of fruit, and hanging down upon the walls, with other pictures to fill up empty places; the story taken out of Daniel. The last room of the suite was "a fair drawing chamber hung with arras, which parted his Honour's lodging from the other side of the house, that so he might not any way be disturbed." We get therefore in this set of rooms an example of the three principal modes of decorating the walls—by panelling, by hanging with tapestry or arras, and (more seldom) by painting. At Theobalds the hall was decorated with trees, and not only were they furnished with leaves and fruit, but, regardless of the niceties of natural history, with birds' nests too, and so lifelike was the effect that, according to the testimony of a German visitor in 1592,[*] when the steward opened the windows the birds flew in, perched upon the trees, and began to sing—perhaps to express their surprise at finding fruit and nests on the trees at the same time. This realistic treatment was, fortunately, not very common, and it is rather curious that so strong a man as Lord Burghley should have delighted in such embellishments, and others equally puerile in conception.

The more usual way of treating the walls was to cover them either with hangings or with panelling. There are numberless references to the former among the poets of the time. Imogen's bedchamber was "hanged with tapestry of silk and silver"; Falstaff fell asleep behind the arras when he took his ease in his inn, and had his pocket picked; Polonius, when he hid himself in order to overhear Hamlet's interview with his mother, slipped behind the arras, and it was through the arras that Hamlet subsequently made the fatal pass with his sword. The rooms in Spencer's Castle Joyous "were round about apparelled with costly cloths of Arras and of Tours," and the parlour of Alma's castle "was with royal arras richly dight." These hangings were moved from house to house when the family migrated from one abode to another, and in Beaumont and Fletcher's *Wit without Money* there is a lively scene in which a great lady suddenly determines to leave her house in town

---

[*] The Secretary of Frederick, Duke of Wirtemberg. *England as seen by Foreigners in the days of Elizabeth and James I.*, by W. B. Rye, p. 44.

for the country. Amid the confusion which ensues—servants shouting, my lady's sister in much anxiety about her dog, her looking-glass, and her curls—Ralph calls to Roger to help down with the hangings, but Roger declines, as he is unable to leave the packing of his trunks. The hangings at Hampton Court were of the most costly description,* Cardinal Wolsey being an ardent collector, and utilizing the services of his agents

134.—BEDROOM IN DEENE HALL, NORTHAMPTONSHIRE. PLASTER CEILING: TAPESTRY ON WALLS.

in various foreign countries to add to his stores. Three-quarters of a century later much of this splendour was still left, and the German visitor whom we have already seen at Theobalds says of Hampton Court, that "all the apartments and rooms in this immensely large structure are hung with rich tapestry, of pure gold and fine silk."† From this regal magnificence there were numberless gradations down to the "smirch'd, worm-eaten

* *Law*, Vol. I., p. 57.
† *England as seen by Foreigners*, p. 18.

tapestry " mentioned in that conversation between Borachio and Conrade which led to their arrest by Dogberry. The subjects of these hangings were of extreme diversity—scriptural, mythological, and allegorical. There were the stories of Toby, Our Lady, and the Forlorn Son, alongside of those of Priamus, Venus and Cupid, and Hannibal. The story of Esther balanced the Romaunt of the Rose. Christian saints and heathen gods were equally welcome, and always and everywhere, either in foliated borders or forming the subject-matter itself, were the arms of the owner, with angels or amorini to support them, and a convoluted scroll to bear the motto. The allegorical subjects are the most bewildering, and they even puzzled the people of the time, to whom such trains of thought were familiar, for it is expressly said of the tapestry in Alma's parlour that in it there was nothing pourtrayed nor wrought but what was easy to understand. Of course much of the tapestry which was so widely used has now disappeared, or has found its way into the hands of collectors; very little is left in its original positions, even if it remains in the houses for which it was first acquired. There is a fair amount, however, to be found up and down the country, and the effect of tapestry-hung walls in conjunction with a rich plaster ceiling is shown in Fig. 134, from a bedroom in Deene Hall, Northamptonshire.

WOOD PANELLING.

Wood panelling is of a more permanent character than tapestry, or at least is not so easily removed and adapted to fresh situations; and there are many examples left of this mode of clothing and decorating the walls of houses and churches. It was in vogue tolerably early in the century, and there is a contract, printed in the *History of Hengrave*, between Sir Thomas Kytson, for whom the house was built, and Thomas Neker, for " seelyng" the house. This " seelyng" has been mistaken for plastering, but a perusal of the contract shows that it must have been panelling, since some of the rooms are to be " seelyd" their whole height, and others only to the height of the windows, or a certain number of feet high. Stools, benches, cupboards, and portals are also mentioned as part of the work, as well as " the gates at the coming in "; and Sir Thomas is to find all manner of timber, hewn and sawn.

Among the rooms to be thus panelled were the hall, the two parlours, the wardrobe over the cellar, and the two great chambers above the daïs. Seven lodgings, that is bedchambers, were to have portals only; sixteen other lodgings were to be " seelyd " to the pendant's foot, and on the pastry house a wardrobe was to be made, with one close press, and open presses round about. There was to be a fret on the ceiling of the hall with hanging pendants, " vault fashion"; no doubt after the manner of the watching chamber at Hampton Court, which was being built about the same time. Towards these works Sir Thomas Kytson was to provide the contractor with " all the old seelyng, and frets of the old work that is in his keeping."

135.—HADDON HALL, DERBYSHIRE. A CORNER
OF THE GREAT HALL.

The development of wood panelling is of considerable interest. Previous to the sixteenth century, that is in the days of the Gothic manner, the construction was on a substantial scale, the framing being formed of wood up-rights and cross-pieces, measuring, perhaps, four inches by three in section, the uprights being from eighteen inches to two feet apart, and strengthened by horizontal cross-pieces at heights of three, four, or five feet, or thereabouts, according to the height of the room. The spaces thus formed into panels were filled with one piece of board let into the surrounding framing, which was sometimes splayed, but more generally moulded, the mouldings being stopped before they encountered the cross-pieces. The screen in the hall at Haddon (Fig. 135) illustrates this early method of construction, while against it, and clothing the wall and the side of the window-opening, is the seventeenth-century panelling, the development of which will be presently explained. The panels in Gothic work were ornamented either with cusping, such as may be seen in the upper part of the screen at Haddon, behind the antlers, or with paintings, such as still remain in a number of churches, especially in the eastern and south - western counties. Gra-dually, however, the large size of the framework was reduced : instead of being four or five inches thick by three or four inches wide, it became only about an inch or so thick by about the same width as formerly. The panels were made narrower, because it was found easier to get boards ten or twelve inches wide than of a width twice

136.—PANELLING OF THE TIME OF HENRY VIII.

those sizes, and gradually the very long proportion of height to width was lessened, the panels became more nearly square, and eventually they were made of varying sizes and proportions, but rhythmically arranged.

The old idea of moulding or splaying the wood framework was long retained, and practical considerations in the framing of it together gave rise to a particular kind of effect, which is characteristic of the earlier kind of panelling. The framework is composed of vertical and horizontal pieces of wood tenoned together and secured by wood pins. It is obvious that if the edges of all the wood were moulded before it was framed together, it would be impossible to make a neat junction where the pieces crossed, because the continuous moulding on the edge of the one piece would interfere with the proper adjustment of the end of the other which comes against it at right angles. It will be seen by referring to Fig. 136, that on the horizontal rails, which are continuous, the moulding and the splay die out before they reach the vertical pieces, thus leaving a plain surface sufficiently wide for the latter to abut against, whereas on the vertical pieces the mouldings are continued from top to bottom of the panel and stop abruptly against the horizontal rails. The vertical pieces could therefore have been worked in one long piece and then cut into lengths, whereas on the horizontal rails the moulding was worked in lengths to suit

137.—STANFORD CHURCH, NORTHAMPTONSHIRE.
LINEN PANELLING.

the width of the panels—a more troublesome proceeding, and one requiring thought and care. The tendency of all change in workmanship being towards the saving of thought and care on the part of the great body of workers, the next steps in the development of panelling were in this direction. But before following these steps, a reference to Fig. 137 will show how in some cases the horizontal rails are continuous, with the edge-mouldings dying out, while the vertical are in short lengths with continuous mouldings abutting against the horizontal rails; and in others the parts played are reversed, and it is the vertical pieces which run through. It will be noticed that in addition to the edge-moulding, there are others on the face of the rails which, not being subject to interference by the abutting of the cross-pieces, are worked continuously without a break.

In both these examples (Figs. 136, 137), and also in Fig. 138, it will be observed that the panel itself is decorated with some kind of carving. The English form is shown in Fig. 137, where the panels are what are known as linen panels, the

138.—A Panel of the Time of Henry VIII.

decoration taking a form something like folded linen. In the long gallery at the Vyne the walls are panelled with linen panelling, with the addition of coats of arms, or badges, or scrolls bearing a motto (Fig. 19). A later form is seen in Fig. 136, where the design is quite Italian in feeling. The circular panels containing heads became a favourite feature in English panelling about the end of Henry VIII.'s reign, and may generally be ascribed to a date within a few years of 1540. The diamond-shaped panels in the lower part appear to be horizontal panels standing on their ends, and are probably not in their original relation to the others. The two charming dolphins counter-hauriant, if the term may be allowed, carved at the top of a long panel, leaving the lower part plain, give a quaint and pleasing effect (Fig. 138). The presence of dolphins rather points to French influence, for, although no doubt the use of this form started in Italy, it was eagerly adopted by the French, since the dolphin was the cognizance of their dauphin. The door at Castle Rising (Fig. 139) gives another example of the use of heads in circular panels among Italian foliage; but it will be noticed that the mouldings round the panels do not conform to the type already explained, but to one which is a step forwarder in development. Instead

PLATE XL.

HADDON HALL, DERBYSHIRE. PANELLING IN THE
DINING-ROOM (1545)

HADDON HALL, DERBYSHIRE. A SIDE OF THE
BAY WINDOW IN THE DINING-ROOM (1545)

of the mouldings of the continuous horizontal rails being stopped short of the sides of the panels, they are carried on and intersect with them. This intersection is called by joiners a mitre, and a mitred moulding is an advance on a stopped moulding or one that abuts against a cross-piece. It will be seen that in this example, although the moulding is mitred at the top of the pane', it still abuts against the bottom rail. In the panelling from Haddon Hall (Plate XL.) it will be seen that the very simple moulding mitres all round the panels. But in all these cases the mouldings are what are called " out of the solid," that is, the actual framework of the panels is moulded, the consequence being that wherever a moulding had to be stopped or mitred, thought and care were required, and a failure of either involved the injury of a fairly large piece of wood. The next step therefore was to refrain from working a moulding on the solid wood, but to keep square edges to the framework, and after framing up all the panelling with these square edges, to insert round the margin of each panel a

139.—DOOR AT CASTLE RISING, NORFOLK.

small separate moulding planted on to the recessed panel. This saved much time and labour, and consequently expense, and is the method pursued in the present day. Its application may be seen in almost any four-panelled door in an ordinary house.

This latest form, the " applied " mitred moulding, hardly came into general use so early as the time of Elizabeth or

James—indeed, the date of its earliest occurrence is a question of considerable interest. But mouldings mitred on the solid had almost entirely replaced the older form of stopped mouldings by the end of the sixteenth century. By returning to the illustration of the screen at Haddon (Fig. 135), an example may be seen alongside the heavier Gothic work; and another example, with a much deeper and broader moulding, may be seen in an upper room at the same place (Plate XLI.). It is

140.—DOOR AT BECKINGTON ABBEY, SOMERSET.

a provoking characteristic of work of this time that its method of treatment does not give an infallible clue to its chronological sequence. In earlier times the mouldings gave this clue: when once a form was superseded by another, it did not occur again; but in the period now under consideration fashion was not so accommodating, and though on the whole the mitred moulding is later than the stopped moulding and finally superseded it, yet there are early examples of mitring, as in the panelling at the Vyne, which must have been put up before Wolsey's death in 1530, and there are late examples of stopped mouldings in such things as chests, which may be as late as James I. The pewing and pulpit at Haddon (Plate XLI.) have them, and they are late Elizabethan, if not Jacobean, while the panelling in the dining-room, which is dated 1545, is mitred.

The panels themselves, which in early days were decorated with the linen pattern, and subsequently with Italian foliage and heads within circles, became plainer and simpler. In the dining-room at Haddon all the lower panels are plain, while a kind of frieze of ornament is carried round in those next to the cornice. The ornament consists for the most part of coats

PLATE XLI.

HADDON HALL, DERBYSHIRE. WOODWORK IN
THE CHAPEL.

HADDON HALL, DERBYSHIRE. BAY-WINDOW IN
THE DRAWING-ROOM.

Plate XLII.

CARBROOK HALL, NEAR SHEFFIELD

of arms from the Vernon pedigree, but there are also heads in circles, linen panels, initials with true lovers' knots, and other devices. All these are carved in relief, but in later times carving gave way to patterns formed by sinking the groundwork and leaving the design on a level with the face of the panel. There was little or no modelling in the design, and the work could be done by a less skilful hand than actual carving would require.

An example is to be seen in a door at Beckington Abbey (Fig. 140): the same kind of work was often applied to the rails of panelling, the face of pilasters, and other plain surfaces. Another specimen, with a little more modelling in it, is at Nailsea Court (Fig. 141). The services of the carver were, however, by no means dispensed with, and there is a vast amount of richly ornamented panelling up and down the country,

141.—Door at Nailsea Court, Somerset.

both in houses and churches. The monotony of the constantly repeated oblongs was broken by the introduction of pilasters, which were themselves fluted or decorated with patterns.

Carbrook Hall, near Sheffield, which has now fallen from its former estate, has a very fine panelled room, in which the pilasters are richly decorated with various simple patterns (Plate XLII.). They support a carved frieze, above which is a wood cornice, and above this again is a modelled plaster frieze some two feet deep, forming part of the handsome ceiling.

At Benthall Hall, Shropshire, is another instance where the monotony of the panels is relieved by the introduction of pilasters, and it is also lessened by the presence of the large centre panels (Plate XLIII.) with their greater freedom of treatment. The variation caused by adapting the same design to the narrower panel of the door in the middle bay is also a pleasant relief. The intention here was to rely upon the panelling itself for the

142.—Part of Reredos (removed) at Stowe-Nine-Churches, Northamptonshire.

decoration of the room; there was no thought of hanging pictures on it; which, indeed, would be out of place, and would spoil the effect both of themselves and the panelling. It may be doubted whether any of the panelling of the time, even the simplest and the most regularly disposed, was intended as a background for other ornament. It was itself the decoration, although, when perfectly simple, it could be used in a restricted way as a background for pictures. But the fashion of hanging up framed paintings and prints had not yet arisen; when it did arise it rendered wood panelling an inappropriate means for the general decoration of rooms. In the church at Stowe-

PLATE XLIII.

SIDE OF ROOM AT BENTHALL HALL, SHROPSHIRE.

Scale : $\frac{3}{16}$ inch to 1 Foot.

Nine-Churches, Northamptonshire, are the remains of some good panelling which once served as a reredos, but which the reforming and restoring zeal of a late incumbent has now relegated to the vestry. There are fluted pilasters here, dividing panels which increase in richness as they ascend, the upper ones containing boldly projecting heads amid the usual strap-work curls (Fig. 142). Sometimes the panels were made with semicircular heads, which rested upon pilasters furnished with imposts and bases, all the margin being highly ornamented, while the panels themselves were plain, as in the Court pew at Chel-

143.—PART OF THE COURT PEW, CHELVEY CHURCH
SOMERSET.

vey, in Somerset (Fig. 143). There are many instances of the use of these arched panels: the long gallery at Haddon has them in wide and narrow widths alternately; and there is a room in the Red Lodge at Bristol where every panel is arched, the effect thus produced being very rich. At Chelvey the frieze is carved with a continuous pattern, as it was in very many instances, but sometimes it was decorated in a more mechanical way with ovals and oblongs, as at Benthall Hall (Plate XLIII.), and occasionally it was pierced in a very charming manner into a kind of filigree work, as in the remains of a screen at Stowe-Nine-Churches, which has shared the fate of the reredos (Fig. 144). The effect of the frieze in this instance is enhanced by its being slightly curved outwards.

In later days, instead of cutting down the substance of the wood in order to get carving in relief, the projection was obtained by cutting the ornament out of another piece of wood and applying it to the surfaces that were to be decorated.

Some of the ornament at Benthall Hall appears to be treated in this manner. But whatever means were adopted, the end aimed at was the same—namely, an extreme richness of effect: indeed, in some of the panelling and in many of the chimney-pieces the result is bewildering in its intricacy of line.

144.—Part of Screen (removed), Stowe-Nine-Churches, Northamptonshire.

PLATE XLIV.

WADHAM COLLEGE, OXFORD.

CHAPTER VIII.

INTERIOR FEATURES (*continued*).

TREATMENT OF THE HALL, SCREENS, OPEN ROOFS.

ON entering the hall after leaving the courtyard, it was on such panelling as this that the eye rested. The screen which divided the hall from the passage was generally even more richly decorated than the adjacent panelling. Its two doorways were flanked with columns, which carried a complete entablature from side to side of the hall; above this came the panelled front of the gallery, which was surmounted in its turn perhaps by a series of small arches, perhaps by some of the fantastic strap-work peculiar to the time. The spaces between the columns were panelled; every panel here and above was decorated with carving—

145.—THE HALL, KNOLE, KENT.

usually of shields of arms, but where these were not suitable, as in halls of colleges, then with foliage or allegorical figures. Knole House, in Kent, has a good example of a screen with heraldic decoration (Fig. 145). Wadham College, Oxford (Plate XLIV.), has one of comparatively simple character; while for sumptuous effect those at Middle Temple Hall, London, and Trinity College, Cambridge (Plate XLV.), could hardly be surpassed. Woollas Hall, in Worcestershire, has a good screen of simple character. The illustration on Plate XLVI. gives a view of it looking from the hall. The archway leads into the passage called the "screens," in which can be seen the open door of the principal entrance. The gallery has a balustraded front ; it is carried out over the entrance porch, and is lighted by a small window, visible in Fig. 69, just below the oriel. The hall, having a room over it,

146.—WOLLATON HALL, NOTTINGHAMSHIRE. THE ROOF OF THE GREAT HALL (1580—88).

has a flat ceiling, and not an open timber roof. The windows of the hall were usually rather high up, and the walls were panelled up to the sills, but as a rule the sill of the bay window at the daïs end was brought down low enough to afford an outlook. Above the panelling the walls were largely occupied by the windows, the spaces between which were hung with " pikes, guns, and bows, with old swords and bucklers that had borne many shrewd blows" : or they were filled with pictures, of which a considerable number, chiefly portraits, began to be found in large houses. From the top of the windows sprang

PLATE XLV.

TRINITY COLLEGE, CAMBRIDGE.

SCREEN IN THE HALL (ABOUT 1604-5).

PLATE XLVI.

WOOLLAS HALL, WORCESTERSHIRE (1611).
SCREEN IN THE HALL.

the roof, the feet of its principals coming down and occupying part of wall space between them. The principals were still constructed in the old hammer-beam manner, even at so late a date as 1604 for Trinity College, Cambridge, and 1612 for Wadham, but all the ornament is of a late type, and gives a very rich effect, the light glancing upwards against the many surfaces of the pendants and the strong lines of the moulded braces. The roof at Middle Temple Hall, built in 1570, is almost as elaborate and fine as that of the Great Hall at Hampton Court, built some forty years before, but the detail

147.—ROOF OF GREAT HALL, KIRBY, NORTHAMPTONSHIRE (1575).

is later in character. The roof of the hall at Wollaton is peculiar in that it is of the hammer-beam type, although supporting the flat floor of a room over it (Fig. 146). Usually, when there was a room over the hall the ceiling was treated with ornamental rib-work, in the same manner as the other and less lofty rooms: the hall at Knole presents an example of this kind of treatment (Fig. 145). At Kirby there is an unusual form of roof, neither flat nor open timbered, but a kind of barrel-vault formed of four straight faces (Fig. 147); each face is divided into large panels by moulded and cut oak ribs of large size, and each panel has a curved diagonal rib resembling the wind-braces of a Gothic roof. The panels are filled with boarding at the back of the ribs.

The Smaller Rooms.

Leaving the hall for one of the smaller rooms, we find much the same kind of treatment, but here the ornamental ceiling plays an important part in the decoration. The walls were panelled, more or less richly, from floor to ceiling, and were crowned with a carved frieze and projecting cornice, above which started the ceiling ribs. The great chamber at South Wraxall (Plate XLVII.) gives a good idea of the whole effect, but the coved ceiling is somewhat exceptional, and so also is the great projection to the left. This is a mass of masonry required to carry the roofs, but the designer, who found himself obliged to leave it (for this room was contrived in an old house), resolved to face the matter boldly and make an ornamental feature of it. It will be noticed that though the panelling here is quite simple, a good deal of character is obtained by varying the size of the panels in a systematic manner.

In the old Town Hall at Leicester there is a good panelled room (Plate XLVIII.), with a handsome chimney-piece and a special seat for the mayor. The work, which bears the date 1637, is simple in design, but is quite as effective and rather more pleasing than many of the more elaborate effects of the time, in which the impression is conveyed that the designers over-exerted themselves.

Another good example of rather later date is to be seen at the " Reindeer " Inn, Banbury (Plate XLIX.); the panelling itself is simple, but the doorways and chimney-piece are more elaborate, and the columns which occur at the angles of the window-recess impart considerable vigour to the whole effect. The restraint exhibited and the concentration of the ornament on one or two places is a welcome relief from the superfluity of decoration which not infrequently distinguishes the woodwork of this period. In the broken and curled pediments of the doorway and chimney-piece we get a decided indication that the seventeenth century was well advanced when this work was done. The ceiling here is very richly wrought, and the whole room comes as a surprise in its out-of-the-way situation.

Sizergh Hall, in Westmorland, offered a still more elaborate

PLATE XLVII.

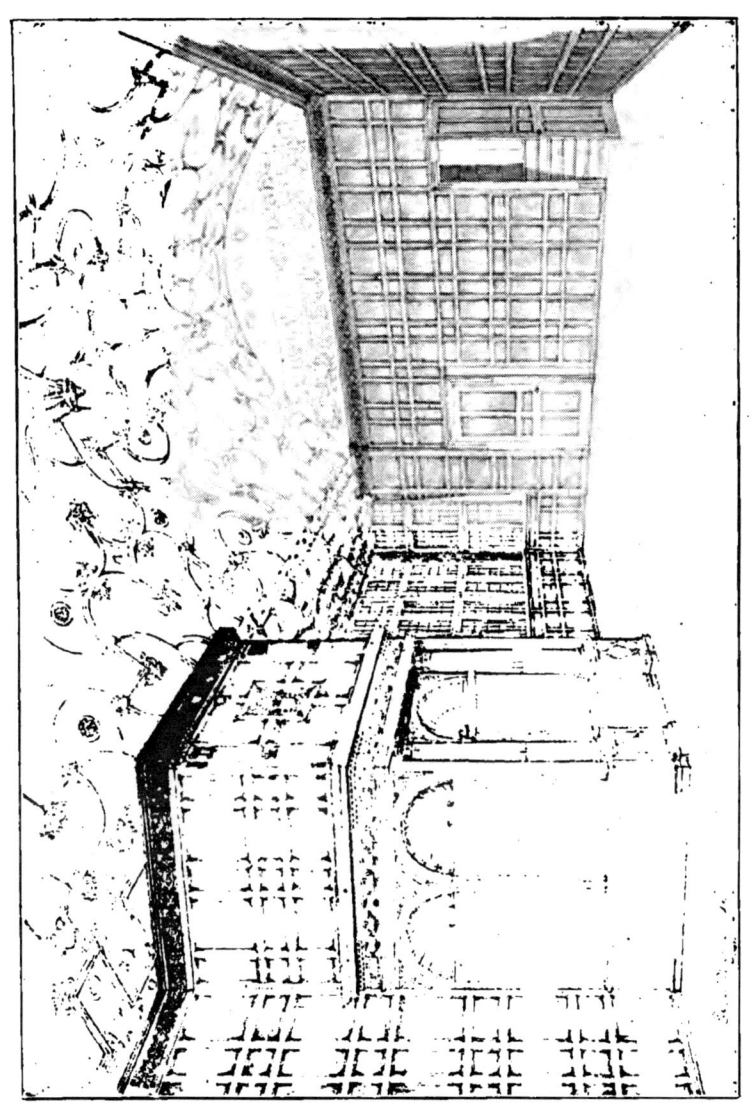

THE GREAT CHAMBER, SOUTH WRAXALL MANOR HOUSE, WILTSHIRE.

PLATE XLVIII.

THE OLD TOWN HALL, LEICESTER
INTERIOR.

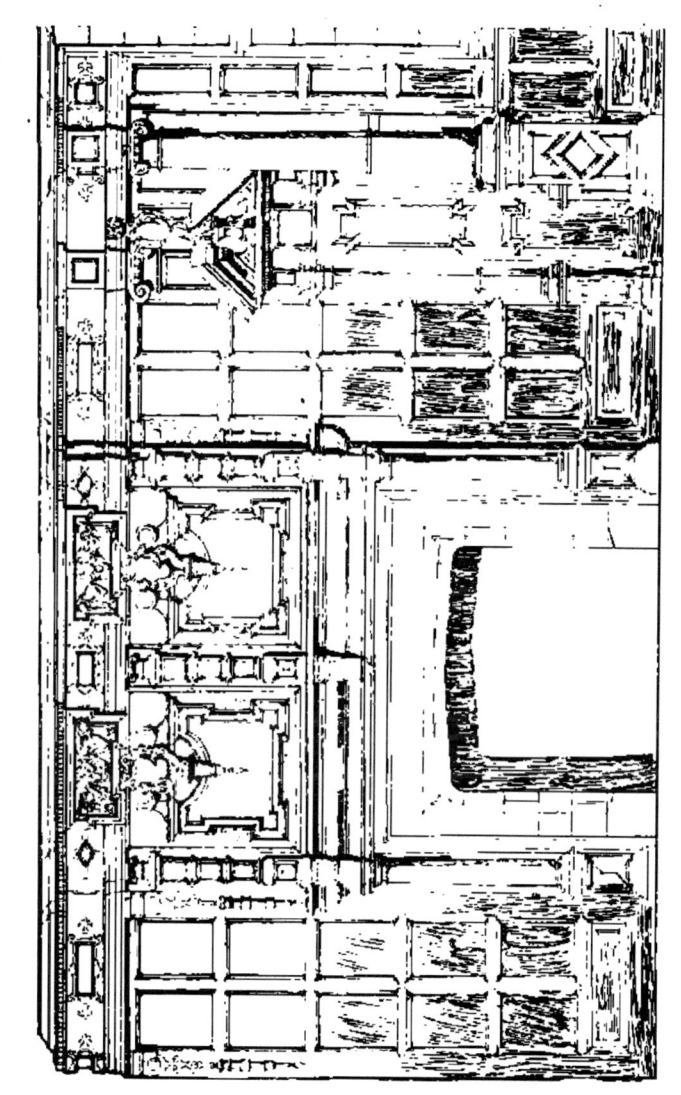

SIDE OF A ROOM, "REINDEER" INN, BANBURY, OXFORDSHIRE.

PLATE L.

This frieze repeats
all round room.

DETAILS OF PANELLING FROM SIZERGH HALL.
(NOW IN SOUTH KENSINGTON MUSEUM.)

Plate LI

BROUGHTON CASTLE, OXFORDSHIRE.
INTERIOR PORCH (ABOUT 1599).

example, which has now been erected in South Kensington
Museum (Fig. 148 and Plate L.). The panels here are not
carved, but inlaid—a method of decoration much in vogue in
Italy, where some exquisite drawing is bestowed upon it, but not
prevalent in England. There are a number of instances in different parts of the country, but, compared with carving, inlay
was seldom resorted to. The domed turret in the corner of the

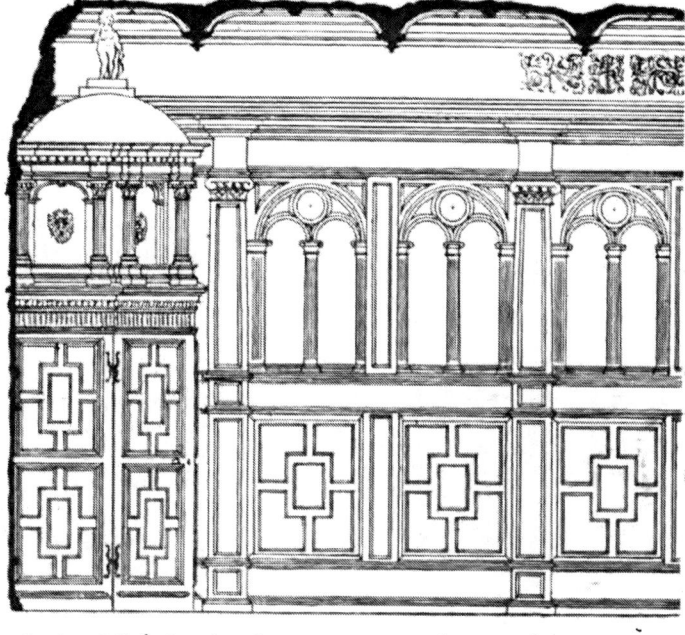

148.—Panelling from Sizergh Hall, Westmorland (now in South Kensington
Museum).

room should be noticed (Fig. 148); it is, in fact, an inside
porch contrived so as to allow access between two other rooms
without having to come through the third. This device in
planning is not of frequent occurrence, but when it was considered necessary much care was taken to produce an attractive
feature. There are several in the southern counties, notably
at Broughton Castle, Oxfordshire (Plate LI.), at the Red
Lodge, in Bristol, and at Bradfield, in Devonshire. This room

at Sizergh presents a fresh type of treatment in the junction of
wall and ceiling. In previous examples the wood panelling
was carried quite up to the ceiling; here it stops short by a
foot or more, and the space thus left is occupied by a modelled
plaster frieze which leads up to the ornamental ceiling. This
method was adopted as frequently as the other; the depth of
the plaster frieze varied a good deal, being in one of the rooms
at Hardwick Hall as much as six or seven feet, and filled
with figure subjects modelled in relief and painted, representing hunting and other woodland scenes: the space below
the frieze is covered with tapestry instead of panelling
(Plate LII.).

DOORS.

Doorways presented another opportunity for the display of
design. At Sizergh the door is merely a portion of the

149.—DOORWAY, ABBOTT'S HOSPITAL,
GUILDFORD, SURREY (1627).

panelling on hinges, the porch
in which it is hung gives it
the requisite importance; but
as a rule the doorways were
surrounded with a large
amount of decoration. In
important houses they were
flanked with columns or pilasters, were surmounted with
a frieze and cornice, and often
with a pediment; obelisks
stood over the pilasters; the
frieze was fluted or carved or
adorned at intervals with
heads; some convenient panel
was filled with the owner's
arms; nothing was omitted
that an extravagant fancy
could suggest (Plate LIII.).
At Levens Hall, in Westmorland, there is a fine panelled
room with a richly orna-
mented doorway (Plate
LIV.), in which fantastic
figures support a cornice whereon is set up a panel for the

Plate LII.

HARDWICK HALL, DERBYSHIRE.

THE PRESENCE-CHAMBER.

PLATE LIII.

DOORWAY IN A HOUSE AT BRISTOL.

PLATE LIV.

LEVENS HALL, WESTMORELAND.
A DOORWAY.

owner's arms, flanked on either hand by a contorted animal.

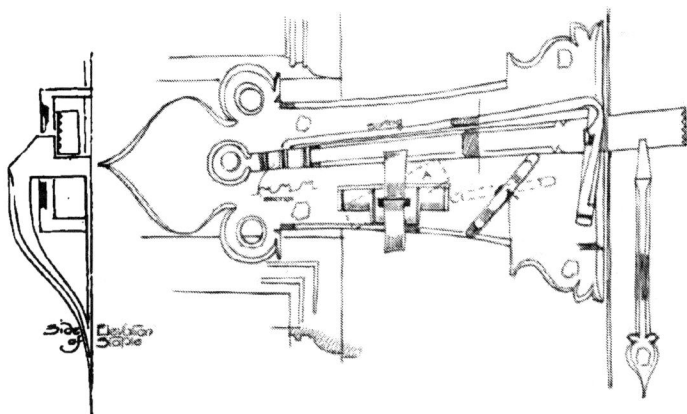

150.—LATCH FROM ABBOTT'S HOSPITAL, GUILDFORD.

In the same district, at Conishead Priory, there is a panelled room of even greater elaboration than this at Levens. Some of the panels are ornamented with mouldings mitred into various patterns, but most of them have niches with pediments or raised panels surrounded with mouldings curved and straight and breaking back in a bewildering manner, while here, there, and everywhere are cherubs' heads and bunches of

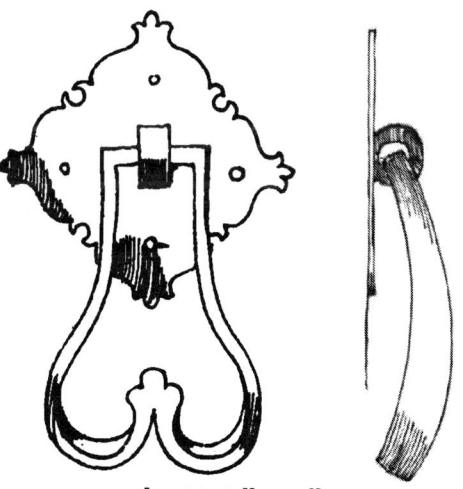

151.—LATCH FROM HADDON HALL.

fruit—the whole effect being rather too bizarre.

Sometimes the embellishment surrounding the door was in stone or even marble, which being less susceptible of minute

detail was more soberly treated. In smaller houses the treatment was naturally less elabo-
rate, but even in places like
St. Peter's Hospital, Bristol,
and Abbott's Hospital at
Guildford, the doorways had
much attention bestowed upon
them (Fig. 149 and Plate
LV.). At Gayton Manor
House, in Northamptonshire,
there is a still simpler treatment, the effect being enhanced
by projecting the door some
inches into the room (Plate
LV.). The hinges and
latches of the doors and the
fastenings of the window case-
ments were of wrought iron,
and were always more or less
ornamental. There were in-

152.—LOCK-PLATES, LATCHES, &c.

variably skill and ingenuity bestowed upon even the smallest

153.—CASEMENT FASTENER FROM HADDON HALL.

piece of work. The latch from Abbott's Hospital, illustrated
in Fig. 150, is an example of a spring latch, that is to say,

PLATE LV.

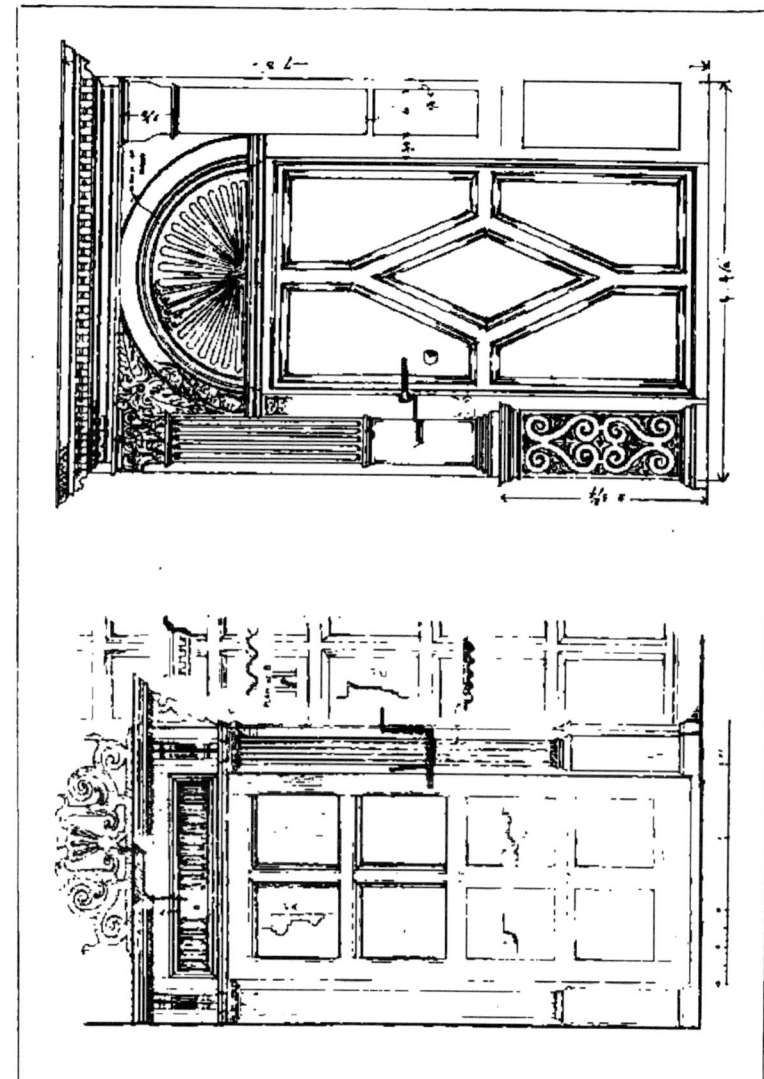

DOORWAY, GAYTON MANOR HOUSE, NORTHAMPTONSHIRE.

DOORWAY, ST. PETER'S HOSPITAL, BRISTOL.

instead of depending merely upon its weight to keep it in its

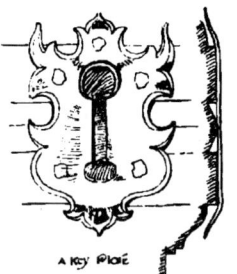

A KEY PLATE

154.—KEY-PLATE FROM ABBOTT'S
HOSPITAL, GUILDFORD.

place, it is furnished with a spring, and the whole of the simple mechanism is displayed to view. The plate to which it is fixed is shaped in suitable places, and the latch and its accessories are also ornamented to a certain extent. On the other side of the door would be a handle, something after the fashion of that shown in Fig. 151, which, however, is at Haddon. It is treated in a similar fashion: the plate is slightly ornamented, and the handle itself is wrought into a

shape at once convenient to grasp and agreeable to the eye. In the casement fasteners a little more ornament was sometimes indulged in, advantage being taken of the fact that the ironwork was outlined against the light of the window. There are two simple examples shown in Fig. 152, and a more elaborate one in Fig. 153. The same treatment was applied to the escutcheons of key-holes, of which examples are shown in Fig. 152 and Fig. 154; the former also exhibits a lock plate and a drop handle and plate. It will be noticed that the whole of this ornament, although in some instances it looks rich, is in reality obtained by the simplest means, which consist in the main of cutting a thin plate of metal into a variety of shapes; there is hardly any modelling about it. This method is characteristic of most of the ironwork of the time; it was only seldom that modelled ornament was indulged in to the extent shown in the knocker and plate illustrated in Fig. 155.

155.—A KNOCKER (1618).

CHIMNEY-PIECES.

Much elaboration was bestowed upon the chimney-pieces, of which, indeed, there are very few simple examples to be met with. They were made of wood, of stone, and of marble.

R.A.   M

Wood and stone were the more usual materials employed, and it is difficult to say upon which the detail was the more minute. The general idea that controlled the designs was much the same in all cases, but the treatment of it varied. The idea was to flank the fireplace opening with columns carrying an entablature consisting of architrave, frieze, and cornice, the projection of the latter forming a convenient shelf. On the top of this composition was another of the same kind, but with smaller columns and of more delicate proportion. The space enclosed between the columns, which in the lower half was the fireplace, was occupied in the upper half by some kind of carved subject. This was very often the arms of the owner, being either those of the family, or his own special achievement. At Boughton House, in Northamptonshire. there is an example of this kind (Plate LVI.). It is fairly simple in design; the centre-piece is the Montagu arms; on the margin of the panel is the motto adopted by Sir Edward Montagu, who caused the work to be done; and in the frieze below is one of the innumerable Latin aphorisms with which houses of this time abound. The fireplace opening occupies the full width between the sides of the chimney-piece, and if the grate were removed, would give a tolerable idea of the appearance of an Elizabethan fireplace, with its cast-iron fire-back delicately modelled, and the fire-dogs, or andirons, to hold the logs in place. This particular fire-back, however, is of a later date. Almost contemporary with this fireplace at Boughton is one at Lacock Abbey (Plate LVII.), equally simple in design, but executed with more refinement. and having a very unusual adjunct in the shape of a hearth-stone ornamented with a pattern inlaid with lead. The two works are likely to be of much the same date, as Sir William Sharington of Lacock died in 1553, and Sir Edward Montagu of Boughton in 1556. At Barlborough, in Derbyshire, there is a fine chimney-piece still fairly simple, in which the upper part is devoted to the owner's personal history (Plate LVIII.). His name was Francis Rodes, a lawyer, and subsequently a justice of the Common Pleas. He married twice. These facts are all set forth on the chimney-piece. His own arms, and those of his two wives, are carved at large, and the names of his wives are printed against their shields. The upper cornice is supported by two caryatides instead of columns, one of whom

PLATE LVI.

STONE CHIMNEY-PIECE FROM BOUGHTON HOUSE,
NORTHAMPTONSHIRE (BEFORE 1556).

PLATE LVII.

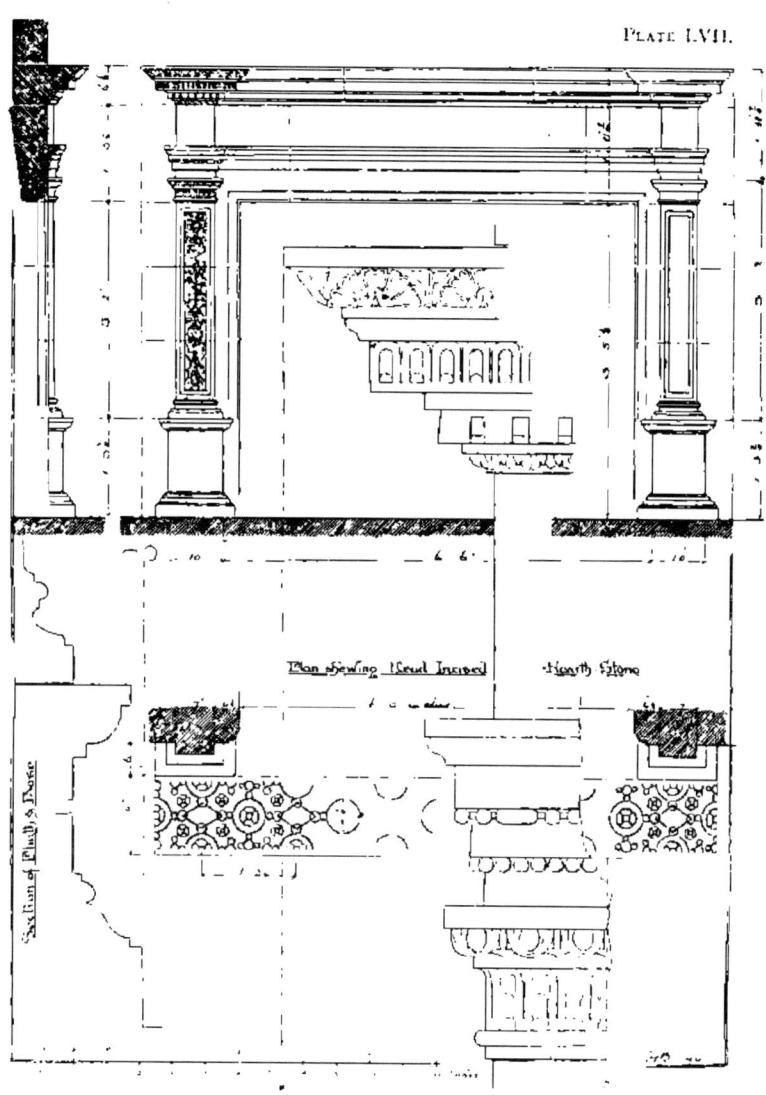

Plan shewing Hood Incised · Hearth Stone

Section of Plinth & Base

STONE CHIMNEY-PIECE FROM LACOCK ABBEY, WILTSHIRE.
(BEFORE 1553).

PLATE LVIII.

BARLBOROUGH HALL, DERBYSHIRE (1584).
A CHIMNEY-PIECE.

PLATE LIX

HATFIELD HOUSE, HERTFORDSHIRE
CHIMNEY-PIECE IN KING JAMES'S ROOM (ABOUT 1612).

PLATE LX.

STONE CHIMNEY-PIECE IN THE GREAT CHAMBER,
SOUTH WRAXALL MANOR HOUSE, WILTSHIRE.

PLATE LXI

represents Justice, in allusion to the calling of the master. At Hatfield House, in a room called after King James, there is a handsome marble chimney-piece, with a large statue of the King in his robes as the centre-piece (Plate LIX.). Here, too, there is an open hearth, with an iron fire-back and handsome andirons. In the great chamber at South Wraxall is a very elaborate stone chimney-piece (Plate LX.), in which the prevailing idea is highly developed. The lower entablature is supported by pairs of caryatides growing out of pilasters, and adorned with bands and swags of flowers. Within the main enclosure is a subordinate margin of mouldings and egg-and-tongue enrichments. The upper part of the composition, though founded on the same idea of columns supporting a crowning cornice, is much elaborated with niches and carved panels. There are no shields of arms, which is rather a curious omission, but instead there are statues of abstract conceptions—Arithmetica, Geometria, Prudentia, and Justitia. The whole effect is extremely handsome, but it is too intricate to be quite satisfactory.

In contrast to this is an interesting chimney-piece in a bedroom at Hardwick Hall, in Derbyshire (Plate LXI.). The material is marble, and the design is unpretending. Its noticeable feature is the panel that serves as overmantel, carved with much grace and spirit. The subject seems to be Apollo and the Nine Muses, though some of the latter appear to have abandoned for the time being the callings over which they presided, in order to join in concerted music. The period of the work is put beyond a doubt by the presence of the royal arms with Elizabeth's supporters, the lion and the dragon, and of the initials E. R. Panels with figure subjects were not uncommon, although they were not often so well executed as this. Scriptural themes were frequently represented, but they did not necessarily imply any special religious character in the house, and often in some of the other rooms of the same house would be other themes of quite mundane inspiration. At East Quantockshead, in Somerset, a house of the Luttrells, one room has in the overmantel the Descent from the Cross, the next a mermaid with scrollwork and flowers, the next the Luttrell arms and the date 1614: others have Christ Blessing the Children; the Lamentation over Jerusalem, with the city in the distance, and a hen in the foreground gathering her chickens

M 2

under her wings; and the Agony in the Garden. Another
house in that district has the Affliction of Job, with the principal figure represented as being in exceedingly poor case.
Occasionally there were no figure subjects, nor even shields,
the panels being quite plain, as in the wood chimney-piece at

156.--WOOD CHIMNEY-PIECE, BENTHALL HALL, SHROPSHIRE.

Ford House, Newton Abbot (Plate LXII.), where the considerable amount of enrichment serves as ornament only, and does
not lend lustre to the family arms. The workmanship is not
of the best, and the details of the design are somewhat poor
and wanting in imagination, especially in the treatment of the
arched panels; but it is characteristic of a good deal of work

Plate LXII.

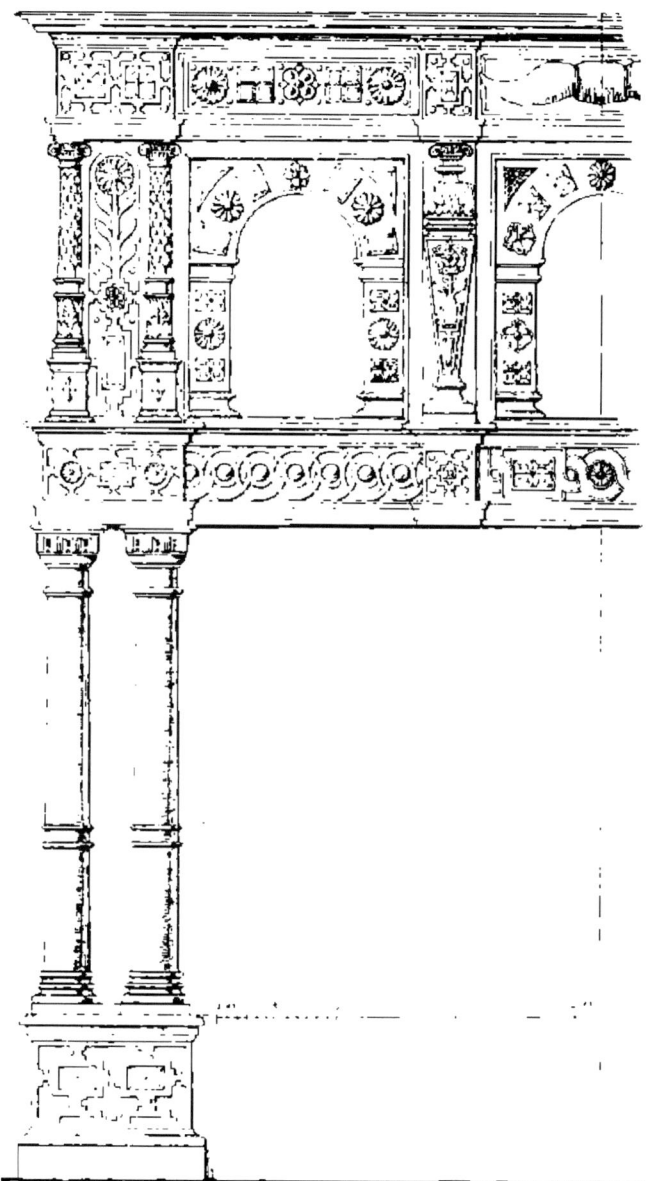

WOOD CHIMNEY-PIECE, FORD HOUSE, NEWTON ABBOT,
DEVONSHIRE.

PLATE LXIII.

STONE CHIMNEY-PIECE, WHISTON, SUSSEX.
(NOW OUT OF DOORS.)

Plate LXIV.

BOLSOVER CASTLE, DERBYSHIRE

of the time.   The chimney-piece at Benthall Hall (Fig. 156) is far more beautifully conceived.   It departs from the regular treatment in the disposition of the main panels.   There is great freedom about the play of the strap-work and figures surrounding the cartouches, and if it be compared with the panelling in the same room (Plate XLIII.), it will be seen that while preserving the same general idea, there is a special richness about this part of the work which is quite appropriate to it as being the chief feature of the room.   It will be seen that here, too, the car-touches in the upper panels bear coats of arms.   At Whiston, in Sus-sex, there is a stone chimney-piece which has got excluded from the house, and now adorns an outside wall.   It is of unusual design (Plate LXIII.), but the family arms form the centre-piece, and are flanked by

157.—STONE CHIMNEY-PIECE, BOLSOVER CASTLE, DERBYSHIRE.

figures of warriors in recesses divided by small, elegant columns. In the upper part is a circular panel containing two subjects, of which it is difficult to decipher the meaning ; the figures, however, are in violent action.   Bolsover Castle contains some of the most striking examples of chimney-pieces to be found in the country.   They are all in stone or marble, and have a variety and originality of design which are quite remarkable. Two of them are illustrated on Plate LXIV.   There are also a number of small ones fitted into corners of the rooms

(Fig. 157), and it will be seen that the walls against which the
chimney-piece is placed are faced with stone to receive it, and
that this plain stonework is surrounded with a moulding against
which the wood panelling stops.

There was a chimney-piece of unusually good design and
workmanship in the palace of Bromley-by-Bow : it is now in
the South Kensington Museum (Plate LXV.). The composition does not quite follow the usual lines, inasmuch as the
upper part, or overmantel, is not a repetition in idea of the
lower. Nor is it divided into panels of equal width and height :
the large central panel, which contains the royal arms, is the
dominating feature, and is flanked on either side by a niche of
much less width and height. The upper half is wedded to the
lower by the bosses on the boldly carved shelf, which carry
down the main lines of the columns. The arms are those of
James I., as the second and third quarters are Scotland and
Ireland respectively, and one of the supporters is the Scottish
unicorn. In another house near London, at Enfield, there was
a well-designed chimney-piece, figured in Richardson's *Studies
from Old English Mansions*, in which the royal arms and badges
were the centre-pieces of the composition. The part above the
fireplace was divided by columns into three panels, of which
the middle one was the largest, and contained the arms of
Elizabeth with her red dragon as one of the supporters. Of
the side panels, one was occupied by the rose crowned and the
other by the portcullis crowned. In the smaller panels below
these, and between the pedestals on which the columns rested,
were the royal initials E. R., and a Latin sentence expressing a
pious aphorism. It is not certain whether this house belonged
to the Crown, or whether this display of regal heraldry was a
compliment to the Queen on the part of the grateful owner. In
either case the making of arms and badges the chief objects of
interest in the composition, and the introduction of the Latin
aphorism on a conspicuous panel are quite characteristic of the
time. At Castle Ashby, in Northamptonshire, is a chimney-
piece (Plate LXVI.) treated in much the same way as that from
Bromley. It was not designed for the house, and therefore the
heraldry is not so apposite as usual. The central panel contains
the arms of the owner set in an elaborate framework of fanciful
carving. On either side is a niche containing a figure of one of
the virtues. The columns which support the cornice are richly

BROMLEY-BY-BOW PALACE.

A CHIMNEY-PIECE (AFTER 1603).

(NOW IN THE SOUTH KENSINGTON MUSEUM.)

PLATE LXVI

CASTLE ASHBY, NORTHAMPTONSHIRE.
A CHIMNEY-PIECE.

carved in low relief, as also are the mantel-shelf and the friezes below it. On the lower of the friezes the family arms are repeated, and in the centre is the crest. The opening of the fireplace is flanked on either side by a female figure, which changes in a provoking way into strap-work and the semblance of a pilaster. The whole effect is rich, and the principles dominating the composition are at once recognizable, but the details are too fantastic to be quite agreeable.

Ceilings.

Of all the architectural work of the time of Elizabeth and James, that which was peculiarly English is to be found in the ceilings. It was a development of native tradition, and although, like all other work of the time, it was influenced by Italian models, it retained its individuality with great tenacity, and in no other country can the same special development of design be found. The root-idea of an Elizabethan

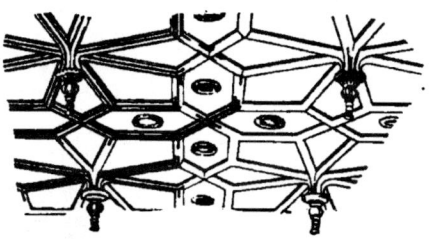

158.—Ceiling of the Presence Chamber, Hampton Court (cir. 1535).

ceiling is to cover the space with a shallow projecting rib forming a more or less regular pattern. The ribs varied in section, and the patterns varied in form. The ribs and the panels they enclosed were sometimes perfectly plain, sometimes highly decorated with modelled work; and between these two extremes were infinite gradations—plain ribs and decorated panels, or plain panels and decorated ribs, the decoration varying from something quite simple to ornament of much elaboration. The plainest examples are sufficient to give character to a room, while the richest are bewildering in the intricacy of the pattern and the minuteness of the detail.

The origin of the idea is to be found in the treatment adopted by the late Gothic joiners. When they had a large flat surface to deal with, they divided it into panels by moulded wood ribs, and they frequently covered the intersection of the ribs with a carved boss or with carved foliage. Their main lines, being

formed of wood, were straight; their panels rectilinear and
often rectangular, the whole treatment being suggested by the
moulded constructional timber of earlier roofs.   At Hampton
Court, in the portions built by Wolsey and Henry VIII., there
are several ceilings of this kind still left.   The ribs are arranged in
simple geometrical patterns with straight lines.   In the watching chamber, at the end of the Great Hall, these ribs are of a
fair size, both in width and depth, and at certain intersections
they are bent downwards to form a pendant after the fashion
prevalent in the stone vaulting of the time (Fig. 158).   Some
of the panels thus enclosed are adorned with a kind of indepen-
dent circular boss formed of a wreath surrounding one of the

159.—BOSSES FROM CEILINGS AT HAMPTON COURT.

royal badges, or even the royal arms.   These bosses are not
carved, but modelled in *papier mâché*, or some similar substance, and they, together with the wood ribs, are secured to
the joists above.   Two of these bosses are illustrated in
Fig. 159, and it is in the wreaths of these comparatively unimportant adjuncts that the only touch of the new fashion is to
be found.
    Other rooms have ceilings of which the ribs are much
smaller in depth and width: the ribs are again arranged in
patterns with straight lines, and at their intersections there are
four small leaves of lead nailed on, the whole junction being
covered with a small plain wood boss, which forms the centre
of the flower.   At other intersections each of the four angles of

PLATE LXVII.

HAMPTON COURT PALACE.
CEILING OF CARDINAL WOLSEY'S CLOSET.

the flat ceiling is occupied with a small modelled head in foliage, all of *papier mâché;* one of these is also shown in Fig. 159. The four insertions taken together form a circle, which is divided into four quadrants by the intersecting ribs (Fig. 160); and the whole arrangement is the first step towards the elaborate decoration which was afterwards introduced, when the facility with which plaster can be worked was recognized and acted on.

Another, though somewhat similar, type of ceiling is to be found in a little room called Cardinal Wolsey's Closet; but here the decoration is more general, and is founded more directly on the Italian manner (Plate LXVII.). The ceiling is divided by wood ribs into rectilinear panels of small size and simple design; the intersections of the ribs are covered, in the manner already mentioned, with a plain wood boss and lead leaves bent down into the angles; each panel is filled with Italian decoration modelled in *papier mâché;* the whole is screwed up to the floor-joists above. The effect is very rich and elaborate. There is also a frieze on the wall which formed part of the design,

160.—PATERA TO A CEILING AT HAMPTON COURT.

although its precise relation to the ceiling can no longer be detected owing to modern alterations. The relation was probably something like what we see to-day (Plate LXVII.), but a close scrutiny shows that the connecting links between the ceiling and the frieze have disappeared; there must have been some kind of moulded cornice. There can be little doubt that the spacing of the panels in the frieze was made to agree with those of the ceiling, and that it had a moulding of some importance at the top to connect it with the ceiling, and corresponding to the border which it still retains at the bottom, on which is painted repeatedly Wolsey's motto " Dominus mihi adjutor." The panels in the frieze are ornamented in a manner corresponding with the ceiling panels, which all contain either a rose or a fleur-de-lys, the devices of Henry VIII. This

ceiling is of great interest, because it is one of the earliest
of a highly decorated kind left to us—for the Tudor joiners
placed little, if any, decoration in their panels; it is more
Italian in manner than any other that survives, and it is formed
of wood ribs and modelled filling, which were made elsewhere
and then brought to the room to be fitted and fixed in position.

From the occurrence of Wolsey's motto in the frieze, it is
probable that this work was done by him; it would consequently date prior to his death in 1530. Richardson, in his
Architectural Remains of the Reigns of Elizabeth and James I.,
gives a large drawing of a ceiling in the Chapel Royal,
St. James's, dated 1540, which is very similar in character to
Wolsey's. It con-
sists of small geo-
metrical panels
formed by wood
ribs, enclosing
rich designs in the
Italian manner,
among which the
King's devices are
constantly· re-
peated, together
with the date,
the initials of
Henry and Anne
of Cleves, and
such mottoes as

161.—PART OF THE CEILING IN THE LONG GALLERY,
HADDON HALL, DERBYSHIRE.

"Vivat rex," "Stet diu felix." If the latter aspiration were
fulfilled, it certainly was not in conjunction with the wife
whose initials are on this ceiling that the wished-for happi-
ness was attained, for she was divorced in July, 1540; and we
therefore incidentally learn that the ceiling must have been put
up in the first half of that year. In addition to the ornament
already mentioned the King's arms frequently occur. The ribs
in this case are broader than those at Hampton Court, and
they are ornamented with a running pattern cast in lead.

These two ceilings are the most Italian in character which
have survived. The type does not seem to have been generally
adopted; but it was rather a simpler one, founded more
directly on Tudor methods, which was developed. The wood

PLATE LXVIII.

DEENE HALL, NORTHAMPTONSHIRE
CEILING OF A BEDROOM.

ribs were replaced by plaster, and in the more plastic material they were no longer kept in straight lines, but were curved into an infinite variety of patterns, more or less intricate. The intersections were sometimes, but not often, covered with foliage; as a rule they were left bare, but where the pattern left a salient angle the lower members of the

162.—PART OF A COVED CEILING AT BECKINGTON ABBEY, SOMERSET.

moulding were carried out to form the stalk of some foliage, as may be seen in the long gallery at Haddon (Fig. 161), and also at South Wraxall (Plate XLVII.). The ribs, which at first were of a section similar to that of their predecessors in wood, soon assumed other proportions: they increased in width and lessened in depth; they sometimes ceased to have any mouldings, and became more like ribbons or straps, as in the example from Beckington Abbey

163.—COVED CEILING, BECKINGTON ABBEY, SOMERSET.

(Fig. 162), but more often they retained their moulded edges, and were ornamented on the flat face with a minute running pattern, such as that at Deene Hall (Plate LXVIII.), and the " Reindeer " Inn, Banbury (Plate LXIX.). The strap-work ribs

did not form such regular set patterns as the others: they
enclosed a panel here and there, but wandered off into spirals
and scrolls, and were emphasized at intervals by little ornamental knobs, such as may be seen in the ceiling of the
gallery at Charlton House, Wiltshire.   It was by no means
necessary for the ceilings to be flat.   Indeed, this kind of
decoration was exactly suited for application to coved ceilings
such as that already seen at South Wraxall (Plate XLVII.), and
that at Beckington Abbey (Fig. 163), where there is not only the
main vault of the ceiling, but also a subsidiary cove at the side,

164.—Part of a Ceiling from Sizergh Hall, Westmorland (now in South
Kensington Museum).

the curved face of which is ornamented with a variation of the
principal pattern.   The end wall of the room is also decorated
in a similar way in the upper part where its shape is controlled
by the curves of the ceiling.   The example at Beckington
Abbey is among the more formal of those where the strap-
work type was employed; there are panels of regular shape,
and the scrolled ends balance one another.   But in some
instances the strap-work conformed in its course to no regular
pattern at all; it twisted and interlaced and bent itself back
upon no system whatever, except that of covering the surface
evenly, and of gathering itself into a knot or of surrounding a

PLATE LXIX.

THE REINDEER INN, BANBURY, OXFORDSHIRE
CEILING.

pendant at regular intervals, the result being that the most
prominent features stand out in regular array from a mazy
background that requires concentrated attention to follow.
There is a ceiling of this kind among the many beautiful
examples at Audley End. These erratic designs were used

163.—CEILING FROM BENTHALL HALL, SHROPSHIRE.

simultaneously with others of much severer character, where
the pattern is of the simplest in structure, and richness of
effect is derived from its frequent repetition, and from the
ornament in the panels. Such an example is to be seen at
Sizergh (Fig. 164), and others, slightly more elaborate, at
Aston Hall (Plates LXX., LXXI.), where the modelling is beautifully delicate and varied. But in both these examples the

proportion is so carefully managed that the shape of the panels, which is the foundation of the design, is not obscured by the patterns which occupy them. The effect is equally rich in both, although the width of the rib and the manner of its decoration are varied. These ceilings are fairly late in date, as Aston Hall was being built from 1618 to 1635, and comes quite at the end of the period under discussion, but they retain all the characteristics of Elizabethan and Jacobean work. Another example

166.—CEILING IN GATE-HOUSE, HADDON HALL, DERBYSHIRE.

of the formal kind is at Benthall Hall (Fig. 165), where the main panels are all of oblong rectangular shape, and are filled with strap-work enrichment surrounding an elliptical boss. The patterns are varied in every case, and exhibit considerable ingenuity in obtaining the same general effect with entirely different disposition of lines. It will also be seen, by comparing this ceiling with the panelling and chimney-piece in the same room (Plate XLIII. and Fig. 156), that they are all *en suite*, and not, as is often the case, designed without relation one to the other.

PLATE LXX.

CEILING OF THE GREAT CHAMBER, ASTON HALL, NEAR BIRMINGHAM (CIR. 1635).

PLATE LXXI.

CEILING OF
"KING CHARLES' BEDROOM"

Section of Mouldings
1/4 full size

Cornice

GENERAL PLAN OF CEILING

Ceiling of Recessed part of Room in plan

Chimney Breast

CEILING OF KING CHARLES' BEDROOM, ASTON HALL, NEAR BIRMINGHAM (CIR. 1635.)

The ceiling at the "Reindeer" Inn, Banbury (Plate LXIX.), is also thoroughly Jacobean, although, from the style of the wood panelling, the room must date from well on in the seventeenth century. Soon after this time the large unbroken space of the ceilings began to be cut up into large panels by cross-beams: the spaces thus formed were still of considerable size, and were decorated in the old manner, as may be seen in a room in the entrance tower at Haddon (Fig. 166), and at Carbrook Hall, Sheffield (Plate XLII.). But it was an easy step to omit this surface decoration, and when that was done, the ceilings became the large coffered ceilings characteristic of the style which followed the Jacobean.

As in the chimney-pieces, so in the ceilings, a favourite method of ornamentation was to introduce the owner's arms and badges. Of the examples given here only two, as it happens, illustrate this custom—the ceilings at Haddon (Fig. 161) and Sizergh (Fig. 164), The square panel at Haddon encloses a shield surrounded by a delicate strap-work border, and bearing

167.—PENDANTS OF PLASTER CEILINGS.

the arms of Manners impaling Vernon, the work having been done by the Sir John Manners who came into possession of Haddon through his marriage with Dorothy Vernon, one of the co-heiresses of her father, Sir George, called the King of the Peak. At Sizergh one of the panels encloses a shield of arms, and others a badge.

There is a very splendid ceiling in the gallery at Blickling, in Norfolk, wherein various badges are introduced, and another at Apethorpe, in Northamptonshire. Others might be named, but the custom was not so widespread in the case of ceilings as of chimney-pieces, perhaps owing to the plasterers having a number of stock designs from which they worked, and which, of course, would not include the arms of any special family. There seems no doubt that the plasterers did have such stock designs, but it is curious how seldom they are found repeated;

hardly anywhere, indeed, can two designs be found which are exactly alike.

Besides heraldic ornament, there was a certain amount of modelled figure subjects of the usual kind—allegorical, mythological, and scriptural; but English plasterers were not very good at modelling the human figure, and it seems to have been generally recognized that a ceiling is not the most favourable position for a close study of detail, and the effect aimed at was

168.—Examples of Plaster Friezes from Montacute, Audley End, and Charlton House, Wiltshire.

one of general richness which did not demand minute investigation—such as, for instance, is necessary to appreciate one of Verrio's painted ceilings—and yet which repaid such scrutiny if subjected to it. Most of the ornament was of a kind which no one would examine unless specially interested—as a draughtsman, for instance, might be ; but in some cases the beautiful modelling induces even the casual visitor to put his neck to inconvenience, as he gladly would do to see the Fish ceiling at Audley End, where the panels enclose a number of excellently modelled fishes and other denizens, real and imaginary, of the ocean, and where the pendants are of unusual beauty. Pendants of more or less projection were another means of adding variety and interest to the design (Fig. 167), and they varied in size from a mere excrescence to an elaborate shaft, supported by figures half human, half foliage, which served to hang the lamp from. This shaft would only occur in the centre of the design, but the lesser pendants were introduced at regular intervals and accentuated its salient points. Another kind of ceiling had no considerable ribs at all, but was covered

169.—PLASTER FRIEZE FROM MONTACUTE HOUSE, SOMERSET.

with a flowing pattern in low relief, so arranged as to fall into a more or less symmetrical design. This is by no means a usual form, but there is an example at Burton Agnes, in York-shire, and another, which stands halfway between the two ideas, in the gallery at Chastleton, in Oxfordshire.

At the junction of the ceiling and the wall was a series of mouldings forming a cornice: these were sometimes in wood and formed the crowning member of the oak panelling, and sometimes they were in plaster. Beneath them on the surface of the wall there was frequently a plaster frieze of more or less depth. Occasionally it was only a few inches deep, as in the drawing-room at Haddon (Plate XLI.), but more usually it was from two to three feet, and in one room at Hardwick it was much deeper, as already mentioned (see Plate LII.). The narrower friezes were ornamented with some kind of running

pattern, the wider ones were divided into panels in various ways, and often displayed the family arms. Examples of the narrower kind in plaster may be seen on Plates LIII. and LXXVI., while others forming part of the panelling are shown on Plates XLIII., XLVII.. and XLIX. Sizergh Hall (Plate L.) has a frieze on the wood panelling and another in plaster above it. Examples

170.—PART OF PLASTER FRIEZE, CARBROOK HALL, NEAR SHEFFIELD.

of different kinds of friezes are given in Fig. 168, and one of considerable depth, and adorned with shields set in large panels, is shown from Montacute (Fig. 169). A fairly deep frieze is to be seen at Carbrook (Plate XLII.), of which a small part of the detail is shown in Fig. 170. An example of the way in which a pattern was fitted into an unusually-shaped space is shown in Fig. 171.

171.—CEILING OF A TRIANGULAR BAY WINDOW AT LITTLE CHARLTON, KENT.

CHAPTER IX.

INTERIOR FEATURES (*continued*).

STAIRCASES, GALLERIES, GLAZING.

THE staircases of the early part of the sixteenth century followed the old fashion, and were of the "corkscrew" type, winding round a central newel. They were built of stone or brick, and were hardly, if at all, ornamented. Then, quite suddenly, the fashion changed, and they were constructed of wood in straight, broad flights, with frequent landings. Everyone who has been up a church tower knows how tiring it is to climb the winding, never-ending steps, unrelieved by anything in the shape of a landing. It is somewhat less fatiguing to mount one of the grand circular staircases of the châteaux on the Loire, the task being lightened by the greater width of the steps and the introduction of more frequent landings. But the management of the landings is one of the great difficulties in a spiral staircase, because they break the regular sweep of the architectural lines. Whether English craftsmen recognized this difficulty from what they saw in France, or whether the idea of improving the circular type did not occur to them, it is impossible to say; but no attempt in this direction was made, unless it may have been at Rothwell Market-house (1577), where a circular staircase of considerable width was intended, although no remains of the actual stairs exist. There seems to be no intermediate type between the stone spiral and the straight flight in wood. In France, and especially in the district of the Loire, the old narrow, difficult steps were wonderfully improved; from being merely a means of ascending, they became elaborate pieces of work, upon which much ingenuity of contrivance and ornament was bestowed. From being two or three feet wide, they became ten or twelve. Instead of curling up a narrow turret, they occupied a considerable tower, and the tower, being one of the chief features of the house, had to be treated with great care. Much fancy was expended upon the internal treatment; a handrail was worked upon the newel,

and wound round it in a continuous line; another projection
formed a plinth, a third served as a cornice; another cornice
followed the sweep of the steps where they rested on the outside

172.—STAIRCASE AT LYVEDEN OLD BUILDING, NORTHAMPTONSHIRE.

wall: everything was done to make the constructional features
serve as ornaments, and the results were some of the most
interesting and curious pieces of stonework that can be seen.
But nothing of the kind was attempted in England.   The

PLATE LXXII.

STAIRCASE FROM BURGHLEY HOUSE, NORTHAMPTONSHIRE.

nearest approach is the stone vaulted staircase at Burghley House (Plate LXXII.), which resembles some of those in France, where the steps are carried in straight flights instead of round a central newel. There is such an instance at the Château de Chenonceaux, where the two straight flights are on either side of a dividing wall, the lower flight merging into the upper by means of winding stairs. These winding stairs were eschewed by English designers, who nearly always kept to straight runs, and at

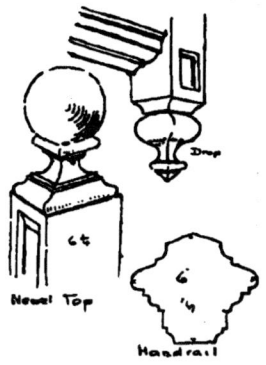

173.—DETAILS OF STAIRCASE, HAMBLETON OLD HALL, RUTLAND.

Burghley the two main flights are connected by a shorter one across the landing. The date of this staircase is not quite certain,

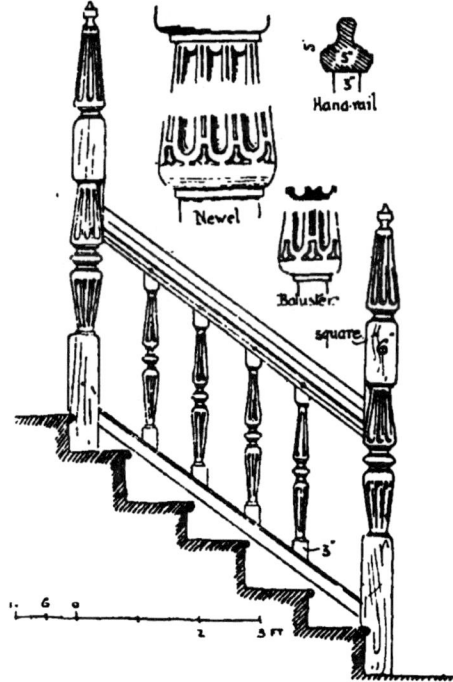

174.—STAIRCASE FROM EAST QUANTOCKSHEAD, SOMERSET.

but it probably belongs to the work which was being done about the year 1556. The idea of stone vaulted stairs, however, did not obtain any hold in England, and there are very few examples to be found. All the finest staircases are of wood, and they seem to have sprung into being without any gradual growth; the connecting links between them and the old corkscrew type, if there were any, have disappeared.

The principle upon which these wood staircases were constructed may be compared to that of the ladder, where the sides of the ladder are replaced by deep and comparatively narrow pieces of wood called "strings," and the rungs are replaced by the treads and risers. One side of this amplified ladder was placed hard on to the wall, the foot of the other was secured into a stout upright post, or "newel," as also was the top: into the same newel that received the top of the first

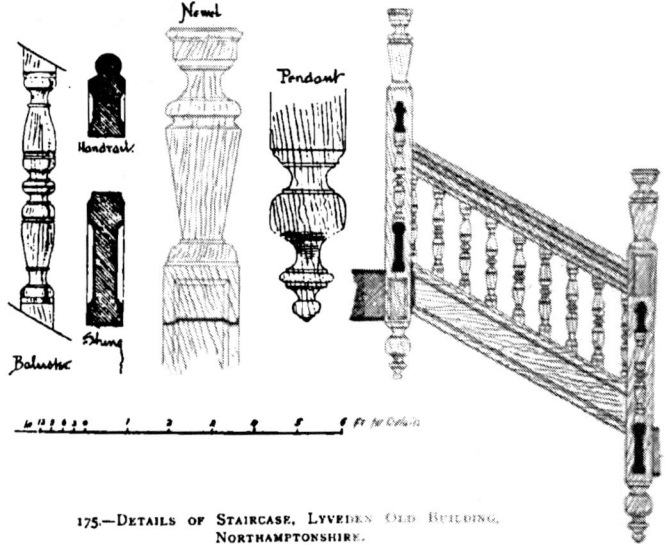

175.—DETAILS OF STAIRCASE, LYVEDEN OLD BUILDING, NORTHAMPTONSHIRE.

string the foot of the second was secured at right angles, and so onwards and upwards as far as the staircase extended. At about two feet above the top of the string, and parallel to it, was the handrail, and between the handrail and the string were fixed the balusters. The top of the first flight leant against a flat landing, on which also the foot of the next flight rested. The construction, therefore, was extremely simple in principle, far simpler than that of the continuous winding flights of the eighteenth century; but the component parts were often highly decorated. All the woodwork was of fairly large dimensions; the newels were six, seven, or eight inches square, the handrail was generally nearly as wide as the newel, the strings were three inches thick or even more, the balusters were

PLATE LXXIII.

PLANS OF STAIRCASES FROM JOHN THORPE'S DRAWINGS IN THE SOANE MUSEUM.

proportionately massive. The flights were five or six feet wide, and comprised usually about six steps, although they were longer when necessity demanded it. The plans on Plate LXXIII. show various arrangements of staircases taken from John Thorpe's collection of plans in the Soane Museum. Nos. 1 and 2 are the most usual types, and of these No. 1 is the more frequent. The space to be occupied by the stairs is divided into nine equal squares, of which those in the corners represent the landings, while the intermediate ones are occupied by the steps; the middle square is the "well-hole." The staircase at Lyveden Old Building, in Northamptonshire, is planned on this principle, and the effect can be seen in the sketch in Fig. 172. The flights in this case consist of seven steps each. This arrangement is very simple, but it necessitates the access to the upper rooms being from one of the comparatively small corner landings.

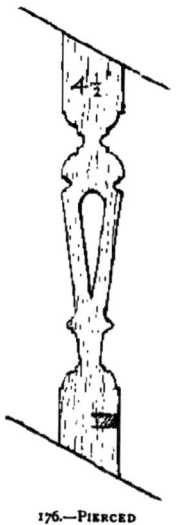

176.—Pierced Baluster.

Another plan, giving a larger landing at the top, is shown in No. 2, and an amplification of the same idea is given in No. 3, where, a larger number of steps being required, the sides have two flights with an intermediate landing. Sometimes the central square, instead of being occupied by an open well-hole, was either a solid block or a shell of masonry, round the four sides of which the steps ascended. Such an arrangement is shown in No. 5, where

Section on line CD

Scale for Staircases

177.—Staircase at Ockwells Manor House, Berkshire.

also may be seen some winding steps in one of the corners; but these winders are not of frequent occurrence, short straight flights being the rule. These four types are those most frequently adopted. Of the others, No. 4 is an instance of the employment of winders, and shows the somewhat unusual

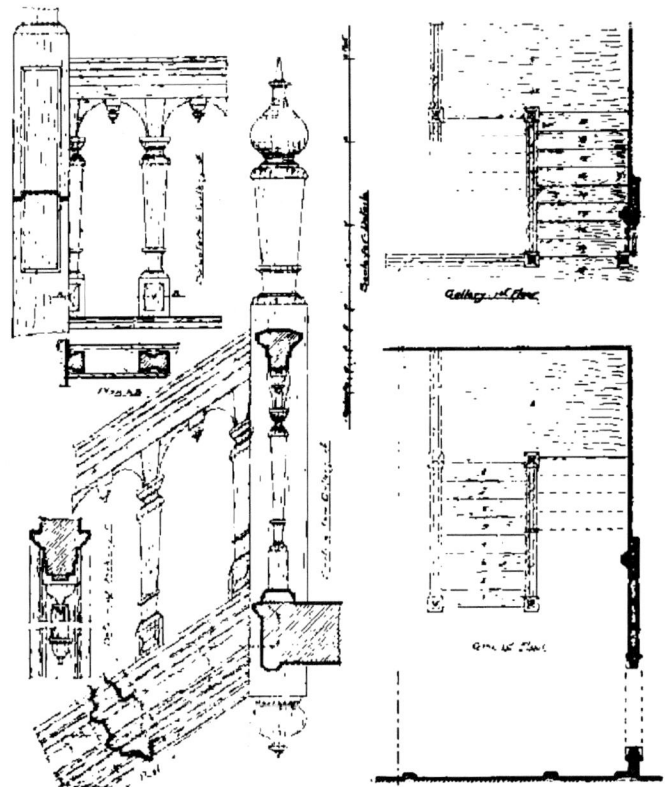

178.—Staircase at Ockwells Manor House, Berkshire. Plans and Details.

arrangement of two lower flights combining into one upper flight; No. 6, being in a turret, consists wholly of winders; and Nos. 7 and 8 are instances of a rather grander style of planning, in which it is evident that considerable effect was aimed at. The plans varied, of course, according to the disposition of the rooms to be reached; the chief characteristics

were simplicity of construction and massiveness of effect.
In the less important houses the work was fairly plain: the
newels were unornamented, except for a shaped top; the string
was moulded at the top and bottom; the balusters were merely
stout turned bars. But there was much variety imparted to

179.—STAIRCASE AT BENTHALL HALL, SHROPSHIRE.

the turning, and while many of the outlines are rather clumsy,
many of them also exhibit considerable subtlety and refinement. To increase the richness of effect the newels were
ornamented either with carving, or with a pattern contrived
by sinking the groundwork, thus leaving the pattern itself
raised and at the same level as the general face of the newel.
The tops of the newel were sometimes little more than round

knobs, as at Hambleton Old Hall (Fig. 173), and a house at
Warwick (Fig. 180); but more often they projected far above
the handrail and were shaped in a variety of ways, of which
four examples of varying degrees of elaboration are given
from East Quantockshead (Fig. 174), Lyveden Old Building
(Fig. 175), Ockwells Manor House (Figs. 177, 178), and the

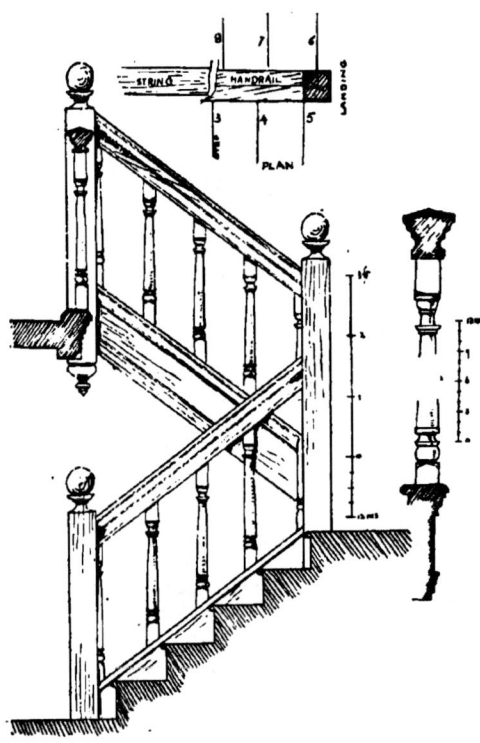

180.—STAIRCASE AT WARWICK.

Charterhouse
(Fig. 181). They
were sometimes
made the pede-
stals upon which
figures were
placed—such as
boys playing in-
struments, as at
Hatfield ; or
warriors in
various guises,
as at Blickling;
or the animal
sacred to the
particular family
concerned, and
hallowed in their
sight by being
borne in their
coat of arms.
The newels at
the Charter-
house carry a
crest by way of
finial (Fig.
181). Then the
outer surface of
the outer string would be also carved (Figs. 179 and 181),
or decorated with a pattern ; and the balusters would sometimes be flat pieces of wood shaped and pierced in a variety
of patterns (Fig. 176). Sometimes, instead of balusters there was
a series of arches springing from small columns and following
the upward rake of the stairs; as at Ockwells Manor House
(Figs. 177, 178), and the Charterhouse (Fig. 181). Or, again,

the balustrade would consist of woodwork cut and slightly carved into a version of the favourite strap-work pattern, like that

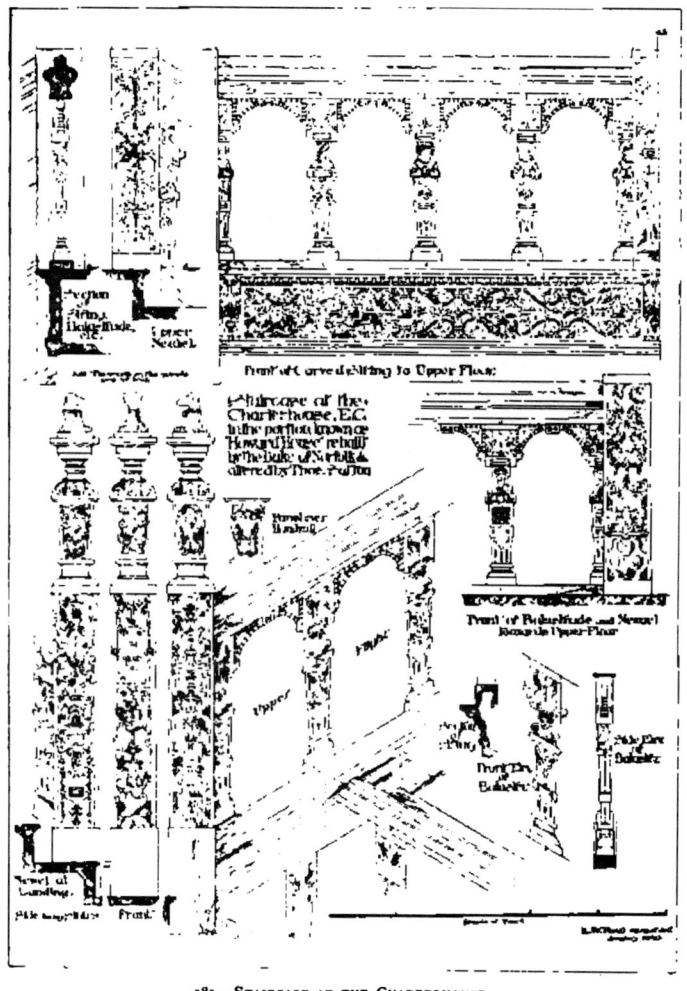

181.—Staircase at the Charterhouse.

at Benthall Hall, Shropshire (Fig. 179). Not infrequently the space at command forbade the arranging of the flights at right angles to each other; the second flight then returned side by side with the first. In such cases either the newels were increased in width sufficiently to take both the handrails, or the handrail and string intersected each other in the way shown on Fig. 180. Occasionally, when a little space divided the flights, the great newels were carried up and joined to each other by wood arches, as in the instance of a staircase at Audley End (Plate LXXIV.): this kind of treatment occasionally produced a most intricate result, of which a careful study is required in order to make out what are its component parts.

There was no end to the variety which the workmen imparted to the simple constructional features which were the groundwork of the design. The points which were always aimed at were breadth of way, ease of ascent, massive appearance, and very frequently richness of effect. The series of stout newels going up and up in a long procession, each crowned with a handsome finial or heraldic animal, alone is enough to lend stateliness to the staircase; and when these are supplemented with quaint balusters, or a row of arches, or, as in later days, with a carved foliated filling, beyond which is seen the highly ornamented string of the upper flight, the whole effect is particularly striking. As a rule the flights were short, from six to eight steps being considered enough between the various landings, but the number varied according to the height to be attained and the space at command.

These fine staircases were clearly made for show as well as use, because it not infrequently happens that having reached the first floor, which was their chief object, they sweep upwards with equal grandeur to the next, where there are only insignificant attics. The upper staircase, however, although it leads to no important room, would be in full view of those who came to the first floor; and it was on this floor that some rooms were placed which were the resort of all who were staying in the house—namely, the Great Chamber and the Long Gallery. The great chamber was, among princes and nobles, the presence chamber, where they received guests. It was the "Great Chamber of Estate." In smaller houses it answered much the same end as the drawing-room of the present day. Even so inconsiderable a person as Slender, who was a small squire, had a great chamber in

PLATE LXXIV.

STAIRCASE AT AUDLEY END, ESSEX.

his house, which he took care to mention casually in the course of his controversy with Falstaff as to the picking of his pocket.

THE LONG GALLERY.

The Long Gallery is a feature peculiarly characteristic of the times of Elizabeth and James. Mention has already been made of this apartment, and of the fact that not a few houses were specially planned so as to obtain a gallery of great length. Some of them were extravagant in this respect, the length being as much as eight and ten times the width. At Buckhurst House the gallery was 254 feet long by 16 feet wide, at Ampthill 245 feet by 22 feet, but it is not quite certain that these were not divided into two lengths each. John Thorpe shows the gallery at Slaugham Place to be 200 feet by 27 feet, Audley End probably 190 feet by 27 feet, Holdenby 140 feet by 22 feet, Aston Hall 140 feet by 18 feet, Copthall 136 feet by 22 feet, Burghley 128 feet by 18 feet, and Wollaton 100 feet by 18 feet. Others, to which there are no names, are 200 feet by 20 feet, 150 feet by 25 feet, and 150 feet by 17 feet, besides many of 80 feet in length by widths varying from 10 feet to 21 feet. The purpose of such a long apartment has never been fully explained : it may have been for exercise ; it may have had its origin from reasons of display or in imitation of royal palaces, where its use as an ante-room to the royal closet is easily understood ; or it may have been merely a development in planning dictated by fashion, each person vying with his neighbour to obtain a long room. But, however this may be, no Elizabethan or Jacobean house of any size was without its long gallery, which was ornamented in the same way as the great chamber, the parlours, and the hall. The walls were either hung with tapestry or panelled, the ceiling was richly moulded, the fireplaces, of which there were two or three in the length, were large and elaborate. The porch of the house was often carried up to form a bay window in the middle of the length, and advantage was taken of other opportunities to break up the extreme length by projections at the side. It was almost always on the topmost floor, where space was of less importance for other purposes ; but as many of the houses were only two storeys high, it was usually easy of access, and, of course, it was approached by one, or oftener two, of the principal staircases. The room at Haddon, now called the ballroom, is in reality the long gallery (Plate LXXV.). It is 110 feet 6 inches long by 17 feet 4 inches wide, and its extreme length is broken along one side by three large projecting bays, the middle one of which, measuring 15 feet by 11 feet 6 inches, is itself large enough for a fair-sized room. The legend of the elopement of Dorothy Vernon from this "ballroom" is a modern invention which confuses the public mind in regard to the household arrangements of that period, for Dorothy's father, who greatly embellished Haddon, lived during the prevalence of the Late Tudor style, and had no such huge apartment: it was her husband who fashioned this long gallery in Elizabeth's time, and adorned it in the manner then prevalent. This may seem a small point to insist on, and to the general public no doubt it is; but to the student, whose imagination naturally clings to the picturesque legend, it is important to realize that the work in the "ballroom" was not done by Dorothy's father, who belonged to the Tudor era, but by her husband, who belonged to the Elizabethan. But leaving this point, it may be remarked that the gallery is panelled with unusual richness, and the ceiling is felt to be in harmony with the rest of the work, although the moulded rib is but small, and the pattern it makes is simple. It may also be noted that there is but one fireplace in the whole length of 110 feet, which must have been quite inadequate, according to modern ideas.

The gallery at Aston Hall (Plate LXXVI.) is a fine example of its kind. The walls are panelled from the floor nearly up to the ceiling, only sufficient space being left above the wood-work for a plaster frieze. The panels have an arched enrichment in each of them, in accordance with the fashion prevalent in King James's time, and they are divided into bays by shallow pilasters, fluted above, and ornamented with imitation rustic work below. The ceiling is of great richness, and itself goes a long way towards "furnishing" the room. There is a row of windows down one side, and a large one at the end. The Hall is now used as a museum, and the rail, which occupies a conspicuous position in the illustration, serves to protect the articles exhibited.

Although it is tolerably certain that Sir George Vernon had no such room as the long gallery, it is not quite clear that

PLATE LXXV.

HADDON HALL, DERBYSHIRE.

THE LONG GALLERY.

PLATE LXXVI.

ASTON HALL, WARWICKSHIRE.

THE LONG GALLERY (ABOUT 1635).

houses in his time were all without them, for at Hampton
Court, in the time of Henry VIII. and Jane Seymour, there
was the Queen's long gallery, which was 180 feet long ·by
25 feet wide, lighted on both sides, and having, like Haddon,
three bay windows down one side, the middle one of which
was not square but circular.* But although the
palace had such an apartment, there is no evidence
that the smaller houses in general possessed them
until the time of Elizabeth, when they became
of universal adoption.

GLAZING.

The windows in the gallery at Hampton Court
were glazed with heraldic glass displaying the
arms, badges, and mottoes of the King and Queen.
This was in accordance with the custom of the
time, the principal windows being generally more
or less filled with heraldic devices relating to the
family who owned the house.   Much of this
splendid decoration throughout the country has
disappeared, but enough is left to show that the
treatment of the glass followed the same lines as
the carving of stone and wood.   In the early part
of the century it consisted of dainty foliage, vases,
candelabra, scrolls, and the quaint animals with
attenuated bodies, which are characteristic of
Italian ornament.   Toward the end of the century
these were replaced with the strap-work and the
great bunches of fruit and flowers which we owe
to Dutch designers. A small part of an early
pattern from Ightham Church is illustrated in Fig.

182.—PORTION
OF GLAZING
FROM IGHTHAM
CHURCH, KENT.

182 ; among the Italian vases and flowers is the
English portcullis, the badge of the Tudor family,
more particularly of Henry VII.   A good example of the later
treatment, when the Dutch strap-work was in vogue, is given in
a panel from Moreton Old Hall on Plate LXXVII.   The strap-
work is merely an ornamental border to the shield bearing the
family device, and is treated in the same way as that which surrounds most of the shields on the tombs of the period.   There

* *Law*, Vol. I., p. 182.

is a fair amount of sixteenth century glass to be found up and
down the country, but it is mostly in small pieces, either saved
from the wreck of larger windows, or consisting of detached coats
of arms. The finest display of the later glass that has survived
is that in the dining-room of Gilling Castle, in Yorkshire,

183.—Glass Panel from one of the Windows at Gilling Castle, Yorkshire (1585).

where there are several large windows full of beautiful heraldic
glazing. Much of it was the work of a Dutchman, Bernard
Dininckhoff, who signs one of the panels with the date 1585
(Fig. 183). The hall of the Middle Temple also has some good
heraldic glass which is dated 1570. There were good English
glaziers both before and after Dininckhoff's time. At Hengrave
the old glass, dated 1567, was the work of Robert Wright,

PLATE LXXVII.

GLASS PANEL FROM MORETON OLD HALL, CHESHIRE.

Plate LXXVIII.

PATTERNS FROM "A BOOKE OF SUNDRY DRAUGHTES."
BY WALTER GEDDE (1615).

who was paid £4 for the "making of all the glasse wyndows of the Manour-place, with the sodar, and for xiij. skutchens with armes."* In the year 1615 one Walter Gedde published a book of pattern glazing called " A Booke of Sundry Draughtes. Principally serving for Glasiers; And not Impertinent for Plasterers and Gardiners: besides sundry other Professions. Whereunto is annexed the manner how to anniel in Glas; And also the true forme of the Furnace, and the secretes thereof," in which he gives 103 pages of designs for lead glazing of varying merit, out of which four have been selected for illustration on Plate LXXVIII. Few, if any, of these designs have survived in actual execution; such patterns as are still to be found here and there are somewhat simpler in design. It is interesting to observe how Walter Gedde considered that his patterns would be useful to plasterers for the groundwork of their ceiling-designs, and to gardeners for the ornamental beds and knot-work with which they embellished their gardens.

The finest examples of painted glass of the early part of the sixteenth century are the splendid windows at King's College Chapel, which were the work of Englishmen. There are also portions of the beautiful glass from the ruined Chapel of the Holy Ghost at Basingstoke, still preserved at the church of Basingstoke, and at the Vyne; and there are three windows in the apse of the chapel of that house. In addition to these examples, there are several windows at St. Neot's Church in Cornwall, the character of which inclines more to the Perpendicular than the Renaissance; there is the east window of St. Margaret's, Westminster; and there are fragments at Balliol and Queen's Colleges, Oxford, and at St. James's, Bury St. Edmund's.† The ornament forming the background to the figures in these windows is all similar in character to that which adorns other work of the same period.

---

* *History and Antiquities of Hengrave,* by John Gage.

† See *The History of Design in Painted Glass,* by N. H. J. Westlake, 1894, in which are numerous drawings of portions of the glass mentioned in the text.

CHAPTER X.

MISCELLANEOUS WORK.

HOUSES IN STREETS, SCHOOLS, MARKET-HOUSES, &C.

THE houses built in towns followed much the same lines as those erected elsewhere in general treatment, but the plan was of course restricted by the situation of the house, and by the fact that it could not derive light from the sides. The fronts were often constructed of wood and plaster, and the upper floors were corbelled out over those beneath in the same fashion as had been customary for many years. Owing to the nature of their materials most of these houses have disappeared through fire or decay. Others have been swept away in the improvements which inevitably accompany prosperity in a town; others have been altered to suit the changes and development of trades. There are not many examples, therefore, to be found except in out-of-

184.—HOUSE FORMERLY IN NORTH STREET, EXETER.

the-way places, or in districts of large towns from which the main stream of business has been diverted. There are a few examples in the older parts of Bristol and York, for instance, but they have been much mutilated and altered. Some years ago there was an unusually good specimen in North Street, Exeter (Fig. 184), but it has now disappeared. Here the columns on the storey above the bays were particularly good both in proportion and in general effect, and there was an unusual amount of richness bestowed upon the carving of the corbels and the strings and cornices. Towns near the coast seem to have been richer in houses of this kind than those further inland. The Buttermarket at Dartmouth is a good specimen: the first floor is carried on

185.—House in the High Street, Canterbury.

columns, thus forming a covered walk; the bay windows are supported by boldly-carved corbels fashioned, some like fabulous animals, some like human figures. Ipswich has some excellent examples of carved strings and beams; it was customary to enrich the faces of the large beams which carried the projecting storeys, and a considerable amount of fancy in design and dexterity of execution were expended upon them. In the eastern counties generally there is some capital work to be found, both in wood and in modelled plaster. Canterbury has

a few remains, one of which, of somewhat late date, is shown
in Fig. 185. The general treatment of the windows on the
first floor is in accordance with Jacobean methods, but the
handling of the boldly-modelled plaster-work above them
points towards the latter half of the seventeenth century as the
time of its execution. Two of the objects aimed at in these
street fronts seem to have been to get plenty of light and to
introduce bay windows. In the example from Canterbury, the
whole front of the first floor is occupied with windows, and

186.—OLD HOUSE, HIGH TOWN, HEREFORD.

there are two bays introduced in the range which serve as large
corbels to the straight front above them. Another example,
from Oxford (Plate LXXIX.), also shows the whole front of
two floors occupied by window space. But this front is gabled,
and has one large bay window in the centre, which is covered
by a broken pediment embracing a kind of dormer, all enclosed
within the lines of the gable itself, which, however, has undergone some alteration since it was first erected. The difference
in the treatment of the arched lights in the several floors should
be noticed. Another variety is to be seen in a house in Stratford-on-Avon (Plate LXXIX.), where the general disposition

PLATE LXXIX.

HOUSE AT STRATFORD-ON-AVON, WARWICKSHIRE.

HOUSE IN THE HIGH STREET, OXFORD.

is rather simple, but all the woodwork is highly ornamented. The main beams which carry the projecting storeys are carved in the manner already mentioned as being prevalent at Ipswich. Here, again, there is a bay window on the first floor helping to carry the storey above it, and another projecting window on the top floor, the upper corners of which are hidden behind the barge-boards. The same general treatment is to be seen in an old house in the High Town at Hereford (Fig. 186), where the excellent effect is produced by very simple means. The woodwork of the framing is all straight, but it is massive, and not much less in width than the plaster panels. The upper storey projects far enough to give good shadow, which is varied by the shallow bays just beneath it. The gables have heavy carved barge-boards, and in each of them is a bay window, the top of which, unlike the example from Stratford, is free from interference by the barge-board. The pendants between the bays on the first floor are of the ordinary pierced pattern. In considering these specimens from busy towns, it should be remembered that they have all been more or less restored.

The fashion of building with timber on the narrow streets of the time was felt to be dangerous, and in the year 1605 a proclamation was made in London that the fore-front and windows of all new houses within the city and one mile thereof should be of brick or stone. The old houses, however, were left until the great fire of 1666 swept them away: it was these charming half-timbered dwellings which afforded the chief fuel for that huge bonfire.

In Thorpe's book there are several plans drawn for "London. Houses." One (on page 18) is entitled "Three houses for the city, or for a country house at 8 parts to the inch." It shows a row of three houses, two of which have a frontage of 33 feet each, while the third has 24. The plans are very rough and unfinished, but they show alternative ways of providing the accommodation. One house has a hall and kitchen on the front, and a parlour, staircase and buttery at the back, while a "vault" is contrived in the centre in a most insanitary manner. The second has the hall and buttery to the front, the stairs at one side, and the parlour and kitchen to the back. The third (having only 24 feet of frontage) has merely an entrance passage and kitchen to the front, and a parlour at the back, while the staircase is opposite the front door—the plan being a forerunner

of the type which later became of universal adoption. The
second part of the title, indicating that the plan might be used
for a country house, is rather obscure, inasmuch as no redistri-
bution of names among the rooms shown could have converted
them into a workable plan for a single house. Another plan (on
pages 135, 136) is called a " London house of 3 breadths of
ordinary tenements." It has a frontage of 51 feet, thus giving

17 feet as the
breadth of an
ordinary tene-
ment. With such
a frontage, it is of
course a much
better house than
those already de-
scribed for the
city. It was en-
tered at one end,
the entry commu-
nicating with a
narrow yard
which gave access
to the garden in
the rear. The
hall looked out
into the street, as
also did the par-
lour and buttery.
At the back were
the winter par-
lour, the kitchen,
and the stairs,
with the larder
under them. The
rooms were not

187.—Corbels, "King's Arms," Sandwich, Kent.

large, the parlour being 18 feet by 13 feet, and the winter parlour
15 feet by 12 feet: as usual, much space was occupied by the
large fireplaces. The first-floor plan is not given, but on a
higher storey appears an open leaded terrace along the street
front, behind which is a narrow and low gallery (only 5 feet to
the rafters) extending the whole length of the house, and again

behind that there are "sundry lodgings for servants, etc."
There are no means of fixing the date of the plan, but it appears

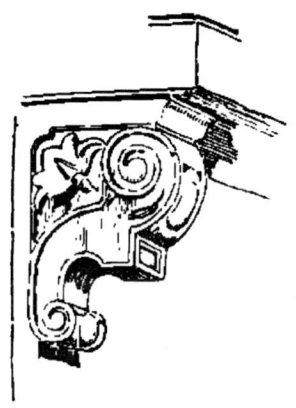

188.—CORBEL AT CANTERBURY.   189.—CORBEL AND PENDANT AT CANTERBURY.

to have been prepared for Sir Thomas Lake, who was clerk to
the signet in 1595, and a Secretary of State in 1616. If we are
to presume that a high official complied with
the proclamation as to houses being of stone
or brick, the date would be prior to 1605, for
although the ground floor is shown with stone
walls, those of the upper floor are only of wood
and plaster.

There is one other plan for a town house; it
is called "A London house, Lady Derby,
Channell Row" (page 110). It is the plan of
a much finer house than any of the foregoing, and as it is built round a courtyard,
there were no special difficulties in providing
light and air. It follows the usual type of large
houses, having a central entrance, from which
a flagged path leads across the court into the
screens of the hall. The staircases, chapel,
winter parlour, kitchen and other rooms are

190.—CORBEL, ORTON
WATERVILLE,
HUNTINGDONSHIRE.

grouped round the court in the ordinary way, the only difference being that those which occupy the sides of the court
have no windows on their outside walls, but only such as look
inwards into the court itself. The restrictions imposed by the

fact of the house being a " London house " are therefore very
slight.   The " Channell Row " where this house was built was
probably the street of that name in Westminster.   These plans
of Thorpe's are of considerable interest, as they show the first
steps taken towards developing a plan suitable for the confined
spaces available in large towns.

Reverting to the smaller examples under consideration, we
find that a great
variety was intro-
duced into the
corbels which
caried the projec-
ting floors; many
of them were
grotesques after
the fashion of that
on the " King's
Arms " at Sand-
wich, in Kent
(Fig. 187), others
were simpler, like
the examples from
Canterbury (Figs.
188, 189), while
others, like that
from Orton
Waterville, Hunt-
ingdonshire (Fig.
190), combined
both ideas. But
the characteristic
common to them

191.—The " Swan " Inn, Lechlade, Gloucestershire.

all is boldness,
both of size and treatment.   They generally had a spiral about
them in one form or another, varied by foliage or projecting
bosses, or some variation of the strap-work *motif*.   The great
corner-posts of such houses as formed the corner of a street were
often wrought with a remarkable amount of care.   They were not
only of sufficient size to make suitable angle-posts, but they were
brought out at the top in a diagonal manner in order to support
the storey above, which overhung the lower one on both faces ;

an instance of this treatment may be seen in the example from
Sandwich (Fig. 187).   In some places it was customary not only
to bring out the face of each storey beyond that of the one
below, but to bring the whole house out over the footwalk.   The
Rows at Chester are a well-known example of this practice.
The Long Row on the great market-place of Nottingham is
another instance, but here the arcade has been almost entirely
re-built, one of the last specimens of a Jacobean front having
recently been removed in the course of making a new street.

In stone districts the local material was chiefly employed, and
all through the small towns and villages of Somerset, Wiltshire,
Oxfordshire, Gloucestershire and Northamptonshire charming
little examples, such as the "Swan" Inn at Lechlade (Fig. 191),
may be found here and there.   The idea is of the simplest—a
door in the middle, with a bay window on each side, crowned
with a gable.   But the disposition of the small windows, the
treatment of the door, and the change from the canted side
of the bay to the square base of the gable afforded opportunities
for variety and for careful treatment sufficient to render these
minor examples well worth attention.

MARKET-HOUSES, SCHOOLS, ALMSHOUSES, &C.

Most of the work of the sixteenth and early seventeenth centuries
which has come down
to us is to be found
in houses ; but there
are a certain number
of other buildings
left, such as town-
halls, market-houses,
schools, and alms-
houses. Of alms-
houses, or hospitals, as
they are often called,
there are some excel-
lent examples in many
parts of the country.
Ford's Hospital, in
Coventry, built in

192.—DESK IN ALMSHOUSE, CORSHAM, WILTSHIRE.

1529, is an extremely good specimen of Late Gothic woodwork; St.

193.—ALMSHOUSES, CHIPPING CAMPDEN, GLOUCESTERSHIRE.

John's Hospital, Rye, is another.   The almshouses at Corsham, in Wiltshire, are not only very picturesque outside, but con-

194.—MARKET-HOUSE, SHREWSBURY.

tain some capital woodwork inside, of which a read-ing-desk is illus-trated in Fig. 192. A n o t h e r s e t, equally substan-tial and of greater extent, is to be found at Chipping C a m p d e n, i n G l o u c e s t e rshire (Fig. 193).   The w o r k i n t h e s e places is simple a n d substantial ; there is no display of ornament, un-less perhaps over the entrance, where the donor would place his

arms with a certain amount of flourish, partly in carving, partly
in inscription; there are no elaborate ceilings nor chimney-pieces,
but tables, desks, and chairs of careful design and workmanship

195.—MARKET-HOUSE, WYMONDHAM, NORFOLK (1617).

have survived in places, and these simple buildings are often
valuable in affording examples of plain, unpretentious work.

There are not many town-halls of this period to be found.
Civic life did not express itself in concrete form in nearly so
pronounced a manner as, for instance, in the Low Countries

during the period under consideration, and as it is doing at home
at the present day. The most striking example of a town-hall
of the time is the picturesque Guildhall at Exeter, which
has a richly-ornamented front projecting over the pavement
and carried on arches. But there were a great many market-
houses built. The finest of these, so far as design and
workmanship go, is the well-known Market-house at Rothwell,
presented to the town about the year 1577 by a neighbouring
squire, Sir Thomas Tresham, but left unfinished owing to the
donor being harassed on account of his zeal as a Roman

196.—MARKET-HOUSE, CHIPPING CAMPDEN, GLOUCESTERSHIRE.

Catholic. Like most market-houses, this building was to have
consisted of an open market-hall on the ground floor, with a
room over it. There is a good example on a larger scale at
Shrewsbury (Fig. 194), substantially built in stone, with mullioned windows and an ornamental parapet. The ground floor
serves as a covered market, and the upper floor is carried
on open arches. At Wymondham, in Norfolk, is a smaller
specimen (dated 1617), serving the same purposes, but it is
built of timber and plaster (Fig. 195). The upper floor stands
on stout posts and brackets, set some two feet within the
outside face, and is approached by a quaint wooden staircase.

PLATE LXXX.

There is a one-storey market-house at Chipping Campden (Fig. 196), built of stone, with arches on each side; the five down the long side are supported on pillars, and have a gable over every alternate arch, while the two at each end are divided by a short length of wall and have a gable over each, thus securing a pleasant variation of treatment: the detail throughout is quite plain. There were also a few market and village crosses erected at this time, but there are not many examples to be found: one of the best is at Brigstock, in Northamptonshire (Plate LXXX.), where its situation in an open space, and backed by stone-built and thatched cottages, renders it a quaint and pleasant feature. The shields at the top bear alternately the royal arms and Elizabeth's initials, E. R., with the date 1586.

During the reign of Edward VI. a large number of schools

197.—School at Burton Latimer, Northamptonshire (1622).

were founded, and there are numerous examples left of those built during the next fifty years. There is a good specimen of the late sort at Shrewsbury; and of the smaller kind, such as were founded in villages, that at Burton Latimer, in Northamptonshire, is one of the quaintest (Fig. 197). Its features are quite simple; mullioned windows, on which are inscribed the date 1622, and the names of donors or, as we should now call them, subscribers; steep gables with finials at the foot; the ordinary excellent chimney of the district, and a rather elaborate doorway surmounted by a curved gable; such are the means employed to produce this attractive little building.

Of other kinds of buildings, which come under no class because there were so few built, may be mentioned the pretty little mill at Bourne Pond, near Colchester, and the Hawking-tower in Althorp Park, Northamptonshire. The former (Fig. 198) is built chiefly of flint, but mixed with the flint are bricks, tiles, and stones. The stone embellishments are somewhat elaborate and varied, and the curious curved and broken outline of the gables points to the Low Countries as

the source of its birth. The mill is dated 1591, and bears the arms of its founder, who was a citizen of the adjacent town of Colchester. The Hawking-tower at Althorp is probably unique (Fig. 199). It was built by Robert, Lord Spencer, in 1612 and 1613, and is said to have been erected by him as a token of gratitude for having been raised to the peerage ; but if so, the acknowledgment fol-lowed the event at an interval of ten years. There is no suggestion of the kind in the only inscription upon it, which runs thus, "This Staninge was made by Robert Lord Spencer 1612 et 1613." It not only bears the arms of Lord Spencer, but also those of the sovereign, very cleverly modelled. The plan (Fig. 200) comprises on the ground floor an entrance, a room with a fireplace, and a staircase, which leads up to the floor above, where the walls were pierced with a number of arches, through which the spectators could watch the sport.

198.—MILL AT BOURNE POND, COLCHESTER, ESSEX (1591).

These arches have been built up in order to render the place habitable, and one or two rooms have been added at the back

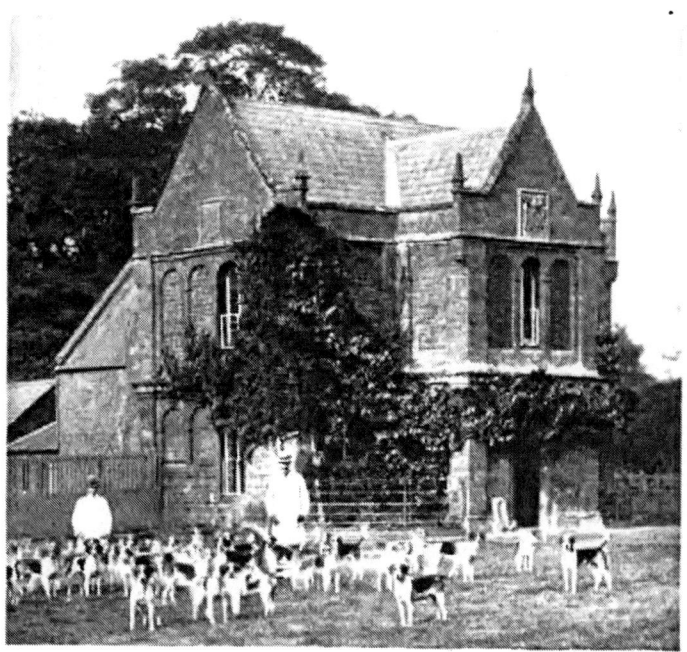

199.—HAWKING-TOWER, ALTHORP PARK, NORTHAMPTONSHIRE (1612—13).

with a like purpose, but a little care enables the original arrangements to be made out with tolerable certainty.

At Scole, in Norfolk, a very curious survival of the old classical *motifs* was to be seen, till the end of last century, in a great sign erected in 1655 for the " White Hart " Inn (Fig. 201). The hart itself lies couchant on the middle of the main beam, beneath a pediment supported by Justice and Plenty, two qualities for which the host may be excused

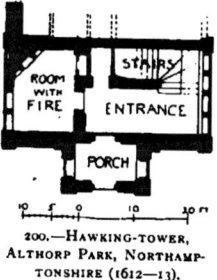

200.—HAWKING-TOWER, ALTHORP PARK, NORTHAMPTONSHIRE (1612—13).

if he considered his house noted. On one side of the centre-piece stands Actæon, about to be torn in pieces by his dogs, to whom

201.—THE SIGN OF THE "WHITE HART" INN, FORMERLY AT SCOLE, NORFOLK (1655).

he is supposed to be addressing the Latin legend beneath him : " I am Actæon, know your master." On the other side stands Diana, and beyond her is Time, about to devour his child, beginning with its hand ; beneath him his identity is made quite clear by the sentence "Tempus edax rerum." In the frieze below the beam are two figures representing (probably) Bacchus and Gambrinus, supported on either side by coats of arms. Angels and lions hold further coats of arms. There is Cerberus with his three heads, while numerous bunches of grapes, men blowing horns, and other devices suitable to the purpose occupy the rest of the space. The whole design might have come from the fertile brain of George Gascoigne, who was responsible for most of the entertainments at Kenilworth when Queen Elizabeth paid her celebrated visit there nearly eighty years before this sign was erected. The fundamental idea which underlay all design of the time was to combine strong classic feeling with picturesqueness of expression.

Work in Churches.

It has already been stated that there is no ecclesiastical architecture of early Renaissance character in England.   There

202 —Chichester Tomb, Pilton Church, Devonshire (1566).

were a number of churches built during the first thirty years of the sixteenth century, but they are all Gothic in treatment. The influence of the Renaissance on certain features to be found in churches, such as chantries and tombs, has already been dealt with.   It remains to glance at the changes that

R.A.   .   P

occurred in church fittings as the century grew older. Although
no churches, or extremely few, were built after the Dissolution
of the Monasteries, still the Elizabethan and Jacobean squires
were not backward in embellishing the ancient structures, and
there are plenty of screens, pulpits, font-covers, and particularly
tombs, to be found all over the country, although it cannot be
denied that under the influence of the revival of Gothic feeling
which took place about fifty years ago, a great deal of Elizabethan and Jacobean work was either destroyed, or removed
to the vestry, into which confined space it was made to fit by
a ruthless exercise of the axe and saw.

203.—From one of the Foljambe Tombs, Chesterfield Church, Derbyshire (1592).

The progress of style in tombs has already been traced to a
certain extent in dealing with the early stages of the Renaissance
movement. It has been shown how the old idea of the altar
tomb, with recumbent figures, lingered on till quite late in the
sixteenth century. In the closing years, however, it became
fashionable to place the figure, still recumbent, beneath an
arched canopy, upon which was lavished an extraordinary
amount of ornament. The arch itself was coffered and adorned
with bosses and stiff flowers of various kinds. It was flanked
with columns which carried an entablature, above which again
rose a superstructure displaying the family arms, and so designed
that with its supporting obelisks and detached figures it formed
a more or less pyramidal finish. The back of the tomb

above the figures, and enclosed by the arch, was usually occupied by a tablet setting forth the name and qualities of the defunct person, together with his alliances, if they were thought at all worthy of record ; and round this tablet was a frame of strap-work of intricate design filling up the remainder of the space, and decked with all manner of delicate ribbons and garlands. In every suitable place appeared the arms of the chief person concerned, or those of his wife, or some notable family to which they were allied. The whole monument was brightly coloured, where the use of different kinds of marble did not render such embellishment unnecessary, and the effect was striking in the extreme. The nobleman and the squire of Elizabeth's days had each a very high

204.—Tomb of G. Reed (d. 1610), Bredon Church, Worcestershire.

opinion of his family, and of his own importance in the scheme of the universe, and nothing would have pleased him better than to see the monument under which he was buried. Some of these great tombs are pretentious in idea and poor in design, but some of them are full of delightful detail, consistent in scale, varied in

P 2

treatment, and beautifully modelled. There is a good example
in the Chichester tomb at North Pilton, in Devonshire (Fig. 202),
which departs from the usual arched type, and which, if it were
erected soon after the death of those whom it commemorates,
in 1566, is quite an early example of the use of strap-work.
The detail of this monument, shown on Plate LXXXI., is
of unusual delicacy, and the elaborate frame which encloses

205.—TOMB OF SIR WM. SPENCER (D. 1609), YARNTON
CHURCH, OXFORDSHIRE.

the black marble
panel is handled
with a delicacy
and lightness of
touch too seldom
met with. The
Foljambe tombs
in Chesterfield
Church, Derby-
shire, are treated
with considerable
originality. One
of them (dated
1592) is in the
form of a sar-
cophagus, and is
adorned with
beautifully model-
led carving (Fig.
203). These ex-
amples are of un-
usual excellence.
The tomb in
Bredon Church
(Fig. 204) to G.
Reed, who died

in 1610, and that in the Spencer aisle at Yarnton (Fig. 205) to
Sir William Spencer, who died in 1609, are specimens of the
ordinary treatment of arched monuments. As time went on
this kind of tomb became much coarser in design. The detail
was less refined, and the recumbent figures were placed no
longer in a simple and dignified attitude, with faces turned
towards the sky and with hands folded in the attitude of
prayer; but they were placed awkwardly on their sides, leaning

PLATE LXXXI.

PILTON CHURCH, NORTH DEVON.
DETAIL OF THE CHICHESTER TOMB.

PLATE LXXXII.

SCREEN AT TILNEY ALL SAINTS, NORFOLK (1618).

on their elbows, sometimes lodged in precarious positions on
a kind of shelf, sometimes with cheek resting on the hand, as
though, in the words of Bosola in the *Duchess of Malfi*, "they
had died of the toothache." All dignity and romance were
eliminated from the work, and the Jacobean squire appeared
in death what he frequently was in life—a very commonplace
creature.

There were
many screens
erected during
the early years of
the seventeenth
century. The
finest specimens
are at St. John's
Church, Leeds,
and at Croscombe
in Somerset, near
Wells, in both of
which churches
most of the wood-
work is of this
period, including
the excellent oak
seats. The
general effect of
the richly orna-
mented wood-
work at Cros-
combe, including
the pews, the pul-
pit, and the lofty
screen, is unusu-

206.—PULPIT, WORTH CHURCH, SUSSEX (1577).

ally striking. But in many churches in different parts of
the country screens may be found of more or less importance. A good example is illustrated from Tilney All Saints,
in Norfolk, near King's Lynn (Plate LXXXII.), which bears
the date 1618 in a little panel over the central arch. The
design, it will be seen, is somewhat unconstructional, for
the main posts of the lower part are not carried up to
support the crowning cornice, but terminate in obelisks,

leaving the cornice to be carried by turned balusters; the effect being to render the upper part rather insecure in appearance. There is a screen at Stonegrave, in Yorkshire, of simple but rather unusual design, in which the detail is very carefully managed. Although it is dated 1637, its general character places it in the category of Jacobean work.

207.—PULPIT, BLYTHBOROUGH CHURCH, SUFFOLK.

Of pulpits there were a large number erected in Elizabeth's time, and still more in King James's, for in the canons of 1603 a pulpit was ordered to be placed in every church not previously provided with one. Many of these have disappeared, through decay or the fury of Gothic restoration, but there are still plenty left, of which several types are illustrated. There is the elaborate one at Worth Church, in Sussex, dated 1577, built up with columns at the angles. The faces are occupied by niches containing figures of the Evangelists (Fig. 206), and the frieze above bears an inscription in the Dutch language. On the panels between the pilasters of the lower stage is some of the applied carving, previously referred to in treating of panelling.

There is a simpler form from Blythborough, in Suffolk (Fig. 207), which consists of panelling framed together, all the framework and the panels themselves being covered with

PLATE LXXXIII.

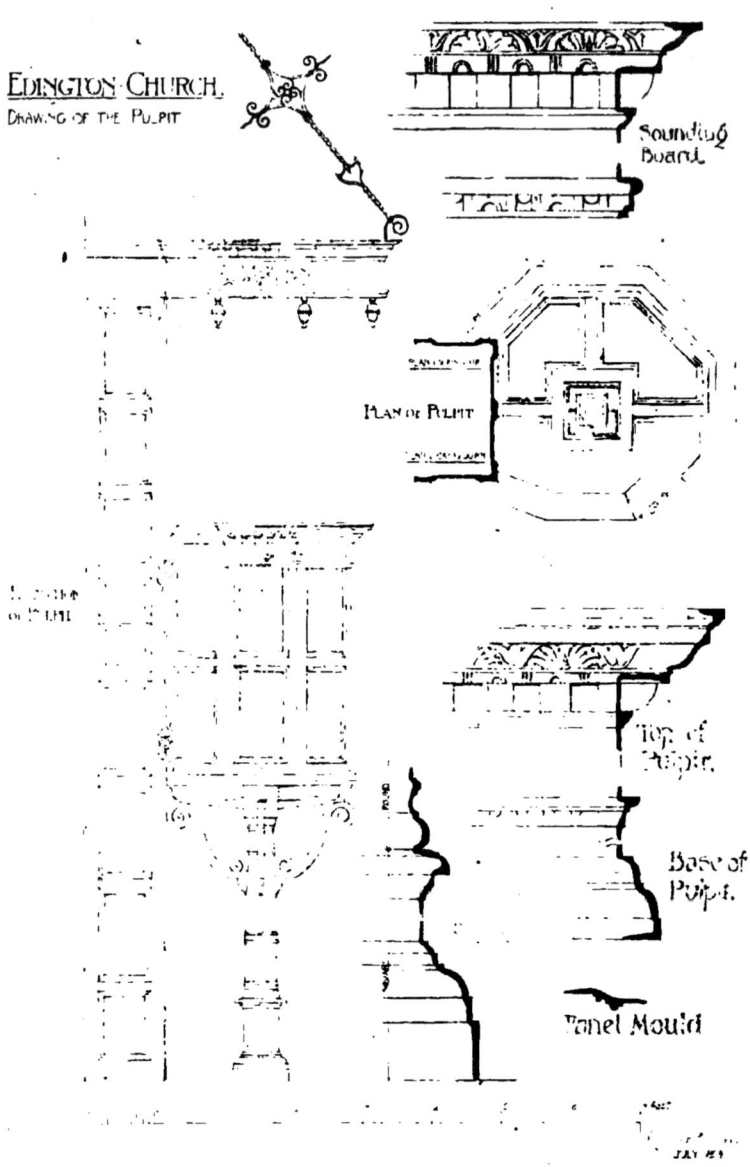

EDINGTON CHURCH.
DRAWING OF THE PULPIT

Sounding Board

PLAN OF PULPIT

Top of Pulpit.

Base of Pulpit.

Panel Mould

PULPIT, EDINGTON CHURCH, WILTSHIRE.

carving in low relief. The widely-projecting bookboard is also ornamented on the underside, and is supported by large carved brackets. The pulpit stands on four short posts let into a wood sill and supported by brackets. Another type is to be seen in Edington Church, Wiltshire (Plate LXXXIII.), of simple and elegant design. The octagonal body of the pulpit consists of plain moulded panelling without ornament ; the bookboard forms a cornice, which is slightly en-riched with dentils and carving. The whole stands on a single turned stout post, from the upper part of which spring brackets of simple form.   There is a panelled sounding-board with a carved frieze and an acorn drop at each angle. The whole work ex-hibits unusual re-straints and refine-ment both of design and detail. Of some-what similar type, but rather more florid in detail, and pro-bably later in date, is the pulpit at Ches-terfield Church (Fig. 208).

208.—PULPIT, CHESTERFIELD CHURCH, DERBYSHIRE.

Font-covers of the seventeenth century are also fairly numerous, and a few of them still retain the elaborate bracket from which they were suspended in order to be raised or lowered with little trouble. There is a good specimen of such a bracket at Pilton Church, in North Devon (Fig. 209), of which, however, the upper part, above the tilted hood, is of later date and coarser design : and there is a still finer example at Astbury Church, near Congleton, in Cheshire.

Of the very few churches which were built during the century that succeeded the Dissolution of the Monasteries, the most important was St. John's Church at Leeds. There is nothing particularly striking in the treatment if we except the beautiful wood fittings. The plan consists of a double nave, divided by an arcade, and the stonework details are plain in character and of no great interest. It might have been expected that window tracery would afford opportunities to the ingenious masons of the time; but either they clung to the old traditions, as did the masons employed by Nicholas Wadham on the chapel of his college at Oxford, where in the years 1610—13, they produced windows of excellent Perpendicular character: or else they tried in a half-hearted kind of way to give to the tracery forms in keeping with those used elsewhere. Such an attempt was made in the church of Kelmarsh, in Northamptonshire (Fig. 210), but it had not much to recommend it, nor were other efforts—in the hall at Wadham and a few other places—of such singular success as to lead further in this direction; and the call for church windows being very limited, no development worth mentioning occurred. The most noteworthy attempt to give a new character to window tracery was made in later years (subsequent

209.—FONT-COVER AND CANOPY, PILTON CHURCH, DEVONSHIRE.

to 1634) at the chapel at Burford Priory, Oxfordshire, where tracery founded on ancient precedents, but following lines of its own, was surrounded by a fully-developed classic archi-trave. Elizabethan and Jacobean detail lingered on in out-of-the-way places long into the seventeenth century, and at Compton Winyates, in Warwickshire, the church, which was rebuilt in 1663, has some quaint little bits of stone detail (Fig. 211), in which the old forms have not yet been replaced by the more strictly classic features which were being more and more generally employed.

210.—Window, Kelmarsh Church, Northamptonshire.

Another instance of the survival of ancient forms is to be seen in the woodwork in the chapel at Peterhouse, Cambridge (Fig. 212), where Jacobean balusters of elegant contour surmount panels treated in the Gothic manner and finished at the top with cusping and foliated spandrils. The date of this door is about 1632.

There are not many speci-mens of ornamental plaster ceilings to be found in churches, but at Axbridge, in Somerset, there is such an instance in the nave, where the ceiling is in the form of a pointed barrel vault, with plaster ribs springing from a cornice adorned with strap-work.

211.—From Compton Winyates Church, Warwickshire.

The ribs form a simple pattern consisting mostly of squares of different sizes, and there are large Jacobean pendants and

bosses at intervals; but out of deference to ecclesiastical tradition, the square panels are ornamented with cusps, which give
to the whole de-
sign a rather feeble
flavour of Gothic;
of its kind, how-
ever, it is an in-
teresting ceiling,
and is one among
many indications
of the attention
bestowed upon
churches during
the early years of
the Reformation.
Another indica-
tion is the fre-
quent presence of
texts upon the
walls. They are
generally sur-
rounded with an
ornamental strap-
work border, such
as roused the ad-
miration of the
narrator of an
entertainment at
Antwerp in
honour of the
Duke of Anjou in
1581, when he
commended the
"compartments of
Phrygian work,
very artificially
handled." These

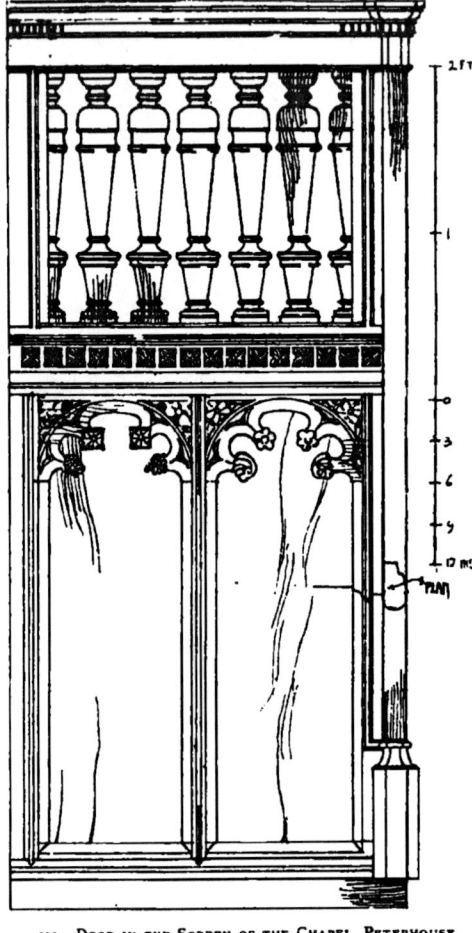

212.—Door in the Screen of the Chapel, Peterhouse,
Cambridge (cir. 1632).

texts seem to have had their origin from a singular circumstance. Queen Elizabeth attended service at St. Paul's on
New Year's Day, 1561, and the Dean, thinking to present her
with an acceptable New Year's gift, caused a number of

beautiful pictures representing the stories of the saints and martyrs to be handsomely bound in a Book of Common Prayer, which he laid upon the Queen's cushion. On opening it, however, she frowned and blushed, and calling the verger to her, caused him to bring the old prayer-book which she had been accustomed to use. At the close of the service she gave the Dean a very uncomfortable quarter of an hour, for having thus gone counter to her proclamation against "images, pictures, and Romish reliques." He excused himself, according to the account, like a lectured schoolboy, and promised that nothing of the kind should occur again. In consequence of this incident there was a general searching of all the churches in and about London, and the clergy and churchwardens "washed out of the walls all paintings that seemed to be Romish and idolatrous," and wrote up "in lieu thereof, suitable texts taken out of the Holy Scriptures."

CHAPTER XI.

SIXTEENTH CENTURY HOUSE-PLANNING AS ILLUSTRATED BY JOHN THORPE'S DRAWINGS.

ONE of the most valuable sources for obtaining knowledge of the house-planning of the reigns of Elizabeth and James I. is the collection of drawings in the Soane Museum, known as John Thorpe's. This collection has given rise to a certain amount of controversy, and will probably give rise to more, for there are so many objections to any theory which can be advanced as to its origin and use. This is not the place to enter upon the arguments for or against any particular view; but as it may be advisable to adopt some kind of working hypothesis, that which best fits the facts seems to be this—that the drawings were drawn in a large book (with the exception of some few which were stuck in), and that by far the greatest number, if not actually all, were drawn by John Thorpe.* There were two men of this name, father and son, and both may have had a hand in it. But whether this hypothesis be accepted or not, it is certain that all the drawings were made during the closing years of the sixteenth century or the opening years of the seventeenth, and that they represent either surveys of buildings then existing, or designs for new ones, or exercises in ingenuity of planning. Whatever else we may or may not have, we have here the Elizabethan and Jacobean ideas of what houses were or ought to be, what accommodation they should contain, and how it should be disposed. In this respect the collection is particularly valuable, because we get everything at first hand ; we see some designs in course of development, and others as they were finished, and entirely free from the manifold alterations which houses themselves have necessarily undergone in the course of three centuries. We also get in the elevations, or "uprights" as they were then called, the designer's ideas of how the houses were to appear ; but in this respect we do not

* The arguments in support of this view are given in a paper by the author, published in the *Architectural Review* of February, 1899.

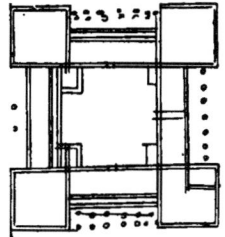

fare so well as with the plans, since the number of elevations is far smaller.

There are, further, a few drawings which may be regarded as studies—studies in perspective, in the five orders, and in the style of foreign architects. For there is no doubt that Thorpe studied books on architecture, both Italian, French, and Dutch, of which a considerable number had been published during the latter half of the sixteenth century. His exercise in the five orders is evidently drawn from an Italian publication, which, however, has not yet been identified. He has copied at least three designs from a French source, one of Androuet du Cerceau's books, "Les plus excellents bastiments de France," published in 1576—79. One of these designs is the Château of Anssi-le-Franc, of which he gives the plan on page 75, and part of the elevation on page 76. The plan is copied accurately except in one or two trifling particulars, and so also is the elevation (Figs. 213, 214); but to the latter he has

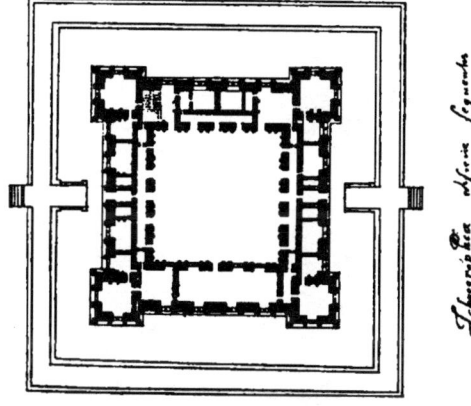

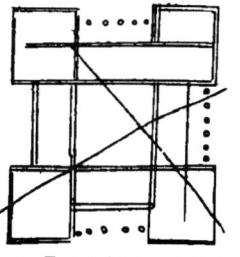

213.—THE CHÂTEAU OF ANSSI-LE-FRANC, COPIED FROM DU CERCEAU (PAGE 75 OF THORPE'S BOOK).

added three sketches of turrets, which do not appear in the original, and which are designed in the Dutch rather than the French style. On each side of the plan he has sketched in pencil the main lines of another plan founded on the original, but which looks as though it were meant to be adapted to English uses. Another plan which he copied from Du Cerceau (on pages 77, 78) is the Château de Madrit in the Bois de Boulogne. This is, with one little exception, line for line like the original, but, curiously enough, here again he has made notes in pencil indicating how he would have adapted it for English habits. The third instance is part of the plan and elevation of the "theatre" at Saint Germain (on pages 165, 166).

214.—The Château of Anssi-le-Franc copied from Du Cerceau, but with three Turrets added (page 76 of Thorpe's Book).

Thorpe was also a student of Dutch publications. On page 24 he has a design entitled "½ a front or a garden syde for a noble man" (Fig. 215), of which the central portion is copied from Plate 20 of Jan Vredeman de Vries's "Architectura, ou Bastiment prins de Vitruve," published at Antwerp in 1577. He

has departed from the original in one or two small particulars;
for instance, he has four-light windows where Vries has two-
light; he has mullions to his dormers where Vries has none;
he has added the final flourishes and pinnacle on the top of the
centre gable which Vries leaves plain, and his treatment of the
windows over the middle arch is different from Vries's; but with

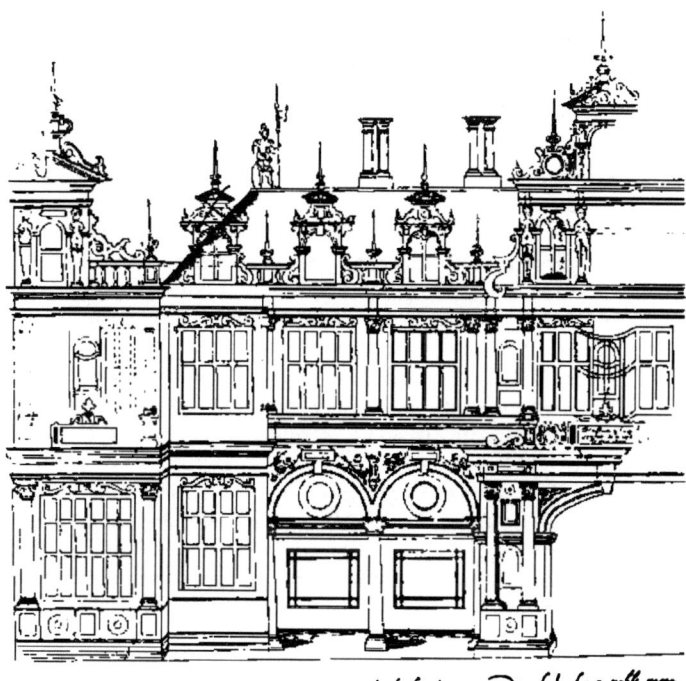

215.—ELEVATION COPIED FROM DE VRIES. THE CENTRAL PORTION IS COPIED; ALL TO
THE LEFT OF THE ARCADE IS ADDED BY THORPE (PAGE 24).

these exceptions the original is followed faithfully as far as to
the end of the arcade, to the left of which the design is Thorpe's
own. Thorpe has written on the panel over the entrance
"Structum ad impensum Dni Sara A° Dni 1600." This is the
only drawing of his which has been traced to Dutch sources,
but nearly all his elevations, of which a few are illustrated in
this chapter, show some hankering after Dutch forms in the
gables. On page 60 of his book he has a few sketches, chiefly

of strap-work gables, which look as though they had been either copied from a Dutch book or inspired by one.

This study of foreign books by one of the designers of the period is a noteworthy fact, and it is equally worthy of note that the study of them seems to have set him thinking, and to have suggested ideas to him, which he jotted down in pencil near the copies which he made from the foreign books. These are not the only instances of this habit, for in other parts of his book are to be seen, by the side of carefully finished plans, hasty sketches of some variation of the same main ideas. Of the foreign books which he studied, some, therefore, were Italian, some were French, and others Dutch: and it is curious to see how the French books seem to have influenced his plans, and the Dutch books his elevations. The French influence on those plans which, so far as we know, were actually carried out, was not strong; but among the plans which may be classed as exercises, are some with towers at the corners, after the manner of those at Chambord, Chenonceau, and Azay-le-Rideau, and a number with square turrets such as those of the Château de Madrit. He may also have derived from the same sources his extreme love of symmetry, and his adoption of the grand manner apparent in some of his designs planned round a court-yard. These French books may, therefore, have influenced his style, but they did not dominate him so much as to cause him to copy the French type of plan in designing an English house. The same may be said of the Dutch influence on his elevations. Only in the one instance already mentioned did he embody a whole piece of Dutch design into one of his own. But in his chimneys, his strap-work gables, and his turrets or lanterns he drew from Dutch sources. And there are two points to notice in this connection—one is that the strap-work gable occurs much oftener in his drawings than in houses actually built; the other is that had these gables been adopted as freely as the eleva-tions would indicate, the houses would have been more Dutch than the Dutchmen's own buildings, for in the latter the stepped gable is far more frequent than strap-work, and produces an entirely different effect.

Let us, however, turn from these speculations to the drawings which compose the great bulk of the book—namely, the plans and (in some cases) elevations which show what kind of building an English house was intended to be, and which ought to be

PLATE LXXXIV.

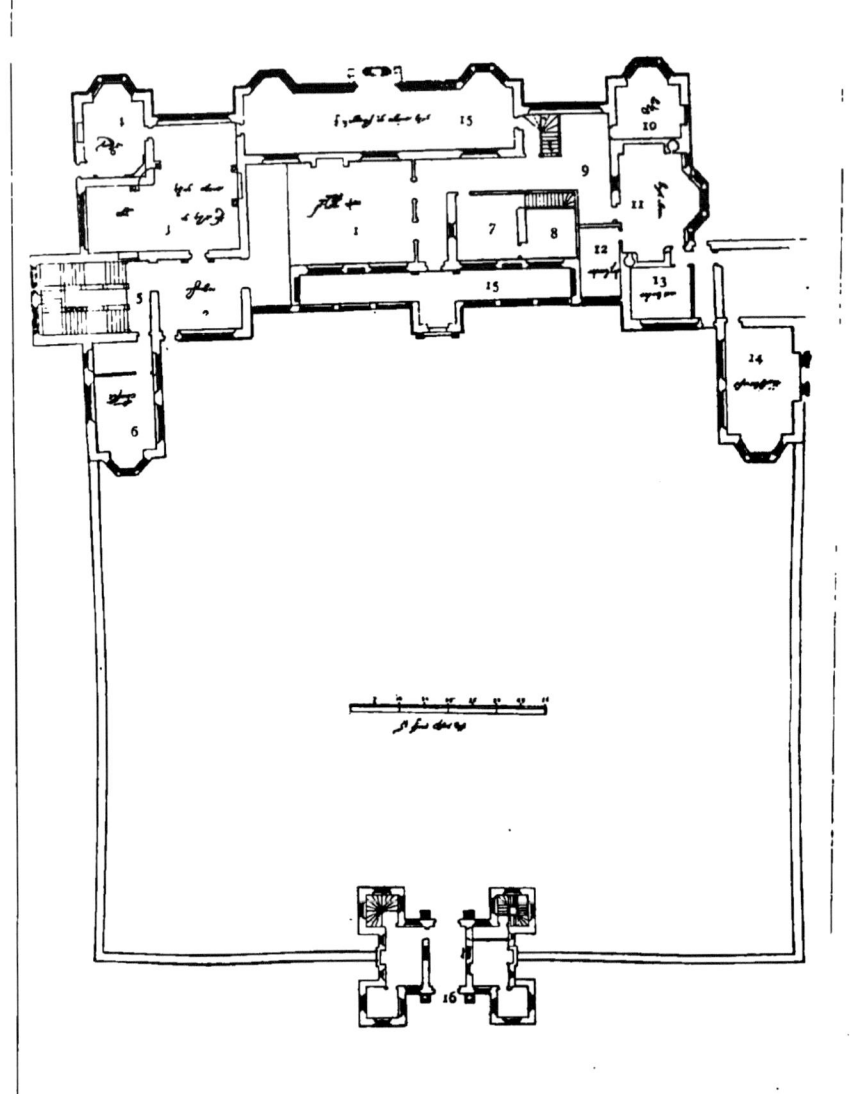

" SIR JARVIS CLIFTON'S HOUSE.
(PAGES 65, 66.)

1. Hall.	5. Grand Staircase.	9. Back Stairs.	13. Wet Larder.
2. Vestibule.	6. Chapel.	10. Lodging.	14. Bakehouse.
3. Parlour.	7. Buttery.	11. Kitchen.	15. Open Arcade.
4. Lodging.	8. Butler's Room.	12. Dry Larder.	16. Gatehouse.

compared with the examples already given in Chapter III. The type of plan made familiar in those examples is the type on which nine-tenths of Thorpe's plans are based. The hall is the centre of household life, the parlour and family rooms are at one end of it, the kitchen and servants' rooms are at the other. But he has a certain number of plans in which the hall shows more or less signs of becoming an entrance rather than a living-room ; the following examples show how the old type gradually changed into the new.

The first plan of the series (Plate LXXXIV.) is named " Sir Jarvis Clifton's House." It shows a large symmetrical house with a forecourt entered through an imposing gate-house fur-nished with a turret at each corner. Directly opposite to this lodge is the porch of the house, which gives access in the usual way to the screens, and thence into the hall, with its daïs shown at the upper end. The bay window at the end of the daïs leads into a large vestibule from which the great staircase and the parlour are approached ; beyond the parlour, at the corner of the building, is an isolated room marked " lodging " (i.e., bed-room). The left-hand wing is occupied by the chapel, which is approached through a vestibule leading out from the foot of the great staircase. This completes the accommodation for the family so far as the ground floor is concerned. On the other side of the hall are the servants' rooms : first, two for the butler with a staircase to the cellar ; then a large vestibule (with a servants' staircase), which leads to another " lodging " ; to the kitchen, with a fine bay window and two fireplaces, one large and one small, each having a little oven close to it ; and to the dry larder : beyond the kitchen is the wet larder, and beyond this is the rest of the servants' department, of which the bake-house occupies a wing balancing the chapel wing. The mouths of the two ovens of the bakehouse are shown, but the paper was too small to allow their full extent to be indicated. There is no upper plan, but from notes on this one it seems that the long gallery was over the arcade at the back of the hall, and that the great chamber was over the parlour and its vestibule. There is an arcade on either side of the front porch, and another between the wings on the opposite side of the house. It is worthy of note that although the front and back façades are of different lengths, each of them is symmetrical in itself. This variation is the result of considerable ingenuity in planning.

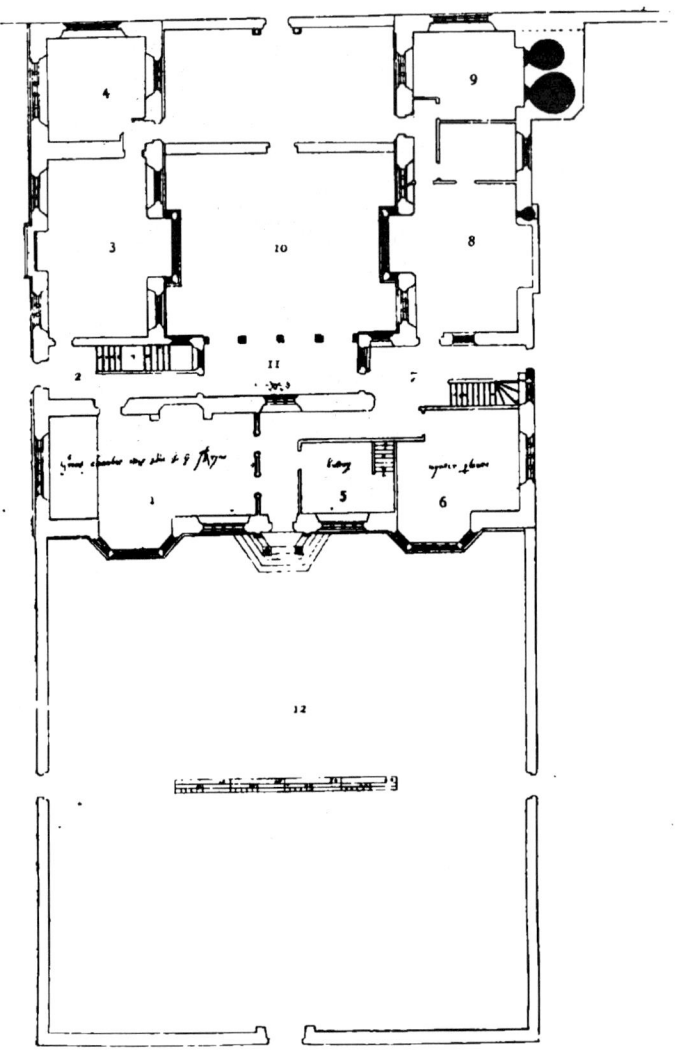

216—An Un-named Plan (pages 117, 118).

1. Hall.	5. Buttery.	9. Pastry.
2. Principal Stairs.	6. Winter Parlour.	10. Inner Court.
3. Parlour.	7. Back Stairs.	11. Open Arcade.
4. Lodging.	8. Kitchen.	12. Outer Court.

The whole plan is worth attention as a specimen of the usual type treated in a broad and dignified manner.

The Cliftons had been seated at Clifton, near Nottingham, for some time prior to the reign of James I.; the family still resides there, but there is nothing in the existing house to connect it with this plan of Thorpe's. Sir Gervase Clifton lived from 1586 to 1666, and was created a baronet in the year 1612. This plan must therefore have been drawn subsequent to that year, as it is entitled " Sir Jarvis Clifton's." There is nothing to show whether it is an original design or a survey of an existing house : the clean way in which it is drawn points to the latter assumption ; but if it is an original design it is interesting as showing at what a late date the old type of plan was still employed.

The next plan (Fig. 216) has no title. It shows a house with a courtyard in front and two long wings at the back, forming a nearly square block. The arrangement follows the established lines : a porch leads into the screens and thence into the hall, which again has the daïs indicated. Owing to the exigencies of the external treatment, the bay window is not placed at the end of the daïs. A door between the latter and the fireplace leads into a vestibule with the chief staircase in it ; beyond is the parlour, with a bay window looking into a small courtyard, and beyond the parlour is another room. On the servants' side is the buttery with its stairs, and then the winter parlour, of which the bay window balances that of the hall. A vestibule containing the back staircase separates these rooms from the kitchen, which has a bay window looking straight across at the bay of the parlour ; beyond the kitchen are two rooms, the first of which is probably a larder, while the other is certainly, on account of the ovens, either the bakehouse or " the pastry." There is an arcade at the back of the front wing, occupying one side of the inner court. The fourth side of this court is enclosed by a wall, but the draughtsman has indicated it in two separate positions, thus making it appear as though there were a solid wing on this side. In this plan, also, the only indication of the upper floor is given in the note written on the hall, " Great chamber over this to yᵉ Skryne " (screen).

The plan shown in Plate LXXXV. has no title, but it has the advantage of having every room named ; and its elevation is also drawn, which was not the case in either of the two

Q 2

preceding examples. The plan follows the familiar lines; it
has a long narrow body, and at each end a long narrow wing at
right angles to it, with a staircase turret at the internal angles.
The porch and screens are in the usual relation to the hall,
beyond which are the parlour and two "lodgings," each of
which has a small inner room attached. The first of these
lodgings is a thoroughfare room, but there is an external door
in the passage connecting the two, which enables the hall to be
gained by crossing the court, thus affording an alternative route
of a kind. On the servants' side of the house are the buttery,
the pantry, the winter parlour, the larder, kitchen, bolting-
house, and pastry. The kitchen has the usual small oven; the
pastry has the invariable two, one somewhat larger than the
other. The two wings are treated symmetrically on the
principal sides (towards the court), one incidental result being
that the pastry gets vastly more light than the kitchen. It has
already been suggested that the winter parlour was placed on
the servants' side in order to be near the kitchen. The bolting-
house was the room where the meal was bolted, that is, sifted.
The "pastry" was, as its name implies, the room in which were
made pies, "cates," confectionery, and the "pretty little tiny
kickshaws" which Justice Shallow ordered when he was furnishing his table for the entertainment of Sir John Falstaff.
The housewives of the time were accomplished in the making
of such dainties. The narrator of the *Progress of James I.* in
1603 remarks upon the delicate fare provided by Sir Anthony
Mildmay at Apethorpe, rendered "more delicate by the art
that made it seem beauteous to the eye; the Lady of the house
being one of the most excellent Confectioners in England, though
I confess many honourable women very expert." When Queen
Elizabeth was entertained at Elvetham by the Earl of Hertford
in 1591, a banquet was served in the evening "into the lower
gallery in the garden," when a thousand dishes were served by
two hundred gentlemen, with the light of a hundred torches,
and among the more notable dishes were some *tours de force* in
sugar-work, representing the royal arms, the arms of all the
nobility, figures of men and women, castles and forts, all kinds
of animals, all kinds of birds, reptiles and "all kind of worms,"
mermaids, whales, and "all sorts of fishes": all these, we are
told, were standing dishes of sugar-work. It is not suggested
that the lady of the house herself produced these masterpieces;

PLATE LXXXV.

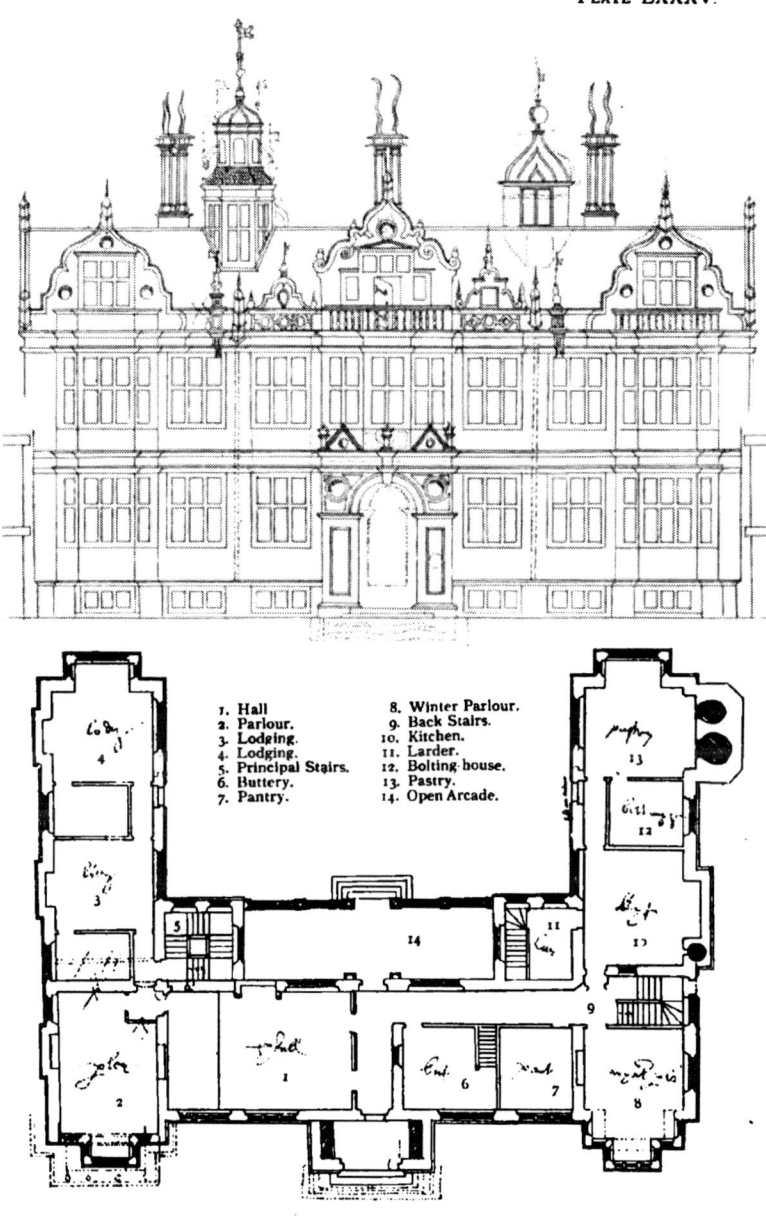

1. Hall
2. Parlour.
3. Lodging.
4. Lodging.
5. Principal Stairs.
6. Buttery.
7. Pantry.
8. Winter Parlour.
9. Back Stairs.
10. Kitchen.
11. Larder.
12. Bolting-house.
13. Pastry.
14. Open Arcade.

UNNAMED PLAN AND ELEVATION.
(PAGES 89, 90.)

PLATE LXXXVI.

"SIR Wᴍ. HASERIDGE."

(PAGES 147, 148.)

1. Hall.	6. Inner Room.	11. Survaying Place.
2. Parlour.	7. Buttery.	12. Kitchen.
3. Principal Stairs.	8. Lodging.	13 Dry Larder (Wet under).
4. Vestibule.	9. Winter Parlour.	14. Pastry.
5. Lodging.	10. Back Stairs.	15. Courtyard.

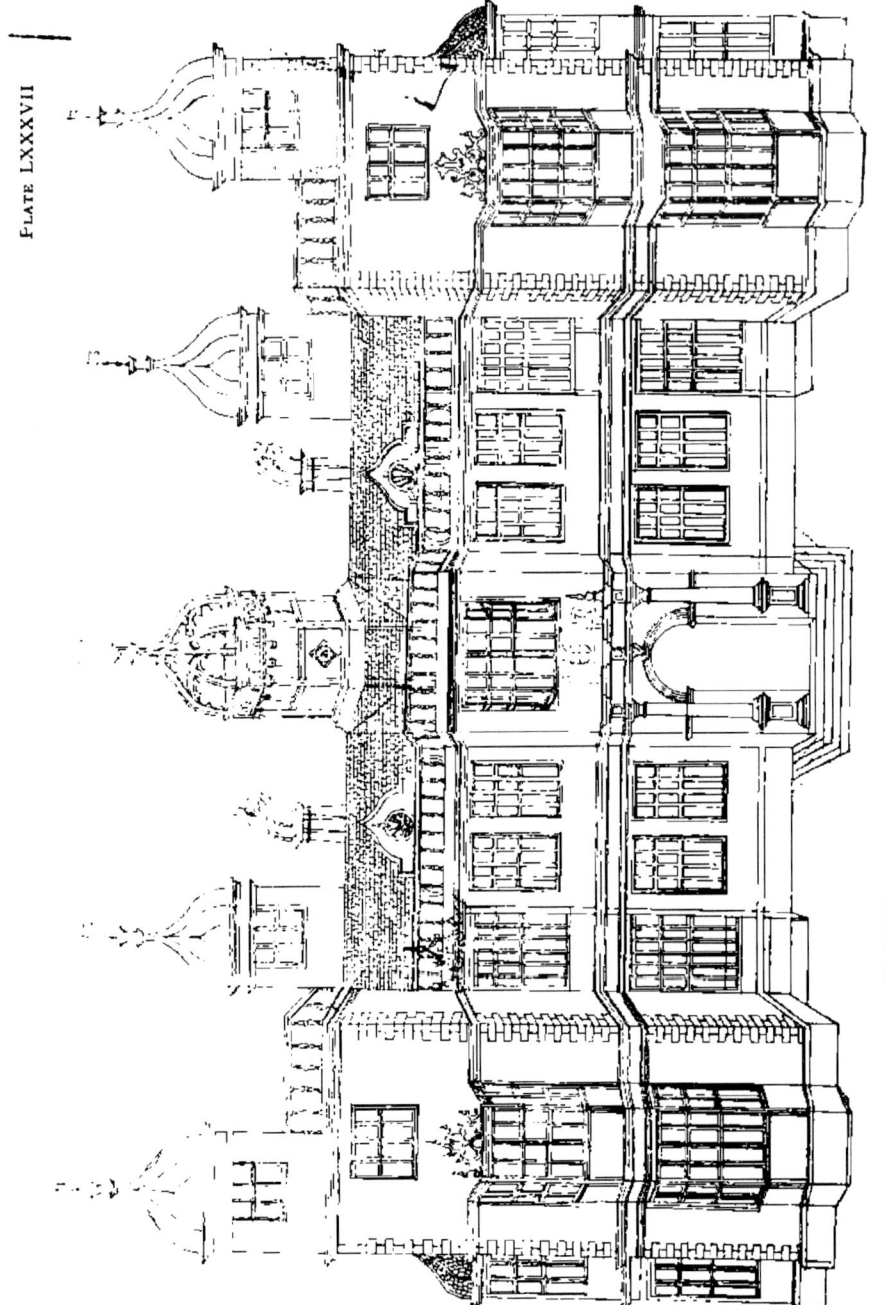

PLATE LXXXVII

ELEVATION OF PLAN ENTITLED "SIR WM. HASERIDGE."

(PLATE 117, 118)

but ladies were certainly skilful in the making of cakes, and it was a recommendation in actual life, as well as in one of the plays of the time, that the heroine could " do well in the pastry."

The elevation is treated, on the whole, in a quiet and dignified manner, but the handling of it from the parapets upwards shows a determination to obtain that picturesqueness of outline which was considered essential. The means to this end are curved gables, quaint pinnacles, and rather elaborate lanterns, of which there are two alternative designs provided, as there are also of the small gables or dormers on the parapet. The type of chimney shown is one of the more reasonable which were employed.

The plan on Plate LXXXVI. shows a slight variation of the usual type, inasmuch as the wings, instead of being narrow and only one room thick, are two rooms thick. In other respects it follows the familiar lines. On one side is the hall with its daïs and bay window ; then the grand staircase and a vestibule giving access to the parlour and a group of two lodgings, the remainder of the wing being occupied by a room which—if the ovens are anything but a repetition of those in the corresponding wing— must be the bakehouse. On the other side of the house are the buttery, a lodging, the winter parlour, the back stairs and vestibule, the kitchen, dry larder, and pastry ; the wet larder, according to a note, is under the dry. There is no arcade here. This plan is entitled " Sir Wm. Haseridge," and the upright (as the elevation was called) has on it the initials D. H. and the date 1606 (Plate LXXXVII.). This is important, as it shows that at that time the old relation of the hall to the rest of the house was still retained. This house, in spite of its title, has not been identified with any existing building. A family of the name of Haselrigge has lived at Noseley, in Leicestershire, since early in the seventeenth century, but the existing house has nothing in common with this plan. The elevation is treated in a simple manner, with very few foreign flourishes.

In the next example (Figs. 217, 218, 219) we have ground plan, upper plan, and elevation : a valuable example, inasmuch as it is one of the few cases in which all three drawings are given ; the upper plan is interesting, as it shows the position of the two chief rooms, the gallery and great chamber. The disposition of the ground floor conforms to the usual type, but is varied so as to enclose a small central court, somewhat after the fashion of Barlborough (Fig. 49) ; but here all the principal rooms are on one floor, whereas at Barlborough the kitchens are in the basement. The accommodation here comprises the hall, grand staircase, and parlour on the one side, and buttery, winter parlour, back stairs, and kitchen on the other. There is a vestibule to the kitchen, which probably would have been

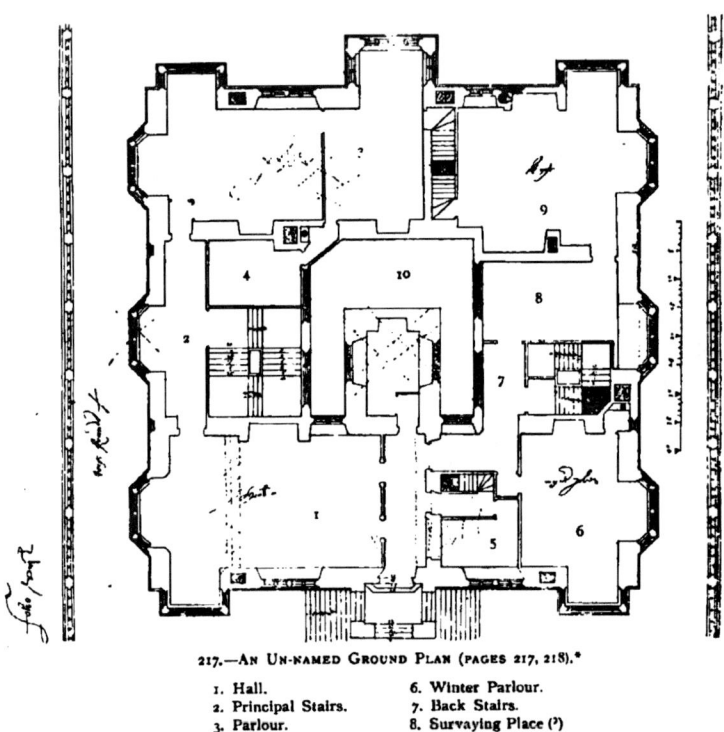

217.—An Un-named Ground Plan (pages 217, 218).*

1. Hall.	6. Winter Parlour.
2. Principal Stairs.	7. Back Stairs.
3. Parlour.	8. Surveying Place (?)
4. Inner Room.	9. Kitchen.
5. Buttery.	10. Inner Court.

called the "survaying place" had it been named, similar rooms being so designated in Figs. 224, 226. The use of the survaying place is not anywhere explained, but most likely it was a serving room, where the dishes were overlooked before being taken to the hall or the winter parlour. There is a staircase from the kitchen which presumably led down to the larders, pantries,

* In order to bring this plan within the limits of the page, the terrace walls on either side have been brought nearer to the house than they are on the origina drawing.

and other subsidiary rooms. The manner in which the middle
bay window on the kitchen side serves to light the vestibule
and the back stairs (through a borrowed light) should be noticed
as an instance of the subordination of the plan to the uniformity
of the exterior. Here, for the first time, occurs an example of
the use of sanitary conveniences: it will be seen that neither
downstairs nor up are they placed in a manner that would be

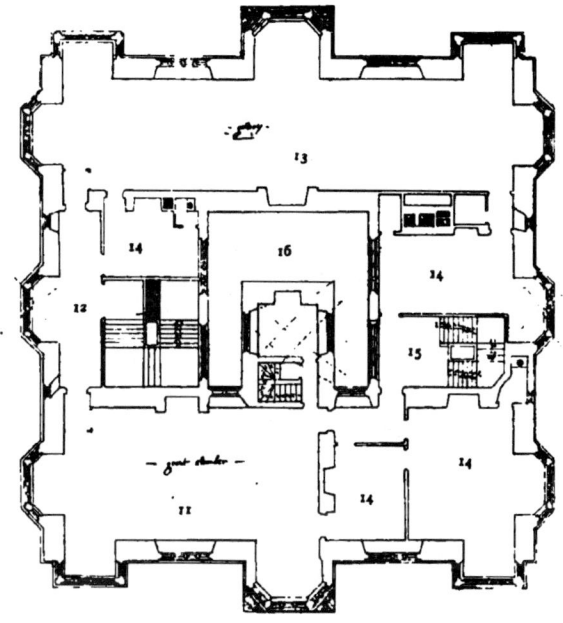

218.—UPPER PLAN OF FIG. 217 (PAGES 217, 218).

11. Great Chamber.   14, 14. Bedrooms.
12. Principal Stairs.   15. Back Stairs.
13. Gallery.   16. Inner Court.

tolerated at the present day. Nor indeed were they arranged
at this period with anything like the same attention to isolation
and means of ventilation which was bestowed upon such places
in mediæval times. The central court is shown with a room
and staircase projecting into it, but this excrescence was very
wisely crossed out, for the court was small enough without it,
and could never have been either cheerful or conducive to health.
The upper plan shows the long gallery, 80 feet long by 20 feet wide,

and the great chamber, 45 feet long by 23 feet wide. To these two rooms nearly the whole space is sacrificed, there being in addition only two fair-sized bedrooms and two smaller apartments, besides those which may have been contrived in the roof. Both the gallery, the great chamber, and the parlour are shown with an inner porch, such as occurs at Sizergh Castle (Fig. 148), and at Broughton Castle, in Oxfordshire (Plate LI.), Bradfield, in Devonshire, and a few other houses. The elevation (Fig. 219) resembles that on Plate LXXXV. It is treated in a simple and unostentatious way, but the most is made of such features as the bay

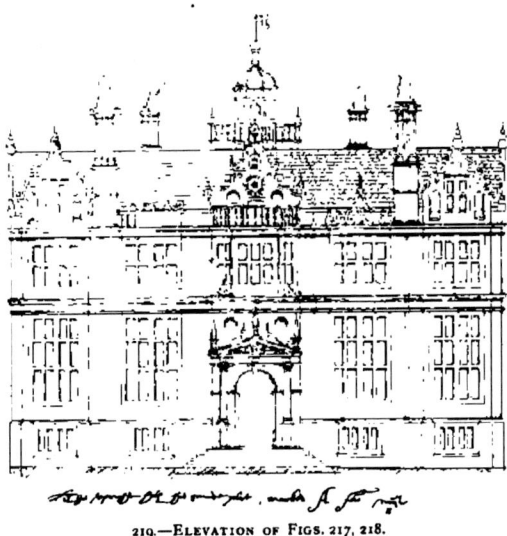

219.—Elevation of Figs. 217, 218.

windows, chimney-stacks, and gables. The latter have the curly outline which is prevalent in the Thorpe collection, but which, as already said, does not appear in the same proportion among such of the actual buildings of the time as have survived. The front chimneys are of the same pattern as those on Plate LXXXV.

The foregoing examples are a few out of a great number which conform to the traditional arrangement of the hall. The vast majority of the plans follow this type, but there are some, which we will now proceed to consider, in which the hall receives a different treatment, thus indicating that important change which resulted in its becoming a place of entrance

instead of what it had been for four centuries—the centre of
household life.

On some of these plans the room which is usually called the
parlour is marked "dy pler" or dining parlour. This shows
that even the eating of meals, one of the functions for which
the hall had always been used, was being transferred from that
apartment to smaller and more comfortable rooms. The heads
of the household, more particularly, sought the quiet of a smaller

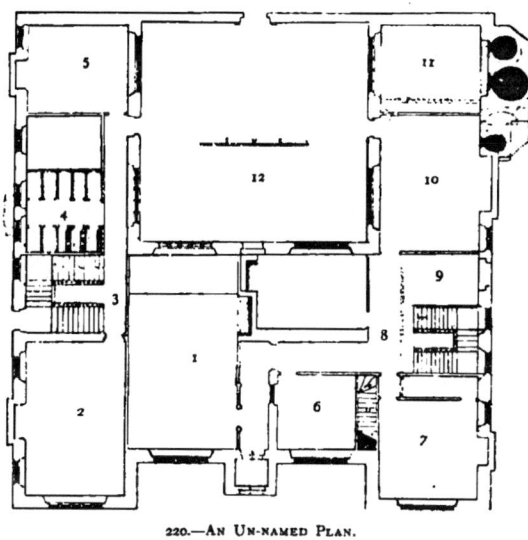

220.—An Un-named Plan.

1. Hall.	7. Winter Parlour.
2. Parlour.	8. Back Stairs.
3. Principal Stairs.	9. Surveying Place.
4. Chapel.	10. Kitchen.
5. Lodging.	11. Pastry.
6. Buttery.	12. Courtyard.

apartment, and with them they took their special friends,
leaving persons of less importance to dine with the household in
the hall. There is a letter from a Mr. Marlivale, of Chevington,
written to Sir Thomas Kytson, of Hengrave, complaining of
having been placed to dine in the hall with the steward instead
of with the superior persons in the parlour. As Sir Thomas
died in 1540, the practice of withdrawing from the great hall
must have begun previous to that date. On one of Thorpe's
plans he has marked a room as the "Servants' dining-room,"

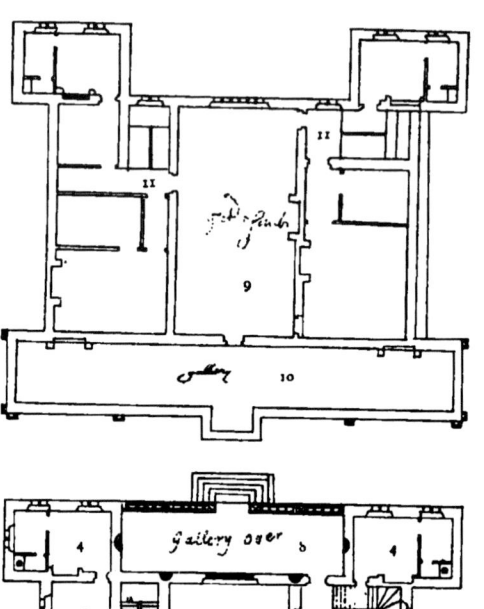

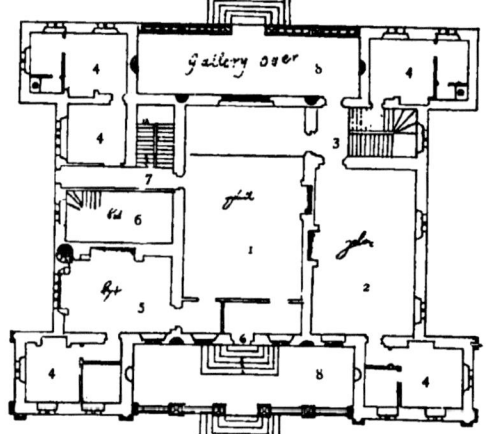

221.—Ground and Upper Plans, un-named (page 85).

1. Hall.	6. Buttery.
2. Parlour.	7. Back.Stairs.
3. Principal Stairs.	8, 8. Open Arcade.
4, 4. Lodging.	9. Great Chamber.
5. Kitchen.	10. Gallery.

11. Stairs.

Other Rooms on Upper Floor are Lodgings.

which indicates a further desertion of the hall, and from the other end. The purposes for which the hall had been used being thus provided for elsewhere, it became no longer necessary to plan it on the old lines. The first change that took place was at the end where the screens were. The screens, indeed, disappeared, and in order to go from the front door to the kitchen department. the hall itself had to be traversed. The following examples show various instances of this change, but in the absence of particulars as to the name and date of most of the plans, it has been impossible to arrange them chronologically : what sequence there is, is a sequence of stages in the development of the new idea of using the hall as an entrance.

The example in Fig. 220 has no name nor any writing upon it beyond the numbers of the stairs. The curious point about it is that the screen is in the side of the hall instead of at the end; otherwise it preserves most of the old arrangements. Although the rooms are not named, they are easy to identify. On the family side are the hall, with its daïs, the parlour, staircase, chapel and "lodgings." On the servants' side are the buttery, winter parlour, back stairs, kitchen and pastry. Owing to the altered arrangement of the screens there is no thoroughfare leading straight from the front door to the court beyond.

In the next example (Figs. 221, 222) we have a further departure from the old type. Screens of a kind there are, but the front door leads only to the hall (through a vestibule), and the hall has to be traversed to gain the kitchen. The buttery is in an entirely novel position, and the tendency

222.—ELEVATION OF PLANS IN FIG. 221 (PAGE 85).

clearly is to preserve the front door for the family, and to relegate the servants to their own entrance. A curious point is that the only way from the kitchen to the buttery, to the upper floor, or to the outside, is through the hall. In spite of these changes the daïs still remains, as though the old custom of dining in the hall survived, notwithstanding the constant traffic which the service of the kitchen must have entailed. The upper plan shows the long gallery—apparently 62 feet long by only 10 feet wide—and the great chamber, 40 feet by 21 feet, which is over the hall. The draughtsman has apparently been led by the symmetry of his arrangements into placing the gallery on the wrong façade in his upper plan. According to a note on the ground plan it should be at the back, and the elevation confirms this disposition. Owing to the situation of the hall it

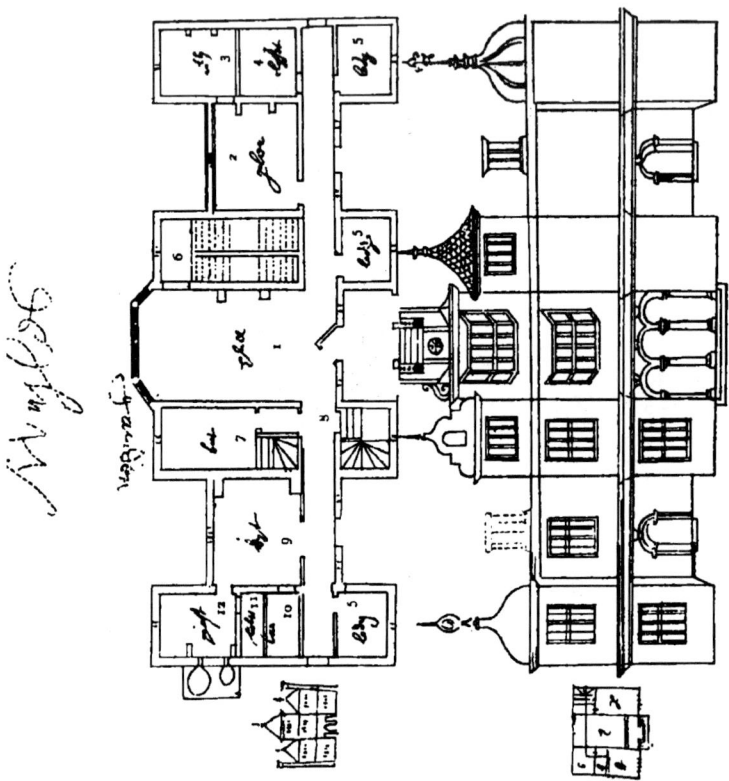

223.—Un-named Plan and Elevation (page 34).

1. Hall.	7. Buttery.
2. Parlour.	8. Back Stairs.
3. Withdrawing Room.	9. Kitchen.
4. Closet.	10. Larder.
5, 5. Lodging.	11. Bolting-house.
6. Principal Stairs.	12. Pastry.

can no longer obtain light from the sides, nor can there be any bay window to the daïs: the only light it receives is from a large window at one end, which must be greatly darkened by the arcade in front of it, carrying the gallery. The great chamber is subject in a less degree to similar disadvantages, receiving

light only from one end. The treatment of the exterior is somewhat after the fashion of Wollaton, but of a plainer kind; there
is a central block
surrounded by
rooms roofed at a
lower level, and at
each corner is a
pavilion. It is quite
possible that this is
merely an exercise
in design, and that
it was never car-
ried out, nor
even thoroughly
digested.

In the next ex-
ample (Fig. 223) the
idea of the entrance
hall is further de-
veloped. The front
door opens into a
passage off which
the hall is ap-
proached, but with-
out a dividing wall.
There is no daïs,
and the parlour is
entered from the
passage instead of
from the upper end
of the hall. The
latter apartment is
still central, and
divides the family
rooms from those of
the servants. There
are fresh designa-
tions bestowed

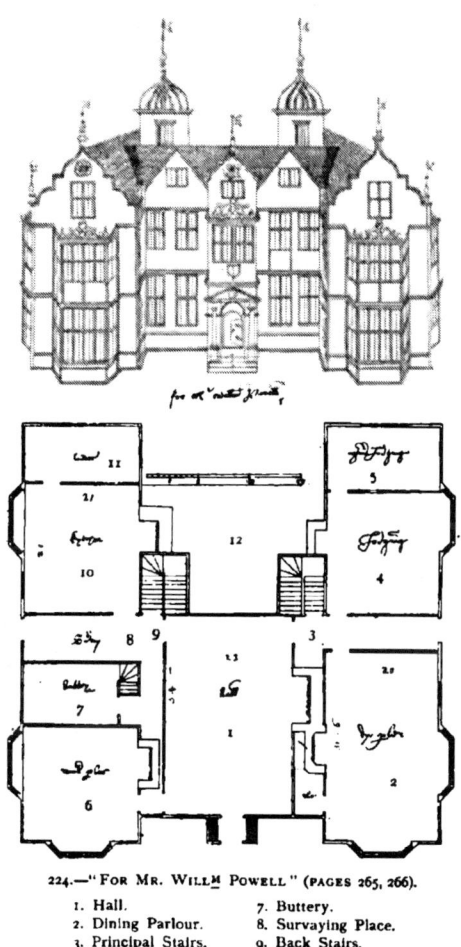

224.—" FOR MR. WILLᴹ POWELL " (PAGES 265, 266).

1. Hall.	7. Buttery.
2. Dining Parlour.	8. Survaying Place.
3. Principal Stairs.	9. Back Stairs.
4. Lodging.	10. Kitchen.
5. Inner Lodging.	11. Larder.
6. Winter Parlour.	12. Court.

upon some of them: the parlour and the lodgings we know, but
in addition to these there is a "closset" and a "wth," or withdrawing room. The buttery is as near to its old position as the

new arrangement allows, and beyond it is the familiar kitchen, with the larder, the pastry, and the bolting-house leading out of the latter. The elevation is again perfectly simple, and calls for no remark beyond pointing out the alternative methods shown of roofing the two central turrets. The sketch plan and elevation should be noticed, jotted down at the side of the main subject, and embodying a smaller version of a somewhat similar idea.

The plan and elevation entitled " for Mr. Willm Powell "

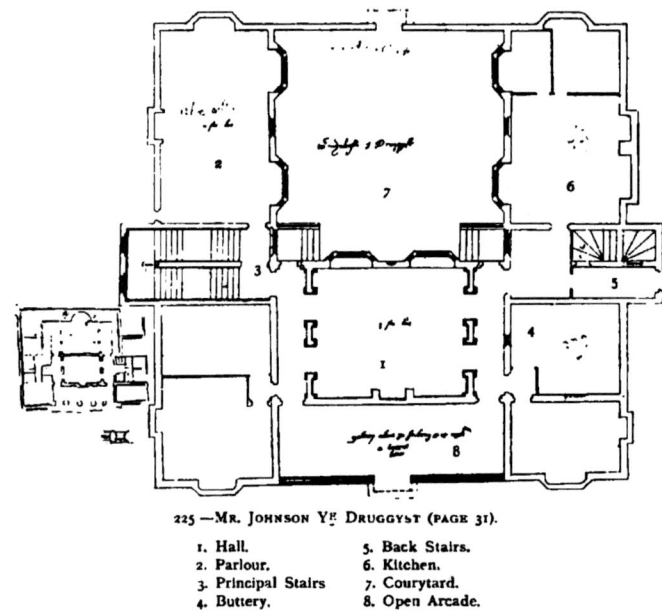

225 —Mr. Johnson Y^e Druggyst (page 31).

1. Hall.	5. Back Stairs.
2. Parlour.	6. Kitchen.
3. Principal Stairs	7. Courytard.
4. Buttery.	8. Open Arcade.

(Fig. 224) have not been identified with any existing building. The elevation is treated more after the English manner, particularly in regard to the gables, than any of the preceding. In the plan the hall is frankly made an entrance hall, without any attempt at making it a living-room. It still occupies a central position, but there are no screens, no daïs, and no bay window. The rooms are all named : the family side includes the dining parlour—now so named for the first time—a " lodging," and an " inner lodging." The opposite wing contains the winter parlour, the buttery, now attached to the servants' entrance, the "survay," or serving place, the kitchen, and larder. The house would seem to be built of wood and plaster, since all the walls are drawn some 6 inches thick, the fireplaces only being of the ordinary thickness.

The plan for "Mr. Johnson yᵉ Druggyst" (Fig. 225) shows a further variation of the hall, which here has a screen and passage at each end. The daïs idea has entirely disappeared, and the bay windows are placed for effect only : the central position is still retained, as also are the two wings, divided into the usual rooms. There are two front doors, one to each passage at the ends of the hall. The buttery occupies the old

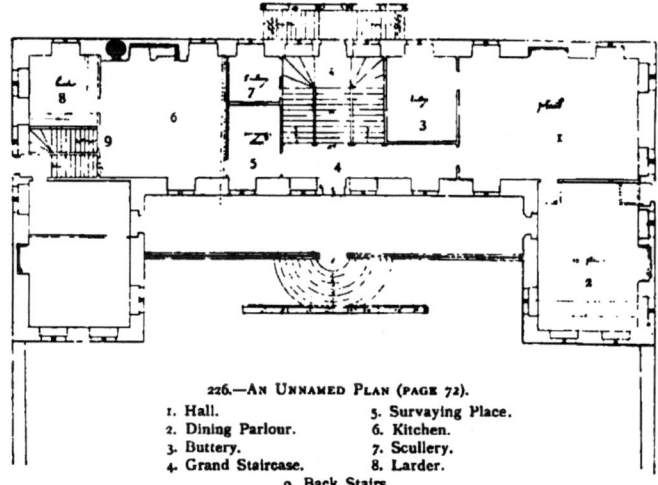

226.—An Unnamed Plan (page 72).

1. Hall.   5. Survaying Place.
2. Dining Parlour.   6. Kitchen.
3. Buttery.   7. Scullery.
4. Grand Staircase.   8. Larder.
              9. Back Stairs.

relation to one of these passages, while the other takes up the space which would formerly have been devoted to the daïs. The relation to each other of the several rooms in the two wings follows the old lines ; it is in the hall that the essential change appears. A note on the plan says that the gallery, 80 feet long and 15 feet wide, occupies the whole length of the front façade, in the centre of which is a turret ; there is also a turret in the middle of each side, over the two staircases. The small sketch at the side of the finished plan should be noticed, as it is another instance of how the draughtsman jotted down a rough variation of the same general disposition of rooms. There is also a sketch for a mullion.

In Fig. 226 is a yet further variation of the treatment of the hall. It is no longer in the centre of the building, but becomes an ordinary thoroughfare room in one corner. The front entrance leads into a corridor, and immediately opposite to it is the great staircase. This is an entirely novel treatment, and indicates a complete revolution in the planning of houses. The hall is no longer the central feature, but gives place to the staircase. For the rest, the old apartments remain; there is the buttery lying between the staircase and the hall, inconveniently mixed up with the family rooms, equally inconveniently cut off from the kitchens. The dining parlour lies beyond the hall and far away from the kitchen, and the kitchen is approached through the "survaying place," and attached to it is a new room, the "scullery." So far as the main lines go, the house is simple and dignified, but the plan is neither so striking nor so convenient as those of the old type.

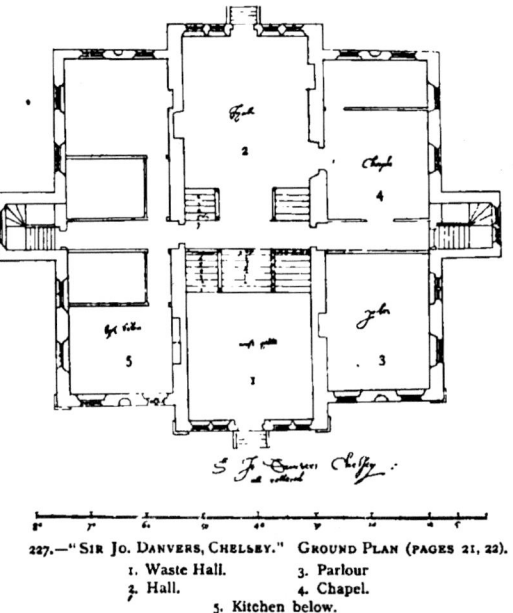

227.—"Sir Jo. Danvers, Chelsey." Ground Plan (pages 21, 22).
1. Waste Hall.   3. Parlour
2. Hall.   4. Chapel.
5. Kitchen below.

The last plan of the series is that of a house for "Sir Jo. Danvers, Chelsey" (Figs. 227, 228), and there are two points to be specially noticed in it—one is that the kitchen and its offices are all underground, the other is that the hall is of the type usual in many Italian houses; it extends right through the house from front to back, and has smaller rooms opening from it on each side. In Italy, the hall and the room over it occupy the whole of this space, and the staircase is among the rooms at the side, but at Sir John Danvers' house the staircase is in the hall itself, thus dividing it into two portions, the outer one of which is named "waste hall," and curtailing the effective space of the chamber over it. The device of placing the kitchen and offices in a basement was not often adopted in English houses; space was generally plentiful, and the native taste was rather in favour of the long and low treatment. But occasionally, where space was limited, or where some special notion controlled the design, as at Lyveden New Building, or where the Italian manner was closely followed, the basement was utilized for the purpose of the kitchens. The sketch-elevation of Sir John Danvers' house points towards a more complete acceptance of classic treatment; it is widely different from the extensive

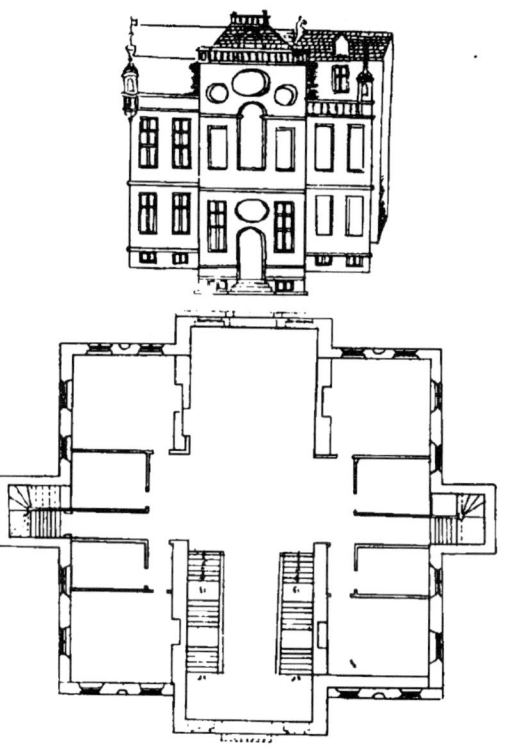

228.—Sir Jo. Danvers, Chelsey. Upper Plan and Elevation (pages 21, 22)

façades and returned wings which are associated with the idea of an Elizabethan or Jacobean house. Sir John built a house (but whether to this particular plan, or not, is not certain) at Chelsea, on the site of one which had been the residence of Sir Thomas More; and he seems to have done so in the early years of the seventeenth century. It is more than likely that he was attracted by the Italian model, since we

R.A.   R

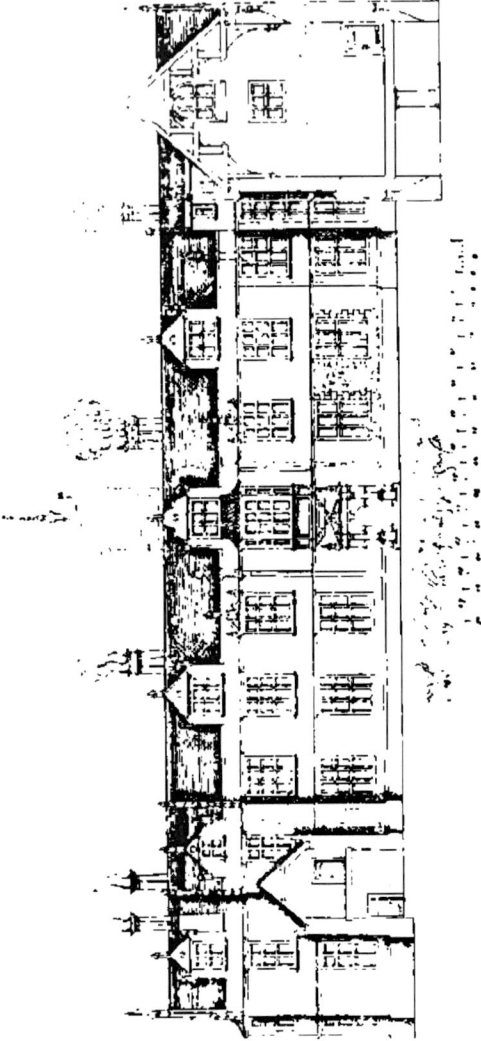

229.—An Un-named Elevation, " ment for one of the sydes of a house about a cort and may be made a front for a house " (page 115).

learn from Aubrey* that " 'twas Sir John Danvers of Chelsey who first taught us the way of Italian gardens. He had well travelled France and Italy, and made good observations. . . . He had a very fine fancy, which lay chiefly for gardens and architecture." There is another rough sketch of an elevation on page 178, accompanied by a plan, where the Italian treatment is still more marked. The centre of the façade consists of two rows of columns, superimposed, and forming an open *loggia* on each floor; they carry a pediment of flat pitch. This sketch is of considerable interest, since it connects Thorpe, who is the representative of Elizabethan and Jacobean design, with the far more Italianized style of his successors.

Two other elevations are illustrated, in addition to those which have accompanied some of the

* John Aubrey's *Natural History of Wiltshire.*

foregoing plans, in order to show the kind of feeling which pervades most of the sketches in Thorpe's book. They are both isolated examples, not attached to any plan, and not named. Indeed, the first of them (Fig. 229) was probably merely a sketch, as it bears the note, "ment for one of the sydes of a house about a cort and may be made a front for a house." It is quite English in character, and is singularly free from the curly gables and fantastic pinnacles which appear on most of Thorpe's elevations, and were derived from Dutch sources. The sections through the wings should be noticed, as this is the only instance in the whole collection in which anything like a complete section is given. The section on the right hand is evidently taken through the hall, and shows its open-timbered roof of hammer-beam type.

The second example (Fig. 230) is nearly as simple in its treatment, but the gables break out into rather extravagant curls. The general treatment, with the large gables, the dormers, and the projecting chimney-stacks, is not unlike that of the west front of Kirby (Figs. 77, 107), but this elevation does not tally with the plan of Kirby, which is not subject to the same accurate symmetry. This drawing bears the note, "The garden syde, lodgings

230.—An Un-named Elevation, "the garden syde, lodgings below and gallery above. J. T." (page 108).

R 2

below and gallery above. J. T.," and as it is initialed by Thorpe, it helps to identify as his many of the other elevations.

One other plan is given (Fig. 231) as an example of Thorpe's ingenuity in planning. .It consists of three rooms arranged within a circular balustrade and surrounded by a circular

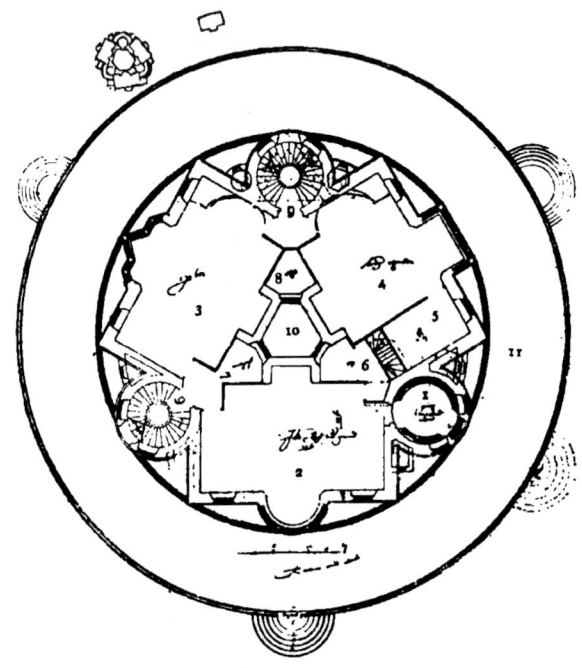

231.—AN UN-NAMED PLAN (PAGES 145, 146).

1. Entrance.	6. Buttery.
2. Hall (Kitchen below).	7. Woodyard.
3. Parlour.	8. Closet.
4. Lodging Chamber.	9. Stairs.
5. Inner Chamber.	10. Open Space.

11. Terrace.

terrace. The angles formed where the three rooms join are occupied by three towers, one of which contains the porch, the other two the staircases. On the ground floor one of the rooms is the hall, one the parlour, one a bedchamber. The kitchen was to be under the hall. It should be observed how the large fireplaces are arranged so as to occupy some of the triangular space enclosed by the three rooms ; and how the odd corners left are devoted to the buttery, a closet, and a wood store. The bay window is different in each room, and is so planned as just to extend outwards as far as the surrounding balustrade. Having thus examined the main features of the design, observe how a number of alternative sketches have been made for filling in with cupboards the angles made by the circular walls of the turrets and the walls of the rooms : observe also that on one of the circular staircases an equilateral triangle has been drawn, evidently as an alternative way of treating the turrets, and observe further how in the parlour and bedchamber a suggestion is made to have a semicircular recess at one end, such as was not infrequent late in the seventeenth century, but which never occurs in an Elizabethan plan. All these points are interesting, because they show how the draughtsman elaborated his design ; and when he had finished this, he sketched a variation of the same idea at the side, in the upper part of the sheet. He was also undecided about the position of his steps on to the terrace, for he drew them first in three sets, opposite to the three bay windows ; afterwards he sketched another set in pencil (shown by dotted lines on the drawing) in a more convenient situation just opposite the porch, and wrote on the old set "Stayres heare," and on the new "or heare." On his main staircases, too, after drawing the steps, he has crossed out three or four and written "half-pace," which means "half-landing."

It will not be uninteresting to add to these illustrations of Thorpe's plans a list of the names of apartments, &c., to be found in his book appended to one or other of the drawings.

Hall.
Parlour.
Dining parlour.
Dining chamber above hall.
The dining chamber.
Winter parlour.
An ordinary winter parlour.
The great parlour with the great chamber over it.
Great chamber.
Gallery.
The long gallery.
Withdrawing chamber.

Lodging.
A nobleman's lodging, *comprising*
    His ante-camera.
    Bedchamber.
    Wood, coal, and privy.
    Servants' lodging.
Officers' lodgings.
A bed chamber.
An inner chamber.
Chaplin.
His study.
Study.

Chapel.
Outward chapel.
Library above.
Buttery.
Butler's lodging.
Pantry.
Pantler's lodging.
Breakfast room.
Kitchen.
The great kitchen.
A privy kitchen.
Dry larder.
Wet larder.
Pastry.
Work room for the pastlers.
Bakehouse.
Privy bakehouse.
Meal house.
Bolting house.
Survaying place.
Scullery.
Spicery.
Trencher.
Pewter.
Milk house.
Brew house.
The boiling house.
Porter's lodging.
Hynds' hall.
Lesser hall for hynds.
Servants' dining-room.
Waiters' chamber.

Waiters' bedchamber.
Steward's lodging.
His clerk.
Brush.
Wood, coal, and stool.
Cellar.
Wine cellar.
A wine cellar and for beer.
Privy wine cellar.
The Queen's wine cellar.
My lord's wine cellar.
A cellar for beer.
Entry.
An entry through all.
Lobby.
Ante-camera.
Closet.
A well light.
A little court for light, &c.
Common vault.
Court.
A tennis court.
A large terrace.
Terrace.
A back walk.
Garden.
Orchard.
Woodyard.
Kitchen garden.
Washyard.
Stable.

CHAPTER XII.

ARCHITECTURAL DESIGNERS OF THE SIXTEENTH CENTURY.

In the foregoing pages examples have been given of the architectural work of the sixteenth century—examples taken from all parts of England, and illustrating all kinds of features. From these it will have been gathered that the same general character pervaded the whole country at any one time, but that there was a great variety of treatment. This variety arose not merely from a difference in arrangement of universally accepted features, or from different methods of handling the same kind of ornament, but from actual differences between the features themselves and between the kinds of ornament, and it points to the employment of men who varied to a considerable degree in the amount of their training as well as in its direction.

It will therefore not be without interest to glance briefly at what is known of the more prominent men who were employed in producing the architecture that has been under consideration, and at the methods which prevailed of supplying designs.

Unfortunately, little detailed information has yet been obtained, or is obtainable, concerning these men, and what we do know about them is neither so full nor so clear as to have emerged entirely from the perplexing mists of controversy and to have attained the serene heights of incontrovertible fact. We know, for instance, that Henry VIII. employed many skilled foreign workmen, especially Italians. But very little work exists at this day which can be pointed out as theirs. We also know that early in the second half of the sixteenth century many Dutch artizans found refuge in England from the rigorous measures of Alva, that licences were given to various towns to receive them, and that a number of other towns petitioned to have strangers allotted to them: most of these towns were situated in the counties bordering on the sea in the East and

South. But masons, joiners, and artificers in the other trades connected with building, do not seem to have been a large proportion of those immigrating.

The most interesting piece of foreign work, inasmuch as it was the first done by Italians in England, can, luckily, be identified in all important particulars, because the contract for it still exists. It was Henry VII.'s tomb, designed, and largely executed, by Torrigiano.* But beyond this tomb, and probably that of Margaret, the mother of Henry VII., and possibly that of Dr. Young in the Rolls Chapel, no English work of Torrigiano's is known. After him came Benedetto da Rovezzano, who partly executed an even more splendid tomb for Cardinal Wolsey, which was to have been placed in the specially erected chapel in St. George's Chapel, Windsor, but which Henry VIII. took to himself on the Cardinal's fall. Wolsey petitioned the King for his own figure —which was to have lain upon the tomb, and could hardly be expected to answer the same purpose for its new owner—and for such other parts as it might please the King to give him. But Henry retained the materials and proceeded to adapt them for his own monument, whereon he and his queen, Jane Seymour, were to have reposed. His queen, however, was soon replaced, and the tomb was still unfinished at his death, and was never carried to completion. Its metal parts were finally melted down by the Parliament Commissioners a hundred years later, but the marble sarcophagus lingered on, and was eventually removed to St. Paul's Cathedral in London, and utilized in the monument of Lord Nelson. Another Italian who was employed by Wolsey, and subsequently by Henry VIII., was Giovanni da Majano, whose name appears in accounts of the time as being paid for certain work; but the work itself has disappeared, except the terra-cotta roundels, containing busts of Roman emperors, built into the walls of Hampton Court. Toto del Nunziata was another skilful Italian whose name appears in accounts, and he is said by Vasari to have built Henry VIII.'s principal palace. This is generally considered to have been Nonesuch, in Surrey, of which there is nothing left, but which, as already stated, must have presented examples of most admirable work in the way of sculpture and painting.†

* See page 12.
† See page 33.

Nicholas of Modena, described as a carver, also worked for Henry, and remained in England for some years after his death, but the work attributed to him is only conjectural. Indeed, the share taken by the Italians of Henry VIII.'s time in the design of English work, is still a matter of controversy to be waged by the learned, and has not yet descended to the more certain level of the text-book. What we do know is, that Torrigiano executed Henry VII.'s tomb under a contract, and that a few other Italians of eminence resided for longer or shorter periods in England, together with a considerable number of their compatriots of less distinction. These men must have exercised considerable influence upon their English companions, and although their own style of ornament did not become universal, they must have prepared the way for the general adoption of the other versions of Italian detail which marked the second half of the sixteenth century.

The same remarks apply to Holbein, although the designs which he executed for work in England are much more numerous than those of any of his contemporaries, and have been identified beyond doubt as his. That is to say, in addition to his pictures, a large number of his drawings remain, principally for articles of goldsmith's work; but the objects themselves have mostly disappeared. One of the largest of his drawings, however, is that of a wood chimney-piece, which, from the initials upon it, was intended for Henry VIII. Some architectural work has been attributed to Holbein, but only on conjecture. Amongst it may be mentioned two gateways at Whitehall, now removed; part of a front at Wilton, in Wiltshire, as well as a little garden-house there; and the splendid screen at King's College Chapel, Cambridge. But there is no actual evidence to connect him with these works, and we should be mistaken in regarding him in any way as an architect in the sense in which we understand the term.

The architect, indeed, as a distinct individual, does not seem to have arisen in those early days: the architect, that is, who not only designed the plan and elevations of the building, but also the details of its various parts and of its ornament. Inigo Jones may be taken as the first Englishman who combined the functions of planner and designer of details; previous to his time the work entailed in the designing of a house was much subdivided, the plan and elevations being provided by the surveyor, and each trade producing its own special details as the work went on. Shakespeare only uses the word "architect" once, and then not in connection with building operations. He gives us, however, a sketch of how to set about building, in the Second Part of King Henry IV. "When we mean to build," says Lord Bardolph, "we first survey the plot, then draw the model; and when we see the figure of the house, then must we rate the cost of the erection. . . . Much more in this great work . . . should we survey the plot of situation, and the model; consent upon a sure foundation; question surveyors." It was the surveyors, such as John Thorpe, who drew the model, which comprised the plans and an elevation, or a perspective view indicating the treatment of more than one front. These drawings were then carried out by the workmen on the spot, who provided their own details. In some of the simpler buildings no surveyor was employed, but rough plans were prepared by the builder himself, not so much to work from, as to indicate, for the purpose of a contract, the general extent and appearance of the building. In others, again, no plans were used, but the work was set out on the spot, and built to the requisite height under the supervision of the master mason. It is almost certain that in some cases only a plan was provided, without elevation; in the Thorpe collection a large proportion of the plans have no elevation to correspond; and Henry VII., in his will, orders his tomb to be placed in the midst of his new chapel at Westminster according to "the plat [*i.e.*, plan] made for the same chapel and signed with our hand." At St. John's College, Cambridge, the contractors who built the second court were bound to erect it according to certain "platts and uprights" (*i.e.*, elevations), thus showing that the "plat" did not include elevations as well as plan.

Such contracts as have been preserved relating to work of the sixteenth century, go to show either that the various tradesmen provided their own designs, or that they were to take some already executed work as a pattern. There were separate contracts for the separate trades, but most of them were with masons, joiners, and glaziers. The masons who built the second court at St. John's were to make the windows after the fashion of those in the court already built. The joiner who fitted up the chapel was to make his work like that in Jesus College and Pembroke Hall, " or better in every point." The joiner who executed the stalls and the fretwork of the ceiling in the chapel at Trinity College, was to make the stalls like those at King's College, while the frets, battens, and pendants of the ceiling were to be made "according to the pattern showed to the master and other of the said College for the said frets, battens, and pendants." The glazier who provided the windows of the hall and chapel at St. John's, was to make them of "good and able Normandy glass of colours and pictures as be in the glass windows within the College called Christ's College."

These contracts are useful because they state expressly the sources whence the design was to be taken; but where the work was not done by contract, such accounts as have been preserved point in the same direction. After the masons had finished the second court at St. John's, including the plastering of the walls and ceilings, there appears an entry in the accounts for the payment of one Cobb for "frettishing" the gallery and the great chamber—that is, for working the ornamental plaster ceiling; and another for the payment of the joiner for the wainscotting of the gallery and for the two chimney-pieces there. No mention is made of any particular design, and the presumption is that the workmen supplied their own. This presumption is stronger in the case of the panelling of the hall at Queen's College, where every item of cost appears, as well as the names of the various workmen employed.

It is interesting to see how the names of the workmen gradually changed. The first entry is on the last day of September, 1531, when Matthew Blunt and Robert Cave were paid for "working on the panelling of the College hall." In November they are joined by one Dyrik Harrison, who does the same kind of work; in December, one Lambert comes, and Matthew Blunt disappears; a few days afterwards a certain Arnold joins them, and subsequently a Peter. In January, Giles Fambeler, carver, is paid for nine capitals, and in February for thirteen more, and he then disappears. But his place seems to have been taken by Dyrik Harrison, who thenceforward is paid, not for ordinary joiner's work, but for carving capitals, shields, arms, and lines of "antique crest" and "antique border," up to the middle of July, when he receives his final payment " by order of the President." In the meantime Robert Cave's name has ceased to be entered, but Arnold, Lambert, and Peter still continue. After Harrison's departure Lambert seems to have done the special work, since in August he gets paid for certain columns and for the " extreme parts of the cresting." His is the last name of the joiners which appears, and in September the work was finished. It would almost seem as though Giles Fambeler, whose name looks anything but English, had been employed for some two months, just to show how the new carving should be done, and that from him Dyrik Harrison, whose Christian name suggests a Dutch connection, picked up a knowledge of the fashionable ornament sufficient to enable him to take Giles's place; and that Lambert in his turn succeeded Harrison. Even if this supposition is larger than the facts warrant, it must have been in some such manner as this that the new forms were disseminated through the country. It is worthy of note that the joiner employed at Hengrave, in 1538, six years after this work at Queen's, was named Dyrik, and it is pleasant to imagine (Hengrave being some five-and-twenty miles from Cambridge) that it might have been the same Dyrik Harrison who had picked up his first knowledge from Giles Fambeler.

In such matters as tombs it is beyond question that the workmen supplied the designs. In the year 1525 there is an entry in the accounts of St. John's of a small sum " given to the master mason of Ely for drawing a draught for my lord's tomb," meaning Bishop Fisher's. In 1533 " Mr. Lee the free mason " was paid for making and setting up the tomb. Upon the Bishop's execution, the monument was taken to pieces and thrown aside, but towards the end of last century the remains were discovered during the process of clearing away the rubbish in an " old disused chapel." A rough drawing was made of them, from which it is evident that the design was quite in the Italian style. ·It shows an altar tomb with a pilaster at each corner, ornamented with arabesques similar to those on Henry VII.'s tomb. The side is occupied by a large panel supported by two amorini, and surrounded with foliage and scrollwork; the end has a shield within a garland. The whole work is described by an eyewitness as being elegant, neat, and ornamented in great taste, from which we may gather that both in design and execution it was a worthy specimen of the style prevalent in Henry VIII.'s

time. We have already seen that it was designed by the
master mason at Ely, and executed by Mr. Lee, the free mason.
If these two were not one and the same man, at any rate there
is no reason to suppose that they were other than Englishmen.*

Some fifty years after Bishop Fisher's tomb was erected,
there was drawn up a contract (in 1581) between the executor
of Thomas Fermor, of Somerton, in Oxfordshire, and Richard
and Gabriel Roiley, of Burton-upon-Trent, "tumbe makers."
The latter agree "artificially, cunningly, decently, and substantially to devise, work, set up, and perfectly and fully finish"
a very fair tomb of very good and durable alabaster stone and
of certain specified dimensions. It is to have on it "a very fair
decent and well-proportioned picture or portraiture of a gentleman representing the said Thomas Fermor," with certain
specified accessories; and also "a decent and perfect picture
or portraiture of a fair gentlewoman with a French hood, edge
and habiliments, with all other apparel, furniture, jewels, ornaments and things in all respects usual, decent and seemly for a
gentlewoman." There are also to be the "decent and usual
pictures" of a son and two daughters with escutcheons in their
hands—somewhat after the fashion, no doubt, of those on the
Bradbourne tomb in Fig. 9. The son is to be in armour and
as living; one of the daughters is to be "pictured in decent
order and as living," the other "as dying in the cradle or
swathes." There are to be four shields, one containing "the
very true arms" of Thomas Fermor; two others his arms and
those of his two wives, severally; and the fourth the arms of
his second wife. They are all to be placed as most may serve
for the "shew and setting forth of the said tomb." Once
again, towards the end, it is stated that all the "devising,
colouring, gilding, garnishing, workmanship, carriage, con-
veying, setting up, and full finishing of the said tomb," is to be
done by the Roileys; but the executor will provide "wains,
carts and cattle" to draw the parts of the tomb to Somerton.
The price for the tomb is to be £40.

It is here expressly stated that the workmen are to do the
"devising" as well as the making of the tomb. The features
which it is to comprise are stated, but the designing and
arranging of them are left to the workmen. It is interesting to

---

* For particulars of these contracts, &c., at Cambridge, see Willis and Clark's
Architectural History of the University of Cambridge, Vol. II.

notice that the male figure is to be the portraiture of a gentleman representing Thomas Fermor, but it does not seem to be
implied that the likeness was to be very accurate. In the case
of the lady, evidently no resemblance was expected, and we are
left to conjecture whether it was the first or the second wife who
was the more nearly represented. All those who are familiar
with Elizabethan tombs will recognize the son and daughter
holding escutcheons, and the child in "swathes," as well as the
four shields bearing the arms of Thomas Fermor and his two
wives. If additional proof were wanted that the design was
left in the hands of the workman, it is to be found in the stipu-
lation that everything is to be placed so as best to " set forth "
the tomb. This important part of the business is not to be
arranged by the executor or any one acting on his behalf, but
by the contracting tomb-makers.

Tombs are comparatively small structures, and might possibly
have been subjects of special custom; but the same custom
prevailed in the building of large houses like Burghley House
and Cobham Hall. When the latter building was in a suitable
condition, the plasterer was sent for in order that he might
submit patterns and models of the ceilings for Lord Cobham
to select from. During a considerable part of the time occupied
in building the earlier portions of Burghley, a number of letters
passed between the foreman and Lord Burghley, in which the
foreman sought instructions from his lordship about many
minute particulars, which would certainly have been settled by
the architect had there been one. Among Lord Burghley's
papers is one showing the plan and elevation of a window,
endorsed in Burghley's own hand " Henryck's platt of my bay
window "; suggesting that, as occasion arose, his lordship
applied to some skilful craftsman for drawings. It is certain
that he made a point of studying books on architecture, for in
August, 1568, he wrote to Sir Henry Norris, ambassador in
France, asking him to provide for him " a book concerning
architecture, entitled according to a paper here included, which
I saw at Sir Thomas Smith's; or if you think there is any
better of a late making of that argument." The enclosure
containing the title of the book is not in existence, so we do
not know what it was; but from this reference we gather that
Sir Thomas Smith (who was a Secretary of State, and had
been ambassador to France) was interested in architecture as

well as Lord Burghley, and that Sir Henry Norris was sufficiently acquainted with the subject to be able to recommend
the latest work dealing with it. Some years later Lord
Burghley was again asking for a French book on architecture,
but this time he gave the title, in phraseology indicating that
he was something of a student of the subject. "The book I
most desire," he says, "is made by the same author, and is
entitled ' Novels institutions per bien bâster et à petits frais,
par Philibert de Lorme,' Paris, 1576." From these instances
it would appear not improbable that had Lord Burghley
lived in the days of Pope, he might have shared with Lord
Burlington the reputation of being one of the foremost architects of the age ; but as a matter of fact he did not pretend
to that distinction : all that he did, apparently, was to direct
the energies of others who had received special training in
architectural matters.

The Henryk who provided the platt of Lord Burghley's bay
window was a Dutch mason in the employ of Sir Thomas Gresham—who built the first Royal Exchange, or Bourse, as it was
called—and he passed backwards and forwards between London
and Antwerp as occasion demanded. Many of the materials
for Gresham's Bourse came from the Low Countries, and were
shipped thence under the superintendence of Gresham's agent,
Richard Clough. Clough's letters from Antwerp, where he was
stationed, give in quaint phraseology a good deal of information
as to the progress of the work which was being prepared over
there both for Sir Thomas Gresham and the more exalted
"Sir William Cecil, the Queen's Majesty's principal Secretary,"
afterwards Lord Burghley. In July, 1566, Clough congratulates
himself on Gresham's liking Henryk so well, and on the work
being so well forward, that when Henryk returns to Antwerp
he can get on with the rest. By the beginning of August
Henryk had arrived, and " your carpenters also, whom I do
mean shortly to return." In the next few letters he is greatly
troubled about " Master Secretary's " paving stones. On the
29th September, he says that he calls daily upon Henryk, who
is looking daily for them, and he has sent a man to the place
where they are in making in order to hasten their departure.
Notwithstanding this, on the 20th October Master Secretary's
paving stones were not come, " but Henryk saith he knoweth
well they will be here within a day or two," and then he will

not fail to send them away out of hand, even if he has to " hire
a small hoy of purpose." But delays in the delivery of goods
vexed the souls of overlookers in as great a degree then as now,
and still on the 10th November " Master's stones are not come,
which maketh Master Henryk almost out of his wit, for I never
fail a day but I am once a day with him, so that they cannot
be long, unless they be drowned by the way." The hopeful
expectation was fulfilled, for a fortnight later Clough writes,
"and as touching Master Secretary's stones, I do not doubt
but that you have received them long since; and that they
have been so long—Henryk saith he could do no more and
if his life had been upon the matter." So the paving stones
were sent off at last, and at the same time Henryk sent a
pattern how they should be laid; it was unnecessary to send a
man, for he thought " that him that paved Master Secretary's
house can so well lay those stones as any that he should send
from hence."

The trying episode of " those stones " being closed, Clough
returns to the subject of the Bourse, and promises to send off
further materials; on the 5th December he says he has shipped
a certain amount " in Cornelius Janson's sprett," and trusts
that before Easter everything will be despatched. Soon after
this, it seems, he went away to get married, and his letters
cease; but in the following April (the 27th) an apprentice of
Gresham's informs him of such matters as had passed in
Antwerp since Clough's departure, among which was the
discharge from the " Prince's men " of two of Gresham's
retainers, whom he intended to send to London " in one of the
ships laden with stone for the Bourse," of which there were
three ready to depart " as to-morrow." As Easter Day fell on
the 30th March in the year 1567, Clough's hope that everything
would be despatched by then was not absolutely fulfilled.

Henryk was now apparently sufficiently at liberty to be
allowed to turn his attention from Gresham's work to Cecil's,
and on the 21st August, 1567, the former writes to the latter,
"As for Henryk, you shall find him so reasonable as you
shall have good cause to be content, and by this post I have
given order for the making of your gallery, which I trust shall
both like you well in price and workmanship." Four months
later, on the 26th December, it was a door for Cecil which was
in question, and as " Henryk my workman " intended to go over

sea after the Christmas holidays, and to stay till April, Gresham desired to know whether Cecil would have his "port (door) set up before his departure, or else at his return." In the following February, Gresham again writes to Cecil reminding him that "Henryk hath lost the pattern of the pillars for your gallery in the country, so he can proceed no further in the working thereof until he have another." He urges Cecil not to fail to send the pattern at once, as Henryk would be back in London by the last day of March at the farthest. This inability of Henryk's to proceed without the "pattern" shows that in this case, at any rate, he did not supply the design. But already four years earlier (in January, 1563) there had been some correspondence between Clough and Cecil about a gallery and a pattern which the latter had sent; and if the two galleries were one and the same, it was probably the old pattern which Henryk had to work to, and there was no need for him to devise a new one. In the case in which Clough was concerned there was some discrepancy in the pattern or instructions sent by Cecil for the pillars and arches, which required correction; he therefore sent back the pattern, so that Cecil might confer with his mason at home. As to a mason going over from Flanders to England, there was no need for it, since the work would be so wrought that it could not be set amiss, besides which a pattern in paper should be sent. The Dutch mason's advice was that the pillars should be made all of one stone, and the arches accordingly, "for they must be made, to be well made, either antique or modern, and this, with the whole pillar, is antique; wherefore according as I shall hear from your honour, so I shall proceed therein." The difference intended to be conveyed between "antique" and "modern" is not very clear, inasmuch as "antique" was the term generally applied in describing work executed in the style which we call Renaissance. But this is a detail which does not affect the general conclusions to be drawn from the whole correspondence, which are, first, that there is no one concerned in these various transactions who acts in the capacity of the architect, but that when instructions are required by the workmen they are sought from the proprietor himself: second, that Dutch workmanship and design were procured by men of eminence in England: and third, that English workmen were thought to be quite as capable of dealing with the worked materials as any that could be sent from abroad.

R.A.   S

The books on Architecture which were published during the sixteenth century point somewhat in the same direction, namely, that there was no all-controlling architect, but that buildings were carried out by co-operation in design as well as execution. At the same time, they make it evident that the idea of the architect as the person who should have chief control had arisen: an idea which took more and more hold until it received its first striking embodiment, so far as England is concerned, in Inigo Jones. Hans Bluom's book on the Five Orders, published at Zürich in 1550, is declared on the title-page to be useful to painters, sculptors, workers in brass and wood, masons, statuaries, and all who require sure measure; no mention being made of architects. The same omission occurs in the English translation published in 1608, which mentions on the title-page free-masons, carpenters, goldsmiths, painters, carvers, inlayers and Anticke-cutters, who must not be taken for anything but cutters of " antique " patterns. The address to the reader professes that the book is offered for the benefit of " Masters, Builders, Carvers, Masons, Lymners, and all sorts of men that love beauty and ornament." The publisher of Vries's book of monuments of 1563 exhorts, on his title-page, all painters, statuaries, architects and masons to inspect, buy and use it; and the same author's book on Perspective of 1604 is addressed to painters, sculptors, statuaries, smiths, architects, designers, masons, clerks, woodworkers, and all lovers of the arts. We have, therefore, the appellation of " architect " introduced, but it is ranked with the statuaries, masons, and smiths; and indeed the term was probably used in its original signification of " master-workman."

There was a book published in 1600, of which the title is interesting, although the contents do not enlighten us in regard to the subject under enquiry. It was called " The hospitall of incurable fooles: erected in English, as near the first Italian modell and platforme, as the unskillful hand of an ignorant architect could devise "; but beyond the use of the word " architect," and the deductions to be drawn from its connection with the " Italian modell," there is no help to be obtained in this quarter.

Some further light is thrown on the term by John Shute. who published his book *The Chief Groundes of Architecture* in 1563. Shute calls himself a " Paynter and Archytecte,"

and in the heading of one of his chapters he speaks of an
"Architecte or Mayster of Buyldings." This is the signification of the term which became gradually accepted, but there
is no evidence that in Shute's time (that is, in 1563) a master
of the buildings was generally employed, or that being
employed he was designated an architect. John Thorpe
was called a "surveyor." Robert Smithson, who died in
1614, fifty years after Shute, is designated in his epitaph as
"architector and surveyor unto the most worthy House of
Wollaton."

All the evidence points therefore to co-operation in design as
well as execution, and while men like Thorpe provided plans
and "uprights," each trade provided its own details. This
view will account for much of what is otherwise very puzzling—
the diversity in character between buildings supposed to have
been the work of the same "architect." The difficulty largely
disappears if we suppose the small scale drawings to have been
supplied by the "surveyor," and then elaborated on the works
by the foreman and the various craftsmen. But that there
was a desire among wealthy patrons to establish an educated
class of "architects" is proved by the Introduction of Shute's
book, for he tells us there that he was sent to Italy by the
Duke of Northumberland in the year 1550 for the express
purpose of studying architecture, and that having there studied
it and amassed a number of drawings and designs of sculpture,
painting, and architecture, he thought good on his return
to set forth some part of them for the profit of others, especially touching architecture. How far Shute himself was able
to put his knowledge to the test of practical experience is not
known, for no buildings are identified as his, and he died in
1563, the same year in which he published his book. He
speaks of his patron having shown the results of his studies
to Edward VI. after his return : Edward died in 1553, and
there were ten years, therefore, during which Shute might have
put in practice what he learned in Italy.

The history of architectural design during the sixteenth
century cannot, therefore, be written round the names of great
men in England as it can in Italy, and in a less degree in
France. Those who do most towards giving character to a
building are those who determine its plan and general outlines ; and the men who did this to our English houses were

the surveyors. Of these John Thorpe is the only one about whom anything much is known; but enough is known to place him in a high rank as a designer. There must have been many others, but their names have disappeared and their fame has evaporated. A list of all those who could be considered architects has been drawn up by Mr. Wyatt Papworth,[*] but the names of those prior to Inigo Jones include patrons, masons, and carpenters as well as surveyors, and the task still remains to assign to each his proper share in the production of the architecture of his day. This architecture was not the work of a single class of men, but resulted from the joint efforts of many minds directing many different tools. High and low, rich and poor, gentle and simple, cultured and uncultured, all combined to the same end, and the authors of the architectural books of the period knew their business when they appealed on their title-pages to so many different artificers.

[*] *The Renaissance and Italian Styles of Architecture in Great Britain,* 1883.

A LIST OF SELECTED WORKS ON
EARLY RENAISSANCE ARCHITECTURE IN ENGLAND.

I. WORKS ON THE ARCHITECTURE OF THE TUDOR PERIOD, &c.

DOLLMAN (F. T.).—An Analysis of Ancient Domestic Architecture in Great Britain. 2 vols. 4to. 1864.

HUNT (T. F.).—Exemplars of Tudor Architecture. 8vo. 1836.

LAMB (E. B.).—Studies of Ancient Domestic Architecture. 4to. 1846.

PUGIN (A.).—Specimens of Gothic Architecture in England. 2 vols. 4to. 1821.

PUGIN (A. and A. W.).—Examples of Gothic Architecture in England. 3 vols. 4to. 1831.

TURNER (T. H.) and PARKER (J. H.).—Some Account of Domestic Architecture in England during the Middle Ages. 3 vols. 8vo. 1859—1877.

II. GENERAL WORKS ON THE ARCHITECTURE OF THE ELIZABETHAN AND JACOBEAN PERIOD; ALSO BOOKS OF REFERENCE, &c.

ARCHITECTURAL ASSOCIATION SKETCH BOOK, THE.
   Old Series. 12 vols. Folio. 1868—1880.
   New Series. 12 vols. Folio. 1881—1892.
   Third Series. Folio. 1893—and in progress.

BLOMFIELD (R. T.).—A History of Renaissance Architecture in England. 2 vols. Imp. 8vo. 1897.

CLAYTON (J.).—Ancient Timber Edifices of England. Folio. 1846.

GOTCH (J. A.).—Architecture of the Renaissance in England. 2 vols. Folio. 1891—1894.

HABERSHON (M.).—Ancient Half-Timbered Edifices of England. 4to. 1836.

HAKEWILL (F.).—An Attempt to Determine the Exact Character of Elizabethan Architecture. 8vo. 1835.

HALL (S. C.).—Baronial Halls and Ancient Edifices of England. 2 vols. 4to. 1850.

NASH (J.).—Mansions of England in the Olden Time. 4 vols. Folio. 1839—1849.

NASH (J.).—Mansions of England in the Olden Time.   4 vols.   4to. 1869.

PAPWORTH (W.).—The Renaissance and Italian Styles of Architecture in Great Britain : A Chronological List of Examples, 1450—1700. 8vo. 1883.

RICHARDSON (C. J.).—Architectural Remains of the Reigns of Elizabeth and James I. Folio. 1840.

RICHARDSON (C. J.).—Specimens of the Architecture of the Reigns of Queen Elizabeth and King James I. 4to. 1837.

RICHARDSON (C. J.).—Studies from Old English Mansions. 4 vols. Folio. 1841—1848.

SHAW (H.).—Details of Elizabethan Architecture. 4to. 1834.

III. WORKS ON THE ARCHITECTURE OF PARTICULAR DISTRICTS, MONOGRAPHS, &c.

COLE (REV. R. E. G.).—History of the Manor and Township of Doddington. 8vo. 1897.

COPE (SIR W. H.).—Bramshill ; its History and Architecture. 4to.

DAVIE (W. GALSWORTHY) and E. GUY DAWBER.—Old Cottages and Farm Houses in Kent and Sussex. 4to. 1900.

ELYARD (S. J.).—Some Old Wiltshire Homes. Folio. 1894.

GAGE (J.).—History and Antiquities of Hengrave. 4to. 1822.

GOTCH (J. A.).—The Buildings Erected in Northamptonshire by Sir Thomas Tresham. Folio. 1883.

HARRISON (F.).—Annals of an Old Manor House. 4to. 1893.

NEVILL (R.).—Old Cottage of Domestic Architecture in South-West Surrey. 4to. 1890.

NIVEN (W.).—Monograph of Aston Hall, Warwickshire. 4to. 1881.
Illustrations of Old Staffordshire Houses. 4to. 1882.
Illustrations of Old Warwickshire Houses. 4to. 1878.
Illustrations of Old Worcestershire Houses. 4to. (?)

PALMER (C. J.).—Illustrations of An Old House at Great Yarmouth. 4to. 1838.

ROUNDELL (MRS. CHARLES) COWDRAY.—The History of a Great English House. 4to. 1884.

TAYLOR (H.).—Old Halls in Lancashire and Cheshire. 4to. 1882.

WILLINS (E. P.).—Some Old Halls and Manor Houses in Norfolk. 4to. 1890.

IV. HISTORICAL AND BIOGRAPHICAL WORKS CONSULTED IN THE PREPARATION OF THIS WORK.

ARCHÆLOGIA : or Miscellaneous Tracts relating to Antiquity, published by the Society of Antiquaries.

ARCHÆOLOGICAL JOURNAL, Vol. VIII. for Contract for Thos. Fermor's Tomb in Somerton Church ; Vols. V. and XXXIX. for Nonesuch Palace.

HISTORICAL AND BIOGRAPHICAL WORKS (*continued*).

ARCHÆOLOGICAL JOURNAL, Vol. LI. 1894. "On the Work of Florentine Sculptors in England in the Early Part of the Sixteenth Century," &c., by Alfred Higgins, F.S.A.

THE GENTLEMAN'S MAGAZINE, August, 1837, for Nonesuch Palace.

JOURNAL OF THE SOCIETY OF ARTS, April 24, 1891. "Decorative Plaster Work," by G. T. Robinson, F.S.A.

TRANSACTIONS OF THE ESSEX ARCHÆOLOGICAL SOCIETY.

TRANSACTIONS OF THE R. I. B. A., May 18, June 8, 1868. "On the Foreign Artists employed in England during the Sixteenth Century, and their Influence on British Art," by M. Digby Wyatt.

WILTSHIRE ARCHÆOLOGICAL AND NATURAL HISTORY MAGAZINE.

ANDROUT DU CERCEAU (JACQUES).—Les plus excellents bastiments de France. Folio. 1576—1579.

ANDROUT DU CERCEAU (JACQUES).—De architectura opus. Folio. 1559.

AUBREY (J.).—Wiltshire Topographical Collections, 1659—1670. 4to. 1862.

BLOOME (H.).—The Book of Five Columnes of Architecture, &c. Translated by I. T. Folio. 1608.

BLUOM (JOANNES, *same as Hans Bloome*).—Quinque Columnarum Exacta Descriptio. Folio. 1550.

BOORDE (A.).—Compendyous Regyment, or a Dyetary of Helth. 12mo. 1542.

BRAUN (GEORGE).—Urbium præcipuarum mundi theatrum quintum. 1582. (For Nonesuch Palace.)

BRITTON (J.).—Architectural Antiquities of Great Britain. 5 vols. 4to. 1807—1826.

BURGON (J. W.).—Life and Times of Sir Thomas Gresham. 1839.

CABALA.—Sive scrinia sacra. Folio. 1691.

DALLAWAY (REV. JAMES).—A Series of Discourses upon Architecture in England. 8vo. 1833.

DIETTERLEIN (WENDEL).—Architectura und Austheilung der V. Seulen. Folio. 1593.

DOLLMAN (F. T.).—The Priory of St. Mary Overie, Southwark. 4to. 1881.

EVELYN (J.).—Memoirs and Correspondence, 1641—1706.

GEDDE (W.).—A Booke of Sundry Draughtes. 8vo. 1612; reissued 1898.

HARRIS (SIR N.).—Memoirs of the Life and Times of Sir Christopher Hatton. 8vo. 1847.

HARTSHORNE (MISS).—Memorials of Holdenby. 1868.

HENTZNER (P.).—Journey into England in 1598. Edited by Horace Walpole. 1797.

KIP (W.) and HARRISON (S.).—The Archs of Triumph, erected in honour of James I. Folio. 1604.

HISTORICAL AND BIOGRAPHICAL WORKS (*continued*).

LAW (E.).—History of Hampton Court Palace. 3 vols. 8vo. 1888—1891.

LETHABY (W. R.).—Leadwork, Old and Ornamental. 8vo. 1893.

NICHOLS (J.).—Progresses, Festivities, and Pageants of Queen Elizabeth. 3 vols. 4to. 1823.

NICHOLS (J.).—Progresses, Processions, Festivities, and Pageants of King James I. 4 vols. 1828.

L'ORME (PHILIBERT DE).—Nouvelles Inventions pour bien bâstir. Folio. 1561.

PEPYS (S.).—Diary, 1659—1669 ; Memoirs and Private Correspondence.

RYE (W. B.).—England as seen by Foreigners in the Days of Elizabeth and James I. 4to. 1865.

SCOTT (SIR GEORGE GILBERT). — Gleanings from Westminster Abbey. 8vo. 1863.

SHUTE (JOHN).—The Chief Groundes of Architecture. Folio. 1563.

STATE PAPERS.—Domestic Series. Elizabeth and James.

TWYCROSS (EDWARD). — The Mansions of England and Wales. Folio. 1847—1850.

VRIES (JAN VREDEMAN DE).—Book of Monuments. 4to. 1563.

VRIES (JAN VREDEMAN DE).—Architectura, ou bastiment prins de Vitruve, &c. Folio. 1577.

VRIES (JAN VREDEMAN DE).—Perspective. Oblong 4to. 1604.

WESTLAKE.—A History of Design in Painted Glass. 4 vols. 4to. 1881—1894.

WILLIS (J.) and CLARK (J. W.).—The Architectural History of the University of Cambridge. 4 vols. 8vo. 1886.

INDEX.

THE END.

BRADBURY, AGNEW & CO. LD., PRINTERS, LONDON AND TONBRIDGE.

Date Due

MAY~~1~~~~1984~~	AUG 6 1980
AUG 2 ~~1975~~	OCT 1 6 1980
DEC 1 1975	OCT 2
~~JAN~~	APR 2 8
	DEC 2 7 1982
	DEC
~~1979~~	APR 2 1 1992
DEC 1 5 1979	MAY 2 4 1992
APR 1 1980	DEC

CPSIA information can be obtained at www.ICGtesting.com
Printed in the USA
LVOW052113200512

282488LV00013B/52/P